Management Gurus and Management Fashions

A Dramatistic Inquiry

Brad Jackson shows in this very readable book that it is predominantly the rhetoric that makes a management guru. He presents a method for deconstructing this rhetoric and demonstrates its explanatory power by convincingly demystifying the doctrines of salvation of several leading gurus.

The book is indispensable reading for all students of management who are interested in explaining the incredible growth of the guru industry. Practitioners who sometimes ask themselves why gurus never live up to their promises, and why management fashions are so short-lived, will also gain a lot of insight from this book.

Professor Alfred Kieser
University of Mannheim

Brad Jackson has written a stunning book. It finally makes sense out of the enigma of management gurus, who continue to flourish despite considerable evidence that their visions are flawed and the application of their advice ineffective. This book is a must for all managers who have shared the fantasy of a guru's rhetorical vision or are tempted to share it. It is a book that is a page-turner and managers who get a copy will be tempted to read it to the end. They should. They will find it enlightening.

Professor Ernest Bormann
University of Minnesota

Since the 1980s, popular management thinkers, or management gurus, have promoted a number of performance improvement programs or management fashions that have greatly influenced both the conduct of organizational life and the preoccupations of academic researchers.

This book provides a rhetorical critique of the management guru and management fashion phenomenon with a view to building on the important theoretical progress that has recently been made by a small, but growing, band of management researchers. Fantasy Theme Analysis, a dramatistically-based method of rhetorical criticism, is conducted on three of the most important management fashions to have emerged during the 1990s: the reengineering movement promoted by Michael Hammer and James Champy; the effectiveness movement led by Stephen Covey; and the learning organization movement inspired by Peter Se~~ and his colleagues.

In addition to its theoretical and empirical contribu ⸲ ⸲late a much-needed critical dialogue between practitioners and academi peal of management gurus and management fashions, and nt and organizational learning.

Dr Brad Jackson is a Senior Lecturer with the Scho Victoria University of Wellington in New Zealand and an A on at the University of Calgary in Canada. He has presented his research to au diences throughout the world and has published articles in the *Journal of Management Studies*, the *Journal of Applied Behavioural Sciences* and *Management Communication Quarterly*.

Management Gurus and Management Fashions

A Dramatistic Inquiry

Brad Jackson

London and New York

First published 2001
by Routledge
11 New Fetter Lane, London EC4P 4EE

Simultaneously published in the USA and Canada
by Routledge
29 West 35th Street, New York, NY 10001

Routledge is an imprint of the Taylor & Francis Group

Typeset in Palatino by Keystroke, Jacaranda Lodge, Wolverhampton
Printed and bound in Great Britain by University Press, Cambridge

British Library Cataloguing in Publication Data
A catalogue record for this book is available from the British Library

Library of Congress Cataloging in Publication Data
Jackson, Brad, 1960–
    Management gurus and management fashions / Brad Jackson.
        p. cm.
    Includes index.
    1. Management—Case studies. 2. Leadership—Case studies.
    3. Executive ability—Case studies. I. Title.

HD31 .J2 2001
658.4—dc21   00–046011

ISBN 0–415–24945–7 (hbk)
        0–415–24946–5 (pbk)

Contents

List of figures and tables

Figures

Tables

Foreword

Chris Argyris

In this book Jackson describes the dramatic increase in consulting activities during the 1990s and argues that these have had an important impact on managing human thoughts and actions, especially in organizations in the private, public, and voluntary sectors of society. He recommends that the consulting practices should be studied more thoroughly and with a scholarly perspective. He also argues that scholars have much to learn from the practitioners, and practitioners from the scholars.

The book represents a fine example of striving to achieve a more fundamental understanding of management consultants and their clients. Jackson begins with a thoughtful examination of the historical and cultural roots of guru behaviour. He helps us to see that however we may wish to evaluate guru behaviour, it has important historical and cultural roots.

Jackson digs deeper into these roots by using a methodology entitled *Fantasy Theme Analysis* which is derived from symbolic convergence theory. He shows that the gurus' actions contain certain basic rhetorical elements that are crucial for their implementation. For example, Hammer and Champy are pragmatists: You must do what we advise because you have no choice. Covey takes a righteous stance: Do as I advise because it is right. Senge's stance is more about effectiveness: You must think about learning because it enhances human and organizational effectiveness. Although these claims may appear to be oversimplified Jackson crafts his argument in ways that show that the core elements are valid descriptions of the gurus' actions.

For example, Jackson examines the action themes that are embedded in each perspective. They include preservation of the self, redemption of the self, and getting control without being controlling. It is action themes such as these that galvanize management actions and hence the initial success of the gurus.

We now come to a puzzle. If these action themes are valued by management, if they have deep historical and cultural roots, why is their life span so short? Why do they become fads that inevitably fade away?

I should like to suggest two explanations. Action themes such as self preservation and redemption, as well as to be in control without controlling, contain inner contradictions. These contradictions surface when attempts are made to implement them. One person's self preservation may become another person's demise. Moreover, both individuals have to face up to the requirements of organizations which are often in conflict with the individuals' actions. These contradictions are recognized by the gurus but are not seen as being built-in. The gurus believe that human beings, being appropriately motivated, can overcome them. Unfortunately, they do not tell us how this can be done.

This leads to a second co-existing explanation. The gurus (less so in the case of Senge) "solve" the puzzle by blaming individuals or organizations. By projecting the responsibility onto others, the gurus bypass becoming aware of their own responsibilities for creating inner contradictions.

For example, gurus espouse participation, empowerment, and personal initiative and responsibility. Yet (with the exception of Senge) they create programs whose successful implementation depends upon the use of hierarchy, unilateral control, and employee limited freedom. Moreover, they do so by being systematically unaware of their inconsistencies and unaware of their unawareness.

Those who attend these programs often begin with an intention to be cooperative and to exhibit their sense of stewardship toward the organization. Soon, they begin to be confronted by the existence of the contradiction. More importantly, they begin to realize that the gurus are unaware of the dilemma. Moreover, if they reflect on their own knowledge and skills, the recipients of these programs soon realize that they too do not know how to overcome these problems. They experience double-binds.

If they do not cooperate, they may be seen as disloyal, if they do cooperate, they do so by reinforcing what they consider to be a sham. They adapt by running silent and deep. And, they deny that they are doing so.

The result is that the gurus, the management, and the employees implement the action themes in ways that maintain them even though the implementation brings to the surface their counter-productive features. One explanation is that when human beings attempt to implement the action themes that produce the counter-productive consequences – they are unaware that they are doing so, and they are unaware that they are unaware. If they become aware, their spontaneous reaction is to blame others and the system. Hence, little genuine learning is possible to solve the basic problem (Argyris 2000).

These explanations assume that the causes of the inner contradictions embedded in the action themes surface when they are being implemented. This means that research to identify and reduce the inner contradictions is not likely to achieve its purpose unless it focuses on the processes of implementation. This in turn requires, I believe, as Lewin has pointed out, the development of sound theory, where "sound" means assigning *implementable* validity equal status to the traditionally recognized internal and external validity. Scholarly consulting can then become the basis for building basic knowledge about advice and improving its effectiveness in everyday life (Argyris 1997).

Chris Argyris
Harvard University
Monitor Company Group, L.P.
Cambridge, Massachusetts

Bibliography

Argyris, Chris (1997) "Failed Theory As A Basis For Scholarly Consulting", *Journal of Social Sciences* V, 3, 4, 5: 809–824.

Argyris, Chris (2000) *Flawed Advice*, New York: Oxford University Press.

Preface

This book stems from research conducted for a doctoral thesis that I pursued on a part-time basis at Lancaster University's Department of Management Learning. My work in executive and management development at the Banff Centre for Management and the University of Calgary served to rouse my curiosity and make me just a little resentful of the remarkable influence and power that management gurus seemed to exert on the management development marketplace. For example, how was it that, in one evening, someone like Anthony Robbins, perennial star of insomniac infomercials, could attract the same number of people to one seminar that it took me to attract in a year to our hundred plus seminars featuring the "cream" of local training talent? Or why was it that, by liberally sprinkling the latest buzzwords into our seminar descriptions, we could boost attendance in an ailing program without necessarily changing its content in any significant way? During the early part of the 1990s I found myself increasingly pondering these and similar questions. While I discovered a number of like-minded people who shared some of my concerns about management gurus and management fashions, there wasn't the impetus to go any further with them.

It was during the course of a routine monthly reconnaissance of the business bookshelves gathering marketing intelligence that I came across Andrzej Huczynski's book *Management Gurus* (1993a) which was also published by Routledge. After eagerly devouring the book over the course of a weekend, I realized that the management guru and management fashion phenomenon could and should be the stuff of a doctoral thesis. In fact, the doctoral thesis might be just the vehicle for tackling and working through some of the questions that had begun to plague my practice as a management seminar organizer. I later found out that this book had, in fact, originated from Andrzej's own doctoral work.

Thus encouraged, I proceeded to explore the literature for more work on the management guru and management fashion phenomena. While I found myself being inundated by material from the business media, I was concerned and somewhat perplexed to find little else on the subject in the academic literature. Gurus and fashions might receive fleeting attention at the beginning of a learned article but were quickly dismissed in customary straw man fashion because of their trivial nature. Most notably, a cottage industry of articles had sprung up in the second half of the 1980s seeking to discredit the work done by Tom Peters and Robert Waterman in the best-selling business book of all time, *In Search of Excellence* (1982). I found myself becoming considerably less concerned about the validity of their work and much more interested in the sources of its massive popularity.

As I began to conduct the research I was heartened by the discovery of a few similarly motivated academics scattered around the globe who were confirmed management guru and fashion watchers. Contact with these individuals encouraged me to present some of my ideas at conferences and to publish some of the better ones in articles. Parts of these articles have found their way into this book. Some of Chapters 4 and 5 have already appeared in the *Journal of Management Studies* (Jackson, 1996b; Jackson, 1999) while some of Chapter 6 has been published in the *Journal of Applied Behavioral Science* (Jackson, 2000). This material has been expanded, updated and refined based on the feedback I received from generous colleagues.

As I wrote my thesis I had a vague idea that I would like eventually to turn it into a book. This thought was appropriately relegated to pipe-dream status until the thesis was properly defended and safely deposited in the university library at Lancaster. I am pleased now finally to have the opportunity to share my thesis with a wider audience and to follow in Andrzej Huczynski's footsteps.

Acknowledgments

In the course of working on this book over the past six years, a great many people have played their part in helping me along the way. I would like to begin by thanking my doctoral supervisor, Professor John Burgoyne, for his sage guidance and support throughout and for encouraging me along with Timothy Clark, to turn the thesis into a book. The members of the Department of Management Learning always made me feel very welcome during my flying visits to Lancaster. I am particularly grateful to Mark Easterby-Smith, Vivian Hodgson, Steve Fox, Anne Lorbiecki, Michael Reynolds, Jill Roberts and Morgan Tanton. Thanks also to Rosamond Pardee for her support and encouragement.

At the University of Calgary, I would like to thank all my colleagues in the Faculty of Continuing Education and Susan Hutton, Tom Keenan and Bill Taylor in particular. My gratitude also extends to the staff of the Management Seminars Area, the Special Sessions Office and TransAlta's Corporate Communications group for putting up with a frequently distracted leader. From the Faculty of Management, I would especially like to thank Pushkala Prasad for allowing me to participate in three marvelous doctoral seminars. I am also very appreciative of the editing prowess of Jo-Anne Andre and the bibliographic support provided by Merrit Penny.

In the closing stages of the book, my newfound colleagues at Victoria University of Wellington's School of Business and Public Management provided me with helpful support and encouragement. Elsewhere in the academic universe I would like to thank the following people who kindly offered support or provided helpful feedback: Eric Abrahamson, David Barry, Ernest Bormann, Doug Bowie, Peter Case, Ann Cunliffe, Timothy Clark, Barbara Czarniawska, Kathy Lund Dean, Michael Elmes, Christopher Grey, Mary Jo Hatch, Shawn Henry, Andrzej Huczynski, Tom Keenoy, Lotte Jensen, Alfred Kieser, David Kirby, Karen Legge, Albert Mills, Kevin Pederson, Anshuman Prasad, Craig Prichard, Graeme Salaman and Alan Thomas.

I would also like to acknowledge Catriona King at Routledge for taking such an enthusiastic interest in the book as well as Gavin Cullen, Sean Daly and Sandra Jones for skillfully steering it to publication.

I am indebted to my parents, Rick and Julie, for the love of learning they instilled in me, their remarkably constructive reading of my work and for driving me around the U.K. to attend conferences and visit departments on so many occasions.

Finally, my wife, Jacquie, who encouraged me to resist the rewards of corporate life and stay in the academic game to get the job done. She was ably assisted by her mother, Mavis, our daughter, Devan, and our son, Colin. My heartfelt thanks to you all for your tolerance, patience and belief in me.

Permissions acknowledgments

The authors and publishers would like to thank the following for granting permission to reproduce material in this work:

The Spieler Agency, NY, for the use of text from *The Fifth Discipline Fieldbook* (Senge et al. 1994), in Table 6.2, 'The five disciplines of Peter Senge's learning organization'.

Table 2.1 adapted from Grint, *Fuzzy Management* (1997) by permission of Oxford University Press.

Every effort has been made to contact copyright holders for their permission to reprint material in this book. The publishers would be grateful to hear from any copyright holder who is not here acknowledged and will undertake to rectify any errors or omissions in future editions of this book.

1 Introduction

Does it matter what church you go to as long as you do the right thing?
If you lock in with Crosby's techniques, you'll get improvement; if you
lock in with Deming, you'll get improvement. Which one is better than the
other? I don't know. I don't think it makes much difference as long as
you're trying something.

(District manager of quality and data management at AT&T,
cited in Oberle, 1990: 52)

We're the only society in the world that believes it can keep on getting
better and better. So we keep on getting suckered by people like Ben
Franklin, Emerson and Drucker and me.

(Tom Peters quoted in *Fortune*, 1996: 33)

Starting out

Management gurus and management fashions have had an important
impact upon my thinking and practice in all three of the roles – manager,
educator and researcher – that I have performed in my professional life.
My initial reading of management guru texts in the mid-1980s was
prompted by a desire as a young manager to understand better what I
was supposed to be doing. Being relatively new to the role and feeling more
than a little insecure about whether or not I was the right person for it,
I turned to the likes of Peter Drucker, Tom Peters and Kenneth Blanchard
for guidance and gleaned more from my reading of them than I had
originally anticipated. In contrast to the stuffy, formulaic introductory
management texts that I was reading for my introductory management
classes, these writers made me feel emotionally good about what I was
doing, firing me up with enthusiasm to "get out there and do something".
I remember being particularly excited by the "Excellence" movement
inspired by Tom Peters with his urgent appeal for direct and spontaneous
action, the breaking down of bureaucratic walls and the general sense
of destiny that it instilled in me. As writers like Peters portrayed it,
management was not only the right thing to be doing but it could also be
tremendous fun.

Subsequently, in the early 1990s, as I began to develop my role as an educator, my feelings toward management gurus and the fashions they spawned became more mixed. Working as a program director, I was charged with developing what I thought to be an impressive roster of management seminars that were based on sound adult education principles. In this role, I was struck by the seeming lack of effort with which a management guru could come to town and persuade 900 or so level-headed middle managers to part with the requisite large sum of cash in order to hear a reasonably good facsimile of what he had already said in his book. Strongly encouraged by my superiors not to miss out on this action, I organized a series of videoconferences that featured a total of ten management gurus delivered live via satellite. Sure enough, this generated considerable interest from the local business community. Sitting in the audience at these videoconferences, I found myself quietly railing against the gurus' platitudes, the clichés and the blatant authoritarianism of the event. Conversations with the audience members before and after each presentation revealed a whole suite of reactions ranging from wide-eyed adulation to cynical disgust. Most of those who attended were in the middle of these two poles. While they were mildly impressed with the gurus' presentation, they tended to be guardedly pessimistic about the chances of the gurus' ideas actually being introduced into their workplace, let alone being successfully implemented.

While I was not entirely comfortable with my involvement in this initiative as an educator, and an adult educator at that, I could not help but be impressed by the power and accessibility of the gurus' language. I sensed that, if properly handled, this power might be used to provide a useful starting point to communicate with managers about alternative ways of managing and organizing. We had attempted to start such discussions at the local level by incorporating into the videoconference event a critical local panel, dubbed the "reality check", which was comprised of an academic, a consultant and a practitioner. The fact that this intervention proved neither to be hugely popular with the audience nor to meet its stated goals, gave me a healthy respect for the complex learning dynamics within the guru–follower relationship.

In the mid-1990s, as I began to develop my role as a researcher, my attitude toward management gurus and management fashions transformed yet again. First, as I read more of the academic literature that had addressed management and organizational issues, I realized that many of the management gurus' ideas had been derived from earlier academic research that was considerably more thoughtful and realistic in its claims than what was being presented by the gurus. Second, in becoming familiar with the debates regarding the existence and consequences of "late" or "high" or "post" modernity, I began to appreciate that the guru phenomenon was not something that was necessarily confined to the field of management but was indeed symptomatic of much wider social, cultural and political changes and, as such, could be examined more profitably within that context. Third, with this recognition came a desire to develop an effective critique that could demystify much of the hype surrounding management gurus and, in the process, perhaps enable managers to break the cycle of dependency on the higher authority of the management guru and to begin to privilege the learning that they, and their immediate colleagues, generated from their own lived experience.

The starting point of this book, therefore, was a fundamental and a deep curiosity on my part about the reasons behind the dramatic growth in popularity of management gurus and management fashions as evidenced by expanding business book sections, packed convention halls and grossly inflated speaker and consultancy fees. In my attempts to answer the book's initial question, a whole host of important subsidiary questions emerged, for example: What makes a management guru? How many gurus are there? Why do some management ideas become immensely fashionable while others remain largely ignored? Is it more a function of the idea itself or the persuasiveness of the management guru who is promoting it? Do management gurus consciously set out to become gurus or is it something that is beyond their control? Who are the people who read, watch or listen to them? What are their motives? How do management gurus help them? Is it by providing cognitive understanding, encouragement or reassurance? What is it about the time and place that has created such an extraordinary demand for management gurus and fashions? It is these and related questions which I hope to shed some light upon during the course of this book.

The wider view

The corporate community's predilection for finding, implementing and then disposing of the latest and greatest organizational improvement programs such as Excellence, Total Quality Management (TQM), Organizational Culture, Business Process Reengineering and the Learning Organization, has been widely documented in the business media and commented upon in typically ambivalent terms. On the one hand, journalists continue to play a key role in celebrating and promoting the latest management innovations and the gurus who are their primary champions (Byrne, 1992; Crainer, 1997; Stewart, 1993). On the other, they make a habit of lampooning the management gurus and castigating the executives for their transient flings with "fads", "quick fixes" and "silver bullets" as well as their insensitivity to the financial and human costs that follow in their wake (Bell, 1995; Farnham and Kover, 1996; Thackray, 1993).

The academic community's reaction to this phenomenon has typically ranged from general indifference to outright hostility (Burrell, 1989; Hitt and Ireland, 1987; Thomas, 1989). More recently, however, a number of writers have begun to recognize that the phenomenon itself warrants serious attention from management researchers for several reasons. First, there is the basic fact that, with the widespread adoption of management fashions across all sectors, management gurus have had a tangible impact upon the working lives of employees at all levels within the organization in both material and symbolic terms (Clark and Salaman, 1996; Huczynski, 1993b; Watson, 1994). With a well-honed package of knowledge and a judicious use of communication technologies, a few individuals have been able to exert a dramatic impact upon what is talked about in the workplace, what organizational problems are deemed to be the most significant, and what managerial solutions are the most appropriate to address these. We only have to think of the pervasiveness of the TQM movement throughout North America and elsewhere to get an appreciation for the sheer scale of influence its three "founders" – W. Edwards Deming, Joseph Juran and Philip Crosby – have had upon many lives.

A second reason for researching this phenomenon is that, although the management consulting industry within which management gurus ply their trade is one of the fastest-growing industries, it remains relatively underexplored compared to the other major industries that it claims to serve. For example, there is no general consensus about how large this industry actually is. The Garner Group has estimated that total fees generated in 1994 were $11.4 billion and that this figure is projected to reach $21 billion by 1999 (Micklethwait and Wooldridge, 1996). Alternatively, Nohria and Berkley (1994) estimated that the "management industry" generated $15.2 billion in revenue and employed 81,000 individuals in 1992 while O'Shea and Madigan (1997) pegged it at $25 billion for the U.S. and double that for the entire world. There is a certain irony that we know so little about an industry that purports to know so much about other industries.

Third, academics are beginning to recognize that the conventional wisdom that held that significant new management knowledge was created exclusively within academe and then disseminated to the larger public through management gurus and consultants is no longer an accurate reflection of reality and may need to be turned on its head (Aldag, 1997; Barley et al., 1988; Clark and Salaman, 1996). In providing an alternative source for the acquisition of managerial knowledge that is presented in a direct and more easily consumable form, management gurus could indeed be seen as a threat to the academic's traditional hold on what and what does not constitute managerial knowledge. While there is no doubt that most popular management ideas can ultimately be traced back to the academic literature, since the 1980s an increasing proportion of the academic agenda is now being driven by a "new wave" of management theory (Wood, 1989) which Huczynski (1993a) has labeled "guru theory". This knowledge not only takes on a different form and function but the traditional academic "guarantors" of validity, generalizability and replicability are replaced by the presentation style, credibility and persona of the author. It is, therefore, in the basic interests of management researchers to become better acquainted with the workings of the management fashion industry and to actively engage with it.

The purpose of the book

The main purpose of this book is to build on and add to the emergent theoretical debate about "guru" theory by developing and then applying a rhetorical critique to an empirical study of management gurus and management fashions. The Fantasy Theme Analysis method of rhetorical criticism is used in this study because it is an established method that provides both a descriptive and an explanatory framework for critically examining the main elements of the management fashion-setting process – i.e. gurus, consultants, managers, program, context, etc. – within an integrated rhetorical frame. Fantasy theme analysis is a dramatistically based method of rhetorical criticism rooted in Ernest Bormann's Symbolic Convergence Theory (Bormann, 1972; 1976; 1982b; 1983). This method of rhetorical criticism provides some important insights because it captures the underlying dramatic appeal of the management fashion to the individual manager as well as the role of the management guru in its articulation, legitimation and dissemination. It gets at some of the things I have noted as being important to the gurus' appeal from my experience as a manager and as a programmer.

There is general acceptance within the literature that there is a dearth of detailed and systematic empirical studies of individual management gurus and the fashions that they have helped to foster. Abrahamson and Fairchild (1999) have claimed that their study of Quality Circles is perhaps the first carefully documented study of a management fashion. In the absence of these accounts, academic and media commentators tend to treat both management gurus and management fashions as an undifferentiated collectivity, stressing the similarities between them at the expense of their differences. This book has been written to provide more empirical material, which can hopefully inform the emergent theoretical debate. The subjects of this book are three management guru-inspired fashions that have come into prominence in North America during the 1990s: the "reengineering" movement led by Michael Hammer and James Champy; the "effectiveness" movement spearheaded by Stephen Covey; and the "learning organization" concept that has been popularized by Peter Senge and his colleagues. Each of these fashions and gurus has received considerable media attention, yet they have not been subjected to any form of sustained and systematic academic analysis.

The third major purpose of this book is to develop a rhetorical critique that might engage both practitioners and academics in a critical dialogue about the sources of the underlying appeal of these and other management guru-inspired management fashions and to reflect on the quality of managerial and organizational learning that they have been responsible, either directly or indirectly, for generating. In this respect, I am standing behind Abrahamson's (1996a) plea for scholars not only to devote more energy toward studying the management fashion-setting process and explaining when and how it fails, but also actively to intervene in the process to make it a more technically useful, collective learning process.

The structure of the book

The book comprises eight chapters. In Chapter 2, the literature that has been written about the management guru and fashion phenomenon by both media and academic commentators is reviewed. The first part of the review examines the recent emergence of management gurus as key figures in corporate life and business discourse and the concurrent growth in the management fashion industry within which, it is argued, the guru occupies a central and critical role. This is followed by an assessment of the functions, validity and general efficacy of management fashions for organizational and management effectiveness. The third part of this chapter reviews four different approaches that have recently emerged in the academic literature to explain the management guru and management fashion phenomenon. Chapter 2 closes with a consideration of the relative strengths and weaknesses of these explanatory accounts and lays out some key elements of an approach that could usefully build upon our current knowledge of this phenomenon by focusing on the rhetorical qualities of the gurus' work and the management fashions that they help to conceive.

Chapter 3 builds upon this rhetorically oriented theoretical direction by reviewing a method of rhetorical criticism literature that actively incorporates the key elements of the new approach that are identified in the previous chapter. Dramatistically based Fantasy Theme Analysis (FTA) is singled out as a method that holds some potential for yielding additional new insights into the management guru and management fashion phenomenon. The chapter describes this method's intellectual origins, its empirical applications and the major criticisms that have been leveled at it. It also describes how the method has been applied in this study, explaining the rationale for selecting the cases, the processes by which the data were collected, and the procedures that were used to analyze them.

In Chapters 4, 5 and 6, Fantasy Theme Analyses of each of the three cases are presented. Each of these empirical chapters begins with a discussion of the distinguishing features of the management guru's background and public persona. This is followed by a description of the composition, scale and level of commitment demonstrated by the "rhetorical community" (Bormann, 1972) that has developed around the guru and his vision. Next are presented the main fantasy themes that constitute the unique rhetorical vision that each guru has skillfully developed through a number of media. Each of these chapters closes by highlighting a particular feature of the guru's work that was deemed to be well worth investigating further.

In Chapter 7 an analysis is presented of the similarities and differences between the three management fashions. An assessment is made of the contributions that a dramatistically based rhetorical critique offers for our understanding of the management guru and management fashion and other managerial and organizational phenomena. In light of this assessment, further potentially fruitful theoretical and empirical lines of inquiry are discussed. The book closes in Chapter 8 with a consideration of what can, and should, be done to foster a constructive dialogue between academics and practitioners that can further our understanding both of what drives the management guru and management fashion phenomenon and what we can do to make it more useful to the theory and practice of management learning. I also look at some recent emergent management fashions and how the management advice industry is likely to develop in the near future with particular reference to the changing persona and function of the management guru.

2 The management guru and management fashion phenomenon

On this rainy Monday morning, the quality movement is very much alive and well in Mahwah, N.J. Eighty-eight year-old Joseph M. Juran has arrived for the latest stop in his "Last Word" speaking tour, and the hotel conference room is packed. Fans are eagerly pulling out their credit cards to buy the $25 framed autographed picture, the $50 lucite bow-tie paperweight memento and the $20 canvas tote bag. Others queue up for autographs.

(Byrne, 1993: 43)

Sharing time with Peter Drucker really beats the book reading. It's the human contact feeling to share time with a famous person – like a conversation, not possible before.

(Participant in a satellite videoconference, May 3, 1994)

Introduction

Until recently, the management guru and fashion phenomenon received little serious attention from the academic community. The commentators who did pay attention to it took a dismissive tack, discrediting the gurus and the lack of rigor they brought to their research and taking relatively little interest in the phenomenon itself (Carroll, 1983; Hitt and Ireland, 1987; Thomas, 1989). The media, by contrast, have always provided a rich source of commentary. Prominent business magazines such as *Business Week*, *Fortune*, *The Economist*, *Success* and *Inc.* have all regularly run cover stories or features profiling a particular management guru or describing the latest management fashion or explaining the reasons behind the enormous appeal of the gurus and their business.

This chapter will draw upon both academic and media sources, primarily from North America and the U.K., to provide a comprehensive picture of what has been written to date about the management guru and management fashion phenomenon. The account is divided into four parts. The first part is primarily descriptive, providing information about the origins, definitions and scope of the phenomenon. This is followed by an assessment of what management gurus and management fashions have and have not achieved. The third part of the chapter examines four different approaches that have been developed in an attempt to explain the phenomenon. The chapter closes with a consideration of the relative merits and limitations of each of these explanatory approaches and, in light of these, lays out some parameters for a study that can make a constructive and novel contribution to this rapidly expanding literature.

Describing the phenomenon

The rise and rise of the management guru

According to *The Oxford English Dictionary*, the word "guru" originated in Sanskrit as an adjective meaning "weighty, grave, dignified" (1989: 964). An etymological link has also been made between guru and the Latin *"gravis"*. This is remarkable because its derivative, *"gravitas"*, was frequently used in connection with the nouns "actor" and *"auctoritas"*. The Latin expression *"gravis auctor"* (the important or true authority) also carries the same general sense of a guru as a person of influence who takes the initiative – in other words, a person who can "do" and have an effect on others. The word "guru" was used for the first time in the sense of teacher or spiritual guide in the Upanishads, a series of Hindu ancient commentaries on the sacred scriptures. The idea of a spiritual preceptor to guide one's study of religion and philosophy has been a constant theme in the religion of India since the most ancient times (*Encyclopedia of Religion*, 1987). Spiritual preceptors have appeared in many forms including the *rshi* ("seer"), the *muni* ("sage" or "silent one"), and later as *acarya, brahmana* and *swami*. However, the figure of the guru has most dramatically captured the attention of the West.

The term "guru" has undertaken an intriguing status passage as it has entered the English language (Jackson, 1996a). *The Oxford English Dictionary* (1989) notes that it is in general and trivial use to describe an "influential teacher", "mentor" and "pundit" (another Hindu word which refers to someone who is learned in Sanskrit and in philosophy, religion and jurisprudence). The dictionary cites numerous yet isolated references to the usage of the word guru since the British first made contact with the Indian subcontinent in the early seventeenth century. It was in the 1960s, however, with the counterculture's widespread engagement with Eastern mysticism led by the likes of Allen Ginsberg, Gary Snyder and Alan Watts, that the word entered popular everyday discourse (Roszak, 1969). Indeed, the dictionary cites a reference in 1967 from *The New Scientist* to Marshall McLuhan as one who "is (or is about to be turned into) one of those gurus whom the United States hungers for more than most nations" (*New Scientist*, 1967: 559).

In contemporary mediaspeak, the title "guru" is accorded to anyone who is recognized as having developed a distinctive level of expertise in one of a number of ever-expanding spheres of human endeavor. On a daily basis we are exposed through the mass media to "fitness gurus", "literary gurus", "investment gurus", "diet gurus", "computer gurus", and "personal growth gurus". We should not be surprised to find that the term appears to be applied indiscriminately and broadly because it has considerable appeal for journalistic discourse. For example, in acknowledging that gurudom has become a "crowded profession", *The Economist* (1994a) provided a somewhat tongue-in-cheek "Good Guru Guide" which features an unlikely collection of luminaries including George Soros, Jacques Derrida and Octavia Paz. The word's oral simplicity and internal rhyme further enhance its attractiveness. Peter Drucker has sourly observed, "I ascribe the popularity of this hideous word to its fitting more easily into a headline than its older synonym – charlatan" (cited in Clutterbuck and Crainer, 1990: 235). Moreover, compared to the drab scientism imbued in the term "expert", the word guru connotes a mystical dimension which implies that the expertise has been gained by other than conventional means and is, therefore, infinitely more interesting. Its links to the underground world of religious cults also lends the term a certain sinister power.

The ambiguous nature of the term "guru" enables the journalists who choose to use it to sit on the fence and suspend judgment. They can demonstrate that they are aware that this person deserves attention but should not necessarily be treated seriously. The term can also be applied to considerable derogatory effect when the journalist wishes to put the aspiring experts firmly in their place. Huczynski (1993a) notes that the term tends to be used pejoratively in the British press whereas in North America it is invariably good for consultants' business to be given "guru" status. The extrinsic ambivalence of the term "guru" makes the media as keen to apply the term, as the gurus they anoint are overtly, yet perhaps not entirely, reluctant to take on the guru mantle. Gurus are, therefore, to a certain extent, both beneficiaries and victims of the "media machine" that helps to create them.

The term "management guru" has only recently enjoyed common currency. The earliest references that I have come across in business journals occur in the mid-1980s. The *Financial Times* ran a series of articles under the title "The Guru Factor", which showcased a number of prominent American management thinkers (Dixon, 1986; Dodsworth, 1986; Lorenz, 1986). Since then the term has become the label of choice when journalists discuss particularly influential management commentators be they academics, consultants or practitioners. Perhaps mindful of the ambiguous and value-laden nature of the term, most academics have chosen to use alternative phrases like "popular management writer" or have focused on the "popular business bestsellers". However, a few writers (e.g. Abrahamson, 1996a; Clark and Salaman, 1996; Huczynski, 1993a; Jackson, 1996a) have recognized the significance of the popular term "guru" and, in doing so, are making it acceptable within academic discourse. In doing this we have acknowledged that the term has considerable resonance in the popular realm and therefore warrants some attention.

In the first full-scale academic study to look exclusively into the management guru phenomenon, Huczynski (1993a) observes that management guruship has largely been a North American phenomenon which emerged during the 1980s. Kennedy (1991) has somewhat wryly observed that, despite its Eastern origins, the guru phenomenon is virtually absent in the managerial thought of Japan and the Pacific Rim economies. More recently, Crainer (1998a) has pointed to the emergence of Asian gurus such as Kenichi Ohmae, Ikujiro Nonaka, Kam Hon Lee and W. Can Kim, who are distinguished by their low-key, cerebral styles and the spiritual orientation of their work. In the West, management gurus have not been nearly as successful in Europe as they have been in North America. In addition to the obvious language barrier, the cultural specificity of American management thinking does not translate as readily and can lead to resistance. American gurus have also been exposed to a measure of competition from a new breed of "Euroguru" such as Percy Barnevik, Sumantra Ghoshal, Arie de Geus and Manfred Kets de Vries (*Economist*, 1995a). Huczynski (1993a) notes that, in the United Kingdom, British managers have a strong tradition of learning from experience, which makes them less receptive to the "quick fix" solutions offered by outsiders. It is, therefore, perhaps not surprising that the only three internationally renowned gurus to have emerged from the U.K. – Edward de Bono, Charles Handy and Reg Revans – have all focused on encouraging managers to learn and think more creatively for themselves.

Huczynski (1993a) argues that "guru theory" is the latest in a series of management idea families that have worked their way through the Western management literature during the twentieth century. The earlier families of ideas include Bureaucracy, Scientific Management, Administrative Management, Human Relations and Neo-Human Relations. Huczynski argues that the "guru theory" label he uses to describe this most recent family of management ideas is useful, "since each guru idea relies for its authorization upon the individual who developed and popularized it" (1993a: 38). He also believes that the term "guru theory" aptly captures the desire, on the part of the gurus' followers, to find hidden or tacit knowledge and their willingness uncritically to carry out the guru's prescriptions.

Huczynski (1993a) distinguishes between three different types of gurus: "academic gurus", "consultant gurus" and "hero managers". The academic gurus are those who have a formal affiliation with an educational institution, invariably a business school, as exemplified by Henry Mintzberg, Rosabeth Moss Kantner, William Ouchi and Michael Porter. The consultant gurus are independent writers and advisers such as John Naisbitt, Tom Peters and Gifford Pinchot. Hero managers are those who are, or have been, practicing corporate leaders and are passing on the benefit of their experience. Some notable examples of these are Bill Gates, John Harvey-Jones, Lee Iacocca and Jack Welch.

The most common technique used to define gurus is to distinguish them from two other archetypes – the consultant and the academic. For example, Kennedy suggests that what separates management gurus from mere consultants is their "timing; originality; forcefulness; a gift for self-promotion and perhaps above all else, the ability to encapsulate memorably what others immediately recognize as true" (1991: xviii). On the grounds that it takes one to know one, the British guru John Humble lists the following six essential qualities of a guru: "integrative power, an extraordinary and intuitive sense of timing; longevity; international influence; missionary zeal; and an ability to listen" (Clutterbuck and Crainer, 1990: 236–237). The academic, typified as the bumbling, out-of-touch, unhelpful figure, is frequently used by gurus to demonstrate what they are not. Frederick Herzberg, for example, with thinly disguised venom, suggests that "you can tell whether someone is a guru by the degree of academic jealousy and hostility he engenders" (Clutterbuck and Crainer, 1990: 235). Similarly, Kenneth Blanchard, who brought the One-Minute Manager into everyday managerial parlance, points out that "academics tend to write for their own satisfaction which does not necessarily mean that managers will be prepared to listen" (cited in Dodsworth, 1986: 14). In a somewhat kindlier vein, Kennedy explains that "today's harsh demands of media and marketing combine to make it very difficult for the quiet thinker or teacher to achieve gurudom" (1991: xii).

While most gurus are always quick to distance themselves from being considered consultants and academics, they are, in true contemporary, Hollywood shrinking violet-style, usually reluctant to embrace guruhood. Robert Blake, co-creator with Jane Mouton of the managerial Grid, remarks, "I detest the word guru and feel that it puts an unprofessional stamp on things" (Clutterbuck and Crainer, 1990: 235). Despite their reticence, gurus are handsomely paid for their troubles. While it is difficult to obtain hard data, best estimates suggest that a management guru can expect anywhere from $20,000 to $40,000 per appearance and some 40 to 60 engagements per year (Bell, 1995). Those at the top of the heap command even more for an appearance – Peter Drucker ($50,000), Tom Peters ($60,000) – while Stephen Covey, taking his cue from Frank Sinatra and Liza Minnelli, "four walls the room", collecting 60 percent of the event's gross sales (McConville, 1994). Only retired public figures such as Margaret Thatcher, George Bush and Colin Powell plus a few select rock stars could expect to be better compensated for their efforts.

Given the guru's role in succinctly summarizing complex management ideas and reducing them to their essences, one can't help but be quietly amused by the arrival of a new genre of book which summarizes and translates the key ideas of the management gurus for an increasingly time-conscious and overtaxed yet curious workforce. The first of this genre was the *Makers of Management*, in which the lives and contributions of 29 "men and women who changed the business world" are reviewed

(Clutterbuck and Crainer, 1990). In the *Guide to the Management Gurus*, Carol Kennedy (1991) identifies 33 "real" gurus who have generated original, durable management thinking. Rowan Gibson selects 16 gurus in his book *Rethinking the Future* (1997). By contrast, in *The Guru Guide*, Boyett and Boyett identify 79 gurus from the 1980s and 1990s by reviewing bestseller lists and asking "friends, clients and associates to recommend people whom they thought had unique insights" (1998: viii). In the somewhat ludicrously titled book *Understanding Management Gurus in a Week*, Norton and Smith identify 56 gurus who were selected by "monitoring inquiries received by the Institute of Management's Information Centre, by trawling the views of Internet Surfers and by surveying some of the principal business and management schools in the U.K. to discover the major influences on current management teaching" (1998: 6).

In summary, there does not appear to be a hard and fast rule about what it takes to be a management guru, nor is there any real agreement as to how many management gurus there really are. We can conclude that guru status is a social creation. It is ordained in large part by media attention and implies current or, at least, relatively recent wide-ranging popularity and, by extension, influence among practitioners, consultants and academic audiences. Once achieved, however, there is no guarantee that guru status can be sustained. Ultimately, the most definitive we can be is to say that guruship is in the eyes of the follower.

Surfing management fashions

The corporate community's predilection for finding, adopting and then abruptly dropping the "latest and greatest" organizational improvement programs is a phenomenon that is widely recognized and frequently lambasted in everyday discourse at work and in the business media (Byrne, 1994; *Economist*, 1997, 2000; Farnham and Kover, 1996). New programs and initiatives that seize the corporate imagination on a wide-scale basis are regularly derided as "fads", "buzzwords", "flavors-of-the-month", "quick fixes" and "silver bullets". This tendency has perhaps been most succinctly captured in the term "fad surfing" or "the practice of riding the crest of the latest management panacea and then paddling out again just in time to ride the next one, always absorbing for managers and lucrative for consultants; frequently disastrous for organizations" (Shapiro, 1995: xiii). In its wake, fad surfing has left an extensive and impressive business lexicon which the media attempt to keep track of through the sporadic publication of glossaries (e.g. Chipman, 1993; Gordon, 1996) and dictionaries, most notably, *Business Speak*, the cover of which promises "4,000 business terms, buzzwords, acronyms and technical words: all you need to get ahead in Corporate America" (Schaaf and Kaeter, 1994).

Pascale (1990) estimated that over two dozen managerial techniques have waxed and waned between the 1950s and 1980s. Using the frequency of citations in the *New York Times*, the *Wall Street Journal* and *The Reader's Guide to Periodical Literature*, Pascale depicts the explosion in business fads to very good heuristic effect in a graph that I have seen being used by consultants as a selling piece to demonstrate that they are *au courant* with current organizational programs. Pascale identifies the following business fads, listed chronologically: Decision Trees; Managerial Grid; Satisficers/Dissatisficers; Theory X and Theory Y; Brainstorming; T-Group Training; Conglomeration; Theory Z; Management by Objectives; Diversification; Experience Curve; Strategic Business Units; Zero-Based Budgeting; Value Chain; Decentralization; Wellness; Quality Circles; Excellence; Restructuring; Portfolio Management; MBWA; Matrix; Kaiban; Intrapreneuring; Corporate Culture and One-Minute Managing. What is most remarkable about Pascale's analysis is that approximately half of these fashions have been spawned in the latter half of the 1980s. Business journalist John Byrne observes that "business fads are something of a necessary evil and have always been with us. What's different – and alarming – today is the sudden rise and fall of so many conflicting fads and how they influence the modern manager" (1986: 53).

The Institute of Personnel and Development, the U.K.'s largest HR/Personnel professional body, has listed "fads and fashions" over the period 1969 to 1994 and has noted a significant increase after 1990 especially (Institute of Personnel Development, 1994: 31). Grint (1997) has plotted an exponential rise in the number of articles (listed in *Business Periodicals on Disk*) regarding eight management fashions that have come to prominence between 1986 and 1995: Culture; Leadership; Business Process Reengineering; Outsourcing; Downsizing; Empowerment; TQM and Competencies. Plotting the rise and fall of five management fashions cited in the Wiso database between 1982 and 1995 (Quality Circles, Lean Production, Business Process Reengineering, Total Quality Management and Organizational Culture), Kieser (1997) has concluded that the cycles of management fashions are becoming not only shorter but their peaks are getting higher. Finally, Brickley et al. (1997) have noted a similar bell-shaped curve when plotting the percentage of published business articles mentioning eight management fashions between 1970 and 1996 (TQM, Benchmarking, JIT, Outsourcing, Reengineering, Activity Based Costing, Quality Circles and Economic Value Added). While it is clear that a direct link cannot be made between the number of citations of a particular program and its take-up by organizations and managers, these studies, even when we allow for the inflationary growth of media outlets, do give us some sense of the potential trajectory of influence that these techniques might have had on organizational thinking and practice.

There is a surprising paucity of data regarding the actual use of these management fashions. The primary source of data has come from Bain & Company, a global strategy consulting firm, who, in 1993, launched a multi-year research project to gather data about the usage and performance of management tools. Each year they interview senior managers and conduct literature searches to identify the 25 most "popular and pertinent" management tools. The 1994 survey found that the top ten most commonly used tools were: Mission Statements (94%); Customer Surveys (90%); Total Quality Management (76%); Benchmarking (72%); Reengineering (69%); Strategic Alliances (67%); Self-directed Teams (59%); Value Chain Analysis (27%); and Mass Customization (21%) (Harrar, 1994). The survey noted that there was a wide variety in the degrees of satisfaction that were ascribed to the tools by the executives that were surveyed. For example, while 31% were "extremely satisfied" with Mission Statements, 11% were "dissatisfied". Similarly, 22% were "extremely satisfied" while 13% were "dissatisfied" with Total Quality Management. In terms of the performance of the tools (defined by improved product development time, higher employee skills and morale, and expanded capacity for future growth), the following five were given the highest performance indexes on a five-point scale: Cycle Time Reduction (3.88), Reengineering (3.87); Self-directed Teams (3.84), Total Quality Management (3.81) and Strategic Alliances (3.79). Subsequent surveys have shown that companies are tending to take on more techniques. The average company used 12.7 of these tools in 1994 compared to 11.8 in 1993 (Micklethwait and Wooldridge, 1996: 17–18). The survey has also noted variation between the national averages in take-up of management tools, with Britain leading the way with an average of 13.7 tools compared to the U.S. (12.8), Japan (11.5) and France (13.7).

The rapid growth and turnover of management fashions have been supported and actively promoted by an extensive network of global and local consultants. As Caulkin has observed, the economic model of consulting "dovetails effortlessly in the larger management fashion production line which ties together consultancy, business schools and the business press in an eye-wateringly productive chain" (1997: 33). In 1993, *Consulting News* estimated that some 80,000 consultants ranging from large and single operator businesses sold $17 billion in advice which was 10 percent more than the previous year (Byrne, 1994). The world's largest consulting firm, Andersen Consulting, was growing annually at a rate of 20 percent during the 1990s and in 1995 alone, added 8,000 new staff worldwide (Kennedy, 1996). Byrne has likened this spectacular growth to a

> self-inflating bubble: consultants beget more consulting as they fuel the marketplace with new ideas and management fads. The incantations of these necromancers can make managers worry that their rivals have gotten hold of something more powerfully new – so they had better buy a little corporate juju of their own.
>
> (Byrne, 1994: 61)

The backlash

In evaluating the contribution that management gurus and the fashions they spawn have made to managerial practice, commentators from both the academic and journalistic communities have invariably been negative in their judgments. The most vitriolic critics have given the gurus' work a number of singularly unflattering labels such as "intellectual wallpaper", "business pornography", "shameless narcissism", "behavioral fast food" and "commonsensical in the extreme". The critical offensive has tended to focus on three main concerns: the intellectually impoverished quality of the gurus' thinking, the gap between the promise and practice when the gurus' ideas are implemented, and the relatively poor manner in which organizations have used these ideas.

Many critics have pointed to the tendency of the gurus to oversimplify what, in their minds, is an increasingly complex business reality. In particular, there is a predisposition for each new approach to provide one single answer. For example, in a searing attack on the "one-minute book" genre, Zilbergeld remarks that, "given the American desire for simple solutions to complex problems, it should come as no surprise that there is a receptive audience for books claiming that difficult goals can be reached in one minute" (1984: 6). In a similar vein, Pascale laments that an unintended consequence of the mass marketing of management techniques has been that it has fostered superficiality to the point that "it has become professionally legitimate in the United States to accept and utilize ideas without an in-depth grasp of their underlying foundation, and without the commitment necessary to sustain them" (1990: 19–20). More recently, Argyris (2000) has weighed into the fray with his book, *Flawed Advice*. In the book he argues that most of the advice given by management gurus and consultants is "unactionable" simply because it has too many abstract claims, inconsistencies and logical gaps to be useful to managers as a basis for concrete actions in concrete settings.

Critics from the academic realm have been particularly critical of the rigor and quality of the research upon which the gurus base their findings. Much of the information contained in gurus' texts stems from the direct experiences and observations of the writer – the bestsellers are unapologetically subjective and anecdotal in their approach. As Pierce and Newstrom observe, "the authors . . . are able to proclaim as sound management principles virtually anything that is intuitively acceptable to their publisher and readers" (1990: 6). In their review of Naisbitt's *Megatrends* (1984), Neal and Groat observed that "solid facts as Naisbitt presents them may more appropriately be viewed as a personal exercise in the 'social construction of reality'. The result is a strange but intriguing mixture of objectivity and advocacy" (Neal and Groat, 1984: 121). Similarly, Maidique describes *In Search of Excellence* as a "potpourri of loosely interconnected, and often redundant, vignettes in search of a framework" (1983: 156). Cummings concludes that, overall, "these books offer very little, if anything in the way of generalizable knowledge about successful organizational practice" (Pierce and Newstrom, 1990: 338).

Researchers writing from an explicitly critical management perspective have also joined the swelling ranks of critics. Most pointedly, Burrell has attacked what he ingeniously calls "Heathrow Organization Theory" (i.e. that which is derived from popular management books) for its "crude pragmatism" and "philosophical vacuity" (1989: 307). It is in these books that one finds the most glaring examples of what Burrell describes as the "absent center" in management theory. That is, "a neglect of philosophically informed thinking about one's own beliefs" (1989: 307). Burrell suggests that, because most mid-Atlantic management theorists tend to think with their beliefs rather than about their beliefs, they are offering only a basic pragmatism that is essentially premodernist. Ironically, however, he predicts that the gurus will move contemporary management theory rapidly from its premodernist phase to a postmodernist phase because "consultants like Rosabeth Kantner and Tom Peters have recognized the new zeitgeist and its emphasis on appearance, image and superficiality" (1989: 310).

In addition to attacking the gurus' poorly developed philosophies, a number of academic commentators have accused them of working within a political vacuum. Wood observes that "perhaps the biggest divide between the academic and the 'consultancy' books over recent decades is the former's explicit concern with power and authority and the latter's relative neglect of them and/or tendency to take them for granted" (1989: 380). Ray (1986) and Wilmott (1993) have illuminated the darker side of the corporate culture movement promoted by many management gurus. They note that, by appealing to the sentiments and emotions of their employees, executives have been able to exert a more subtle and potentially more debilitating form of control by ensnaring their employees in a hegemonic system which espouses autonomy or empowerment but discourages multiple values and active dissent. A thriving cottage industry of politically informed critiques has been developed in reaction to specific organizational improvement programs such as Core Competencies (Brewis, 1996; Du Gay et al., 1996), Human Resource Management (Legge, 1995; Townley, 1995) and TQM (Rippin, 1994; Wilkinson and Wilmott, 1995).

A number of critics have also focused their attention upon the performance gap between what is promised by the management guru and what actually happens when the management fashion that he or she is proposing is implemented. Perhaps the best-known instance of this gap was the subsequent performance of many of the companies that were singled out by Peters and Waterman for their "excellence". Five years after the publication of *In Search of Excellence*, two-thirds of the 43 companies that had demonstrated superiority for at least 20 years prior had slipped, expired or were in serious difficulty (Pascale, 1990). A number of academic studies added fuel to the fire by discrediting the empirical data that were used in the book. For example, Johnson et al. (1985) expressed concern that the six performance indices used by Peters and Waterman measure only a firm's financial performance whereas the return to shareholders is a much truer measure of "excellence".

While Peters and Waterman's work clearly attracted considerable academic scrutiny, there is a remarkable dearth of studies that have tried to assess to what extent various management fashions have actually been able to deliver on their economic promises. Several consultant-sponsored studies have concluded that, in the majority of instances, they do not deliver at all. For example, a 1992 survey conducted by Arthur D. Little found that, of 500 American companies studied, only one-third believed that programs such as Total Quality Management (TQM) had had any significant impact on their organization's bottom line (Furlong, 1994). A 1993 survey administered by A.T. Kearney revealed that only 20 percent of 100 British firms claimed that their adoption of an organizational improvement program had yielded any tangible financial results (Furlong, 1994). Nohria and Berkley (1994) polled managers at nearly 100 companies on more than 21 different programs and found 75 percent of them to be unhappy with the results they had generated in their organizations. In their 1995 survey of 787 companies around the world, Bain & Company found that, while 72 percent of managers believed that companies who use the right tools are more likely to succeed, 70 percent of them said that the tools promise more than they deliver (Micklethwait and Wooldridge, 1996). The 1999 survey revealed a general decline in the use of tools which many of the survey participants accounted for by pointing to the universal preoccupation with the new economy and the rise of the Internet (*Economist*, 2000).

These surveys are by no means conclusive but they appear to confirm the conventional wisdom that management fashions generally fail to live up to their expectations. While many critics cheerfully place the blame for this failure at the gurus' feet, a number of others are more inclined to explain the failure by pointing to how organizations have implemented these ideas. For example, Byrne observes that "there is nothing inherently wrong with any of these ideas. What's wrong is that too many companies use them as gimmicks to evade the basic challenges they face" (1986: 53). Likewise, Pascale writes, "overwhelmingly, companies apply them in a piecemeal fashion and shift from one to the another too frequently" (1990: 18).

The tendency to embrace each new bestselling theory wholesale is fittingly described by McGill (1988) as the product of a "Management-Club-of-the-Month" mentality, which he believes is widespread among America's corporate elite. Tom Peters himself is critical of the organizations that have followed him. In an interview he is quoted to have said that

> the difference today is that middle management and even the rank-and-file have read the books. They're committed and enthusiastic about

the programs, but they have come to the realization that the senior level really hasn't bought into it and doesn't want to give up control.

(Stuller, 1992: 21)

Kilmann has likened the search by companies for the organizational "quick fix" to the quest for the Holy Grail. He argues that "single approaches are discarded because they have not been given a fair test", concluding, "it's time to stop perpetuating the myth of simplicity" (1984: 24). To help managers in their quest, Nirenberg (1997) has developed an annotated compendium of 100 management techniques or "power tools".

Not only are companies shifting too quickly from one idea to another but also, in many cases, their strategy has been to hedge their bets by taking on several innovations simultaneously. Edward Lawler, a venerable management guru in his own right, graphically likens this approach to a "gigantic buffet at Sunday brunch" from which the organizations take enormous helpings and end up with "a bad case of indigestion" (cited in Stuller, 1992: 22). When companies pursue this eclectic approach to organizational change, the effectiveness of the individual techniques is undermined because of the organization's inability to get its employees to remain focused over a sufficiently long period. In some instances, these techniques may be incompatible or even contradictory. For example, employees in many organizations have been challenged with reconciling their organization's "customer service" and "downsizing" strategies.

Rigby (1993) has not only expressed concerns about the effectiveness of business fads to meet their stated objectives but has also voiced some strong objections based on the harm that they can cause in organizations. First, he argues that they create unrealistic expectations that inevitably lead to disappointment and the lowering of morale. Second, he says, fads create dangerous shortages of some strategic elements and toxic overdoses of others. Third, they can be internally divisive. In selecting one approach over another, certain departments, by virtue of their function within the organization, will be deemed winners and others losers. Fourth, because fads tend to be programmatic and imposed externally and top-down within the organization, they have an in-built tendency to rob employees of their own initiative. Finally, and worst of all in Rigby's estimation, is the fact that fads undermine a basic tenet of strategy – by simply copying what other organizations are doing, organizations lose a basic source of distinction and, therefore, weaken their competitive advantage within their marketplace.

While the assessment of the management guru and fashion phenomenon has been largely negative, a few commentators have been more positive in their evaluation of its contribution to managerial thought and practice. For example, while critical of the scientific validity of the gurus' work, Maidique (1983) argues that academics have a lot to learn from writers such as Peters and Waterman. Unlike many academics, they demonstrate the importance of being in touch with business realities and priorities. Moreover, they write in such a way that they "engage the reader in the same way they were engaged by their subjects" (Maidique, 1983: 156). In his attack on Thomas's scathing critique of popular management theory or "One-Minute Education" (Thomas, A.B., 1989), Cunningham (1989) castigates academics in general for imposing a false and unhelpful dichotomy between academic and popular texts. By lumping work into one of these two categories, the "59-Second Academics" automatically prejudge the merit of the work and deny the possibility that any work that is popular is worthy of consideration. This, in Cunningham's mind, is a serious abrogation of their duty as management researchers.

Maidique (1983) argues that the message of organizational and managerial revival heralded by these new management thinkers should not be ignored by academia but synthesized into a revitalized academic thrust. Newstrom and Pierce (1989) credit the gurus with the excitement and enthusiasm for organizational change that their bestsellers have generated. They are particularly interested in the role gurus can play as "catalysts" in the further development of sound management philosophies and practices. To insure that this role is properly served, they advocate that managers read widely from both the traditional academic and the nontraditional management literature. They encourage "cautious consumption" of the popular books, urging readers to be critical of the authors' objectivity, validity and reliability. Newstrom and Pierce argue that, if the gurus are read properly, they can make an important contribution to a manager's education.

A few business media commentators have also pointed to the positive contributions that have been made by gurus. Byrne, for example, suggests that "a little faddishness may be helpful because it makes managers think about new ways to do their jobs better" (1986: 61). Certainly, the number of letters that appeared in the weeks following both of his *Business Week* cover stories from managers who were indignantly defending the gurus and fads that he had attacked would lend support to this view. *The Economist* has defended the gurus' work on the grounds that it encourages managers to think about change and to look at what other companies are doing, surmising that "the only thing worse than slavishly following management theory is ignoring it completely" (1994b: 18). Micklethwait and Wooldridge take an "it could be worse" line in their defense of management gurus by pointing out that management theory is still a young discipline and that, "rather than fretting about management theory's excesses, we should be grateful that its adolescence has not been more harmful" (1996: 369).

Camerer and Knez argue that academics have misunderstood the real function that management fashions play for organizations. Taking TQM as their example, they propose that it "solves a coordination problem, moving a firm stuck at a marginally profitable equilibrium to a better equilibrium" (1996: 108). The features of ideas like TQM that are so offensive to academics (i.e. too simple, attention-getting) are the very qualities that executives prize in their quest to get as many of their employees working together on a common cause. According to Camerer and Knez, the fact that management fashions like TQM are used only temporarily and abandoned after a few years need not prove that they are worthless, because, "if the job of TQM is coordinating change then, once the job is done the terminology becomes useless and should make way for a new 'fad'" (1996: 110).

While management fashions have come and gone with reasonably monotonous regularity, there has, since the mid-1990s, been a growing backlash against the management guru and fashion phenomenon. Ironically, this backlash is starting to resemble another management fashion, creating a substantial niche market for a number of anti-guru bestsellers such as *The Witch Doctors* (Micklethwait and Wooldridge, 1996), *Fad Surfing in the Boardroom* (Shapiro, 1995), *Dangerous Company* (O'Shea and Madigan, 1997), *Management Redeemed* (Hilmer and Donaldson, 1996), *Consulting Demons* (Pinault, 2000) and the intriguingly titled, yet ultimately disappointing lampoon, *The Book that's Sweeping America* authored by the "world's #1 business guru" Stephen Michael Peter Thomas (Butman, 1997). The "Consultant Debunking Unit", established by the magazine *Fast Company*, vividly captures and reflects the anti-guru tenor of a new breed of self-sufficient executives (*Fast Company*, 1997). Perhaps most telling of all is Tom Peters' well-publicized capitulation to Dilbert, the satirical cartoon character created by Scott Adams as America's number one management guru (Fisher, 1997).

How do we make sense of this apparent paradox between the continued expansion and success of management gurus and management fashions in the face of a substantial and escalating wave of criticism? Characterizing this conundrum as "the great consultancy cop-out", Caulkin observes that, "of all the paradoxes of the modern business world, perhaps the most remarkable and least satisfactorily explained is the rise and rise of the management consultant" (1997: 32). Burgoyne and Reynolds have probably come closest to advancing a satisfactory explanation. Referring to the management learning industry in general, they argue that

> It is a problem-based area of activity, rather than a solution-based one. Some activities, such as AIDS research and treatment, exist because there is a problem. Others, perhaps like the mobile phone and fax machine industries and markets, exist because there is a solution. There is much to be said for the argument that management learning is a problem-generated (rather than a solution-generated) area of activity. This makes sense not only of the coexistence of growth and criticism in the field, but also of the great variety of approaches and methods used in management education and development.
>
> (Burgoyne and Reynolds, 1997: 7)

This intriguing explanation helpfully reorients our attention away from a general preoccupation with assessing whether or not management gurus and management fashions actually work to a much more compelling question which dwells on problem rather than solution generation. Namely, why do we need them? This is the question to which we now turn.

Emerging explanatory accounts

Paralleling the popular media backlash has been a strong surge in interest on the part of academic researchers in the management guru and fashion phenomenon. A growing number of researchers from North America, Europe and Australasia have begun to look at the phenomenon as an important area of inquiry that deserves serious and sustained attention (Abrahamson, 1996a; Clark and Salaman, 1996; Furusten, 1999; Grint, 1997; Jackson, 1996b; Kieser, 1997; Ramsay, 1996; Spell, 2000). As yet, the research effort is at an exploratory and fragmented stage in its evolution but it has moved beyond basic description to the beginnings of attempts to advance broad explanations for the management guru and fashion phenomenon. Grint (1997) has helpfully identified five types of approaches that have been developed to explain the management fashion phenomenon: the Rational Approach, the Structural Approach; the Distancing Approach, the Institutional Approach and the Charismatic Approach. These he places on a grid that is formed by two sets of axes. The first axis is divided into two sections based on whether the main emphasis of the explanatory account lies with the logic of the approach or with its emotional qualities. The second axis is divided into two sections based on whether the accounts are rooted in an internalist approach, which focuses on ideas or forces within the individual, or in an externalist approach, which focuses upon the significance of exogenous or structural forces. Grint places the Institutional Approach in the center of this grid. However, I would contend that, because it is difficult to separate out work that is conducted using the Institutional Approach from work that uses the Distancing Approach, it makes sense to

	INTERNALIST	**EXTERNALIST**
LOGIC	Rational	Structural
EMOTION	Charismatic	Institutional/Distancing

Figure 2.1 The four approaches to explaining management gurus and management fashions

Source: Adapted from Grint (1997)

combine this body of work and to place it in the externalist/emotional quadrant as depicted in Figure 2.1.

The Rational Approach

The Rational Approach suggests that the primary reason why there are management fashions is precisely because they work. In a highly competitive and turbulent environment, organizations will seek out new ideas in order to survive. Those that select the right ideas, survive; those that don't, fall by the way. For example, Brickley et al. observe,

> As a growing number of large, once-successful companies began to lose opportunities to more flexible and, in some cases, overseas competitors, the opportunity costs of having unresponsive organizations began to show up in declining shareholder returns. This in turn created a broad-based demand for management prescriptions that would enable companies to respond more effectively to the new environment.
>
> (Brickley et al., 1997: 29)

Along the same lines, Huczynski (1993a) argues that the major reason why gurus have been so successful is that they have closely matched their ideas with the needs of individual managers. Gurus have acknowledged and responded to the manager's need for a measure of predictability in an increasingly uncertain world. The gurus provide this by helping the manager to make sense of his or her business environment.

The primary reason attributed by the media for the surge in interest in management gurus and fashions is America's economic context at the end of the 1970s. At that time, Americans became conscious of the threat posed to their well-established position of economic dominance by their international competitors, particularly Japan. The Japanese threat was well documented in Richard Tanner Pascale and Anthony Athos's *The Art of Japanese Management* (1981) and William Ouchi's *Theory Z* (1981). Both authors spoke reverentially of the Japanese approach to management and urged American managers to learn from their competitors. Increased exposure to international competition put tremendous pressure upon American corporations and their managers to respond constructively and quickly. This pressure spurred not only a demand for new and readily implementable management approaches but also a hunger for American success stories. Two consultants, Tom Peters and Robert Waterman, responded accordingly with their book *In Search of Excellence* (1982). The book became America's bestseller in 1982, selling 1.2 million books. Despite being largely reviled by the academic community, it provided a series of entertaining and inspiring case studies of American companies that had thrived in the face of foreign competition. As Freeman observed,

> After the anti-business era of the late 1960's and early 1970's, after
> the recession-shocked later 1970's, after being bullied by Japanophiles,
> after a decade of finger pointing by management experts – managers
> were dead ready for a positive message and simple answers. They were
> primed to soak up the gospel of made-in-America excellence.
>
> (Freeman, 1985: 348)

The enormous scale of the sales of *In Search of Excellence* and Lee Iaccoca's
autobiography (Iacocca and Novak, 1984) indicates that they were not just
required reading for senior executives but also for the general public. As
William Shinker, publisher of Harper & Row's trade division comments,
"whenever in book publishing you can tap into anxiety, the chances are you
will have a book that sells very well and could be a bestseller" (Knowlton,
1989:102). It is this anxiety that was in large part responsible for the
tremendous success of Howard Ruff's *How to Prosper during the Coming Bad
Years* (1979), Douglas Casey's *Crisis in Investing* (1983) and Ravi Batra's
Surviving The Great Depression of the 1990's (1988), all worthy protagonists
in what John Kenneth Galbraith has described as the publishing industry's
"cottage industry in predicting disaster" (Huczynski, 1993a: 40).

The changing demographic profile of the American population has
also served to inflate the market for business and management media. The
well-educated professional segment of society has expanded in recent years.
In particular, an increasing proportion of formally educated individuals
come from the management discipline. More than 75,000 students are
awarded MBAs every year in America, which is 15 times the total awarded
in 1960 (Micklethwait and Wooldridge, 1996). Their book-based training
has insured their continued reliance on and enthusiasm for management
and business books long after they graduate.

The Structural Approach

A number of commentators have highlighted the importance of the socioeconomic, political and cultural contexts within which management
theories and ideas emerge and become widely adopted. In this respect, the
success of a new idea or theory is determined, in large part, by how well it
meshes with the material needs of managers and their organizations at a
particular point in time and the prevailing political environment, cultural
norms and expectations. This approach endeavors to explain the adoption
of management fashions as a cumulative process by which management
alters its control strategies to suit the conditions.

With respect to the influence of the socioeconomic context, Barley and
Kunda's (1992) paper stands out as a landmark study. Their extensive
historical analysis suggests that, since the 1870s, American managerial
discourse has been elaborated in waves or "surges" that have alternated
between "rational rhetorics" (which state that work processes can be

formalized and rationalized to optimize labor productivity) and "normative rhetorics" (which state that employees can be rendered more productive by shaping their thoughts and capitalizing on their emotions). They propose that these surges of innovative discourse are rooted in cultural antinomies that are fundamental to all Western industrial societies, namely, the oppositions between mechanistic and organic solidarity and between communalism and individualism. This pattern challenges the prevailing assumption that American managerial discourse has moved progressively from coercive to rational and, ultimately, to normative rhetorics of control (Bendix, 1956; Jacoby, 1991; Wren, 1972). Barley and Kunda show that the timing of each new wave roughly parallels the broad cycles of economic expansion and contraction circumscribed by the students of long waves (Kondratieff, 1935; Rostow, 1978).

Building on this work, Abrahamson (1997) identifies five different types of "employee–management rhetorics" that have swept through U.S. managerial discourse over the last century: Welfare Work, Scientific Management, Human Relations/Personnel Management, Systems Rationalism, and Culture/Quality rhetorics. Using a similar historical timeframe, he examined two competing theses which, when tested empirically, were found to be complementary. The "performance-gap" thesis, which Barley and Kunda (1992) rejected in their study, states that the popularity of rhetorics that promise to narrow performance gaps fluctuates with the magnitude of these gaps across organizations. The "pendulum thesis" advanced by Barley and Kunda, on the other hand, predicts that the popularity of rhetorics relates to the upswings and downswings in long waves of macroeconomic activity.

In addition to the socioeconomic context, the changing political context has also been seen as an important determinant in shaping what management fashions become popular at a certain time. Closely associated with the threat of international competition in the 1980s was a marked change in America's political and cultural mood. The Reagan era was characterized by a renewed commitment to the entrepreneurial values that had supposedly built the nation and a considerably more positive interest in business and the world of commerce. The "business decade" of the 1980s stood in stark contrast to earlier decades. As Erwin A. Glikes, the president and publisher of *The Free Press*, suggests,

> the role of the corporation in American life was underestimated and undervalued for more than fifty years. It played the villain in the melodrama that American social analysts promulgated to describe what they thought was social and economic reality in America.
> (Cited in Knowlton, 1989: 102)

He adds, "bestsellers may never be the most thoughtful books on a subject, but when it comes to business, they offer convincing evidence that the American dream still casts a spell over the reading public" (1989: 103).

A similar change in mood developed in Britain during the Thatcher era in a nation where the manager had always been attributed an even lower, non-professional status (Watson, 1986). Guest (1990) has suggested that the growth of the human resource management (HRM) fashion in the United Kingdom during the 1980s had much to do with the changing economic and political climate that saw a tendency for policy-makers and corporate captains to look to the United States as a model of good practice. Ironically, because HRM derives much of its fundamental appeal from its alignment with core American values such as individualism, optimism, leadership and the American Dream, Guest suggests it would, inevitably, only ever enjoy limited success in the U.K. While the appeal of HRM may have waned, a number of writers have shown how guru theory, in general, with its clarion call for new, entrepreneurial, anti-bureaucratic forms of organizational administration, resonates powerfully with the enterprise culture fostered during the Reagan and Thatcher eras and continues to be the dominant ethos of the Clinton and Blair administrations (Du Gay and Salaman, 1992; Rose, 1991; *New Statesman*, 1996).

Thrift (1997) has described how major structural changes in the world economy such as the deregulation of financial markets; the exponential growth of information; the growth of a more differentiated production–consumption nexus; and a general speed-up in transportation and communications have all contributed to the rise of a new era of capitalism which he dubs "soft capitalism". A critical element in this transition has been the development and dissemination of a new hegemonic managerial discourse which is "changing the world economy as much as the changing shape of the world economy is changing itself" (Thrift, 1997: 36). Broadly, the new managerial discourse stresses the following themes: the fast-paced changes and uncertainty of the external environment; the need for organizations continually to learn to adapt by being constantly flexible and always in action; challenges to existing knowledge forms; and the creation of organizations that are made up of willing and willed subjects. According to Thrift, the propagation of this discourse has been made possible by the explosive growth in "agents" responsible for its spread across the globe, including management gurus, consultants, business schools, and the business media which form an increasingly powerful "circuit of capital" that has only been existence since the 1960s. This self-organizing circuit is responsible for the production and distribution of managerial knowledge to managers. Thrift notes that, "as it has grown, so have its appetites. It now has a constant and voracious need for new knowledge" (1997: 40). In the same vein, Gee et al. have collectively described the works of gurus as "fast capitalist texts" which "seek to attend as textual midwives at the birth of the new work order" (1996: 24) characterized by heavy competition, privatization, deregulation and customization.

Kleiner (1992) has elaborated on the relationship between the cultural context of the 1980s and the rise of the management gurus. He contends that gurus have actively promoted a "culture of intervention", which is a predominant theme in the contemporary corporate culture of America's large corporations. Those who promote the "culture of intervention" advocate that organizations, like people, can be transformed and perfected through managed social change. Many gurus trace their roots back to the counter-culture movement of the 1960s. The unit of social change may have changed (i.e. from the community to the corporation), but the processes are essentially the same. From his numerous interviews, Kleiner notes:

> A large number of change agents, at one time or another, have dabbled in performance – usually acting or music. And nearly all, including the quality people, have countercultural roots: time spent at an underground newspaper, a Peace Corps outpost, a community organizing office, an EST training centre, or an ashram. Most keep their past hidden from clients, but credit that same past as the source of insights on which they base their livelihood today.
>
> (Kleiner, 1992: 40)

The Institutional/Distancing Approach

The Institutional Approach draws on theory that is concerned with the forces of institutionalization found outside the organization and the internal processes of institutionalization (Burgoyne and Jackson, 1997; Meyer and Scott, 1983; Powell and DiMaggio, 1991). It suggests that organizational decision-makers, especially under conditions of uncertainty and information overload, are forced into taking action that resembles the lead by others in the field. Researchers adopting this approach are, therefore, primarily concerned with "bandwagons" which are diffusion processes "whereby organizations adopt an innovation, not because of their individual assessments of the innovation's efficiency or returns, but because of a bandwagon pressure caused by the sheer number of organizations that have already adopted this innovation" (Abrahamson and Rosenkopf, 1993: 488). Bandwagon pressures take one of two forms: "institutional" pressures, which occur because non-adopters fear appearing different from many adopters, and "competitive" pressures that occur because non-adopters fear below-average performance if many competitors profit from adopting. Both pressures can prove to be highly persuasive, generating strong mimetic behavior and creating isomorphic tendencies within and across specific institutional fields. Strang and Macy (1999) have taken this work further by building a computational model of adaptive emulation which combines arguments about organizational decision-making and institutional mimicry. Running experiments with this model, they show that it is empirically plausible for innovations to be adopted on a wide scale even if they are entirely worthless. Moreover, with the increased use of competitive benchmarking and external consultants, they predict the continued amplification of faddish cycles as firms adopt and abandon "hot" organizational innovations.

Researchers who have chosen to make institutionalization a key motive in explaining the creation, dissemination and adoption of new management programs have tended to utilize the metaphor of the market to organize their accounts. Viewed through the lens of the market, the process is conceptualized as a relatively simple supply-and-demand model by which management ideas, theories and techniques are developed by groups of suppliers and then consumed by a largely undifferentiated group of manager consumers (Alvesson, 1990; Beaumont, 1985; Huczynski, 1993b; Jackson, 1994a; Krell, 1981). In fusing this market metaphor with the equally powerful metaphor of fashion, Abrahamson (1996a) has presented the most comprehensive, and arguably most influential, attempt to conceptualize the business fad phenomenon to date. His model is presented to help scholars better understand the dynamics of "management fashion" which he defines as "a relatively transitory collective belief, disseminated by management fashion setters, that a management technique leads to rational management progress" (Abrahamson, 1996a: 257). These management fashion-setters, identified as consulting firms, management gurus, business mass-media publications and business schools, are characterized as being in a "race" to sense managers' emergent collective preferences for new techniques, to develop rhetorics that describe these techniques, and to disseminate these rhetorics back to managers and organizational stakeholders. Rhetorics, according to Abrahamson, "must not only create the belief that the techniques they champion are rational, but also that they are at the forefront of management progress" (1996a: 268).

Empirical research inspired by the Institutional Approach has tended to take one of three thrusts. First, it has attempted to track and model the diffusion of selected management fashions. For example, Alvarez (1991) has, with an analytical framework that combines neo-institutional theory and the sociology of knowledge, examined the diffusion and reception of the idea of entrepreneurship in the 1980s in three countries: Britain, Mexico and Spain. In their research into three consultant-driven approaches to organizational improvement – Management by Objectives; Organization Development; and Total Quality Management – Gill and Whittle (1993) have identified an "organizational life-cycle" for management ideas. Using a 40-year "panacea cycle", they plotted the relative progress of each of these approaches along a bell-shaped curve that commences with a "birth" stage in which the guru writes a seminal book; then moves to "adolescence" in which consultants and senior managers promote a packaged intervention; to "maturity" during which the approach becomes routinized/ bureaucratized by consultants and internal human resources staff; and then, finally, to "decline", at which point the costs exceed apparent benefits and a new approach is adopted. In their extensive study of the Quality Circle fashion, Abrahamson and Fairchild found that it had a low-popularity latency period that was followed by a wave-like, ephemeral popularity curve. In addition they noted that "emotionally charged, enthusiastic, and unreasoned discourse characterized the upswing of the Quality Circle wave, whereas more reasoned, unemotional, and qualified discourse characterized its downswing, evidencing a pattern of superstitious collective learning" (Abrahamson and Fairchild, 1999: 708).

A second thrust of the institutional research has attempted to shed some light on the dynamics and relationships between various management fashion-setter groups. Diffusion theorists have traditionally assumed that knowledge flows primarily from the academy to the field. However, a study of academic- and practitioner-oriented discourse around the topic of organizational culture revealed that, while the discourses were initially quite distinct, over time, the academics appear to have moved toward the practitioners' point of view (Barley et al., 1988). Similarly, Huczynski (1994) has highlighted the gatekeeping role that business school faculty plays in selecting which popular ideas the students should be exposed to. He tentatively suggests that the ease of teaching and the readily apparent possession of a valuable truth were the two most important considerations.

A number of writers have highlighted the popular press as another key management fashion-setting group. For example, Chen and Meindl (1991) have examined the business media's role in the social construction of the public image of hero managers like Donald Burr of the People Express airline. Specifically, they allude to the role the media play in determining what issues are important, setting the agenda for what the public thinks about, and reinforcing or changing existing beliefs and cultivating perceptions of the nature of social reality. Alvarez and Mazza (2000) have argued that the popular press is a primary factor in diffusing and legitimizing management fads. Their empirical study of the diffusion of the Human Resource Management movement in several Italian newspapers in the last decade has lent some support to their argument that the popular press not only provides management theories and practices with social legitimacy, but also performs some tasks associated with the production of management fads. Elaborating on the fashion metaphor they conclude that while the academic press diffuses management theories and practices as "haute couture", the popular press works the "prêt-à-porter" side. Evidence provided by Spell (2000) suggests that for some management fashions (i.e. Benchmarks and Pay-for-Performance plans) the popular business press may have led the way while for others (i.e. Quality Circles or Peer Review), the reverse was true. He does acknowledge that the relatively longer production cycles associated with academic publishing may have an important bearing on this lag phenomenon.

The book publisher's intermediary role in the diffusion of ideas (Coser et al., 1982) has also been singled out as an important management fashion-setter (Byrne, 1986; Clark and Greatbatch, 1999; Freeman, 1985; Furusten,

1999; Pierce and Newstrom, 1990; Tirbutt, 1989). In accounting for the rapid explosion in the business book market, these writers have noted several characteristics that distinguish contemporary from older business books. The current crop of books are not only more optimistic in their outlook than their predecessors, but they use non-theoretical language, providing managers with what appears to be an easy cure for their organizational woes and a clearly marked pathway toward personal success. Furthermore, the new books are considerably easier to read. Freeman singles out Blanchard and Johnson's enormously popular book *The One Minute Manager* (1983) as a prime specimen of high readability using a scoring system developed by Flesch (1974). The book is full of short sentences, words with few syllables, personal pronouns, and simulated dialogue that enable the typical manager to read it in less than an hour. Told in the form of a fable, the book stood in stark contrast to the relatively sterile format of the traditional management texts.

Contemporary business bestsellers tend not to be fundamentally critical of management or business. Earlier management bestsellers such as *The Organization Man* (Whyte, 1957), *The Peter Principle* (Peter and Hull, 1969) and *Parkinson's Law* (Parkinson, 1957) were satirical in tone, scathingly critical of the corporate status quo and very much in keeping with the predominantly anti-business rhetorical tone of their time. The 1980s bestsellers, by contrast, were more celebratory, stressing the central role that business and industry have to play in maintaining the nation's wealth and global standing and the important contribution that managers make in sustaining this. While business books have been an important component of the management fashion industry, their influence should not be exaggerated. As Thomas (1989) has noted, it would be naive to equate the widespread purchase of any popular management text such as *In Search of Excellence* or *The One-Minute Manager* with either widespread reading, common interpretation, or indeed any influence on the reader's beliefs or behavior. Research by the Management Training Partnership in the U.K. found that 75 percent of the personnel directors that they surveyed bought at least four management books a year. However, only one in five actually read them (Crainer, 1996a: xiv).

A third and considerably less well-developed thrust in institutional research has attempted to examine the processes of idea diffusion within the organization. Specifically, the kinds of questions that are asked in this vein include the following: Who is responsible for introducing new performance improvement programs into the organization? How are the concepts disseminated? Is there a similar cycle of pioneering acceptance, mass application and gradual decline within organizations as there is among organizations? What are the patterns of acceptance of and resistance to new programs? Three studies illustrate potentially useful lines of inquiry for the comparatively underdeveloped intra-organizational diffusion research. In his study of the internal mobilization processes within the 62 "excellent" companies identified by Peters and Waterman (1982), Soeters discovered some strong similarities with the mobilization of "social movements" which he defines as "groups of people who unite or at least interact with one another on the basis of some kind of dissatisfaction or strain" (Soeters, 1986: 303). Repenning (1996) has attempted to model the adoption and use of a program using an explicit disequilibrium perspective that encompasses interactions between many organizational levels within the firm. When simulated, the resulting model suggested that the introduction of an improvement program in an environment of decentralized decision-making might result in unexpected outcomes which, if misinterpreted, may induce actions that result in the demise of an otherwise successful improvement program. Finally, Knights and McCabe (1998b) have observed from their study of bank employees working under a Business Process Reengineering (BPR) work regime, that BPR was neither as simple to implement nor as rational in its content as the gurus claimed. Moreover, BPR did not prove to be as coercive in its control over labor as many critics feared. They concluded that "staff are not simply victims of management control, but are often active participants in the conditions that maintain and reproduce control and the stress and resistance that may follow as a result" (1998b: 188).

The Charismatic Approach

The Charismatic Approach places the figure of the guru squarely at the center of the analysis. Briefly stated, this explanation suggests that, in the face of increased uncertainty and spiraling competition, executives and managers may turn to the charismatic figure of a guru for guidance largely as an act of faith. To whom they turn is dependent on the quality of the guru's "performance" and how effectively he or she appeals and speaks to the executives' needs.

The most successful management gurus have proven themselves to be consummate self-promoters who know how, and are willing, to work effectively with the requisite promotional infrastructure of book publishers, agents, journalists and seminar promoters. It is this ability and willingness that not only creates their initial popularity but also sustains it. Huczynski suggests that gurus and consultants insure that management ideas are constantly upgraded or replaced through what he describes as a process of "planned obsolescence". This enables them to "enter the management idea market with the confidence that a particular product which is selling well today will be displaced at a future time" (Huczynski, 1993a: 285). By conveniently and appealingly packaging their ideas, vendors provide managers with much-needed relief from the need to search extensively for new solutions. Harvey MacKay, author of *Swim with the Sharks without Being Eaten Alive* (1988), is very much in tune with the need for easy access to new management ideas. He believes that "differentiators" such as celebrity endorsements and a money-back guarantee were important to the sales of his book (Barrier, 1990). The book and spin-off products such as tapes, videocassette, train-the-trainer programs and survey instruments have become powerful tools not only for making consultants visible in an increasingly crowded marketplace but also for legitimizing the consultant in the eyes of their customers (Clark and Greatbatch, 2000). The book has, in effect, become an "oversized business card for management consultants" (Brimelow, 1989: 42). As Pierce and Newstrom comment, "through the printed word they hope to provide a unique take-home product for their clients, communicate their management philosophies, gain wide exposure for themselves or their firms, and occasionally profit handsomely" (1990: 3). The importance of having a bestseller was obviously not lost on a pair of ambitious consultants who spent $250,000 buying more than 10,000 copies of their own book, *The Discipline of Market Leaders* (Treacy and Wiersema, 1995; see also Stern, 1995). Many commentators would argue, therefore, that gurus' marketing strategies, however questionable they may be, are frequently a more critical determinant of success than the ideas and concepts they develop.

Clark and Salaman have taken this "marketing strategy" argument and done much to extend and deepen it significantly. They have suggested that the key to understanding the power and impact of gurus is to see what they do as "performance" (Clark, 1995; Clark and Salaman, 1998a). They have shown that the dramaturgical metaphor (Burke, 1968; Goffman, 1960; Mangham, 1996; Mangham and Overington, 1983, 1987) provides a useful framework within which to illuminate the activities of management consultants. Given that the key task of management consultants is to convince clients of their quality and value, impression management is a core feature of consultancy work. While gurus share the same concern with performance and impression management as consultants, the guru's work is distinctive because it is primarily concerned with transforming consciousness and the guru relies heavily on one-way communication in large public arenas to get his or her message across. To properly illuminate the distinctive quality of the guru's work, they argue that a powerful metaphor is required.

Clark and Salaman propose that the guru's performance should be viewed as the functional equivalent of that of the "witch doctor" in tribal societies. Witch doctors and gurus serve to assist their clients with pressing problems, anxieties and stresses but they do this from marginal positions, being both in and out of their respective societies. Following Cleverley (1971), they suggest that the knowledge that gurus and witch doctors use shares properties with magical knowledge – it is developed in order to control the critical uncertainties of the world and is developed through the manipulation of supernatural agencies. By juxtaposing the typical live performance of a witch doctor with that of a management guru, they convincingly portray the similarities in the ways they work. Specifically, they note a "common focus upon the emotional, the generation of threat and risk for all parties, the destabilizing of identities, allied to the repetitive emphasis on simplified, action-focused ritualistic nostrums" (Clark and Salaman, 1996: 104). They conjecture that successful gurus have always known that their success is largely dependent upon the magic and mystery of their performance and have found new and creative ways in which to exploit it.

This dependency was well recognized by the gurus' forebears. In his book, *Religion and the Decline of Magic*, Thomas (1973) has noted the tendency of businessmen in the sixteenth and seventeenth centuries in England to contact wizards and cunning men on such matters as insurance policies, the purchase of commodities and the advisability of loans. Returning to the contemporary world of commerce, the quasi-religious and magical aspects of the gurus' work have also been noted by numerous writers (Fincham, 1996; Huczynski, 1993a; Jackson, 1996b; Sharpe, 1984). In his investigation of prominent British management guru, Eli Goldratt, author of *The Goal* (Goldratt and Cox, 1984) and *The Race* (Goldratt and Cox, 1986), Jones notes that Goldratt's guru-philosophy depends upon both reason and belief for its success. He argues that "the former supplies the logic and rationale for action; the latter generates the faith and commitment required to make fundamental change" (Jones, 1997: 29).

Shifting attention away from the guru's performance to the manager's needs, it is apparent from the literature that executives will bring a new idea into their organization for a number of reasons. They may perceive that the idea can solve a specific problem that they believe to be critical to their company. A new idea may also be adopted to act as a motivational device within the organization. Similarly, it can serve as a vehicle to assist organizational change. The gurus not only motivate employees with their fresh ideas and perspectives but also draw on their personality to legitimize organizational change. As Stuller suggests, "associating the ideas with people serves not only as an identifying or mnemonic device for a corporation's employees, but it also gives the change personality" (1992: 21). Management guru Robert Waterman acknowledges that "consultants are a way around the issues that companies usually put into their 'too hard' basket" (cited in Stuller, 1992: 21). Critical to their success in this role is the new language they bring to the organization through their books, seminars and speeches that can enable employees to look at entrenched problems in a new light. It is, therefore, not surprising to find that a large percentage of business bestseller sales units comes from block orders placed by companies for distribution throughout their organizations (Freeman, 1985).

Huczynski argues that, in addition to fulfilling cognitive and material needs, gurus have appealed to managers' social or externally directed esteem needs by legitimizing their role in society and providing positive role models to follow. In the process, the gurus have served to reassure managers and reduce the feeling of insecurity that is an inevitable fact of managerial life. Huczynski, therefore, proposes that "the growth in the popularity of management guru books and seminars, far from being linked with an upturn in managers' confidence, in fact represents a response to widespread self-doubt among executives, even those at the top" (1993a: 196). Huczynski also discusses how management gurus have been able to address the personal or internal needs of individual managers. In particular, he emphasizes the spiritual or charismatic quality of the gurus' work in motivating and inspiring their managerial audiences (Bass, 1986; Bryman, 1992; Pauchant, 1991). Gill and Whittle (1993) have speculated that the rise and fall of management fashions may be attributed in part to the effect of covert psychoanalytic processes upon organizational behavior (Kets de Vries and Miller, 1984). They sketch out how three common group "fantasies" identified by Bion (1961) and others at the Tavistock Institute – "flight/fight" culture, "dependency" culture and "pairing" or "utopian" culture – all encourage in some way either a dependency on a new management guru or a new management fashion.

While academics have shed considerable light on the charismatic qualities of the management gurus' work, a major weakness of the Charismatic Approach is the lack of empirical investigation that has been conducted into how executives and managers actually perceive and use gurus' ideas. The major reason for this paucity of research is the fundamental methodological and practical challenges that such research questions pose. One example of this type of research was conducted as part of Huczynski's doctoral study (Huczynski, 1991: 473–481). Interviews were conducted with eight managers from the local plant of an American multinational company concerning what managerial ideas they found valuable and why. He found that, with the exception of management control, they mentioned all of the elements that he had identified in his review of secondary sources (i.e. management legitimation, applicability, steps or principles, communicability, unitary perspective, universal application, individualistic perspective, human nature model, contribution/ownership, leadership). Some of the managers interviewed valued new managerial ideas because they were "challenging" (i.e. they were forced to look at things in a different light), while others valued the link or "correspondence" which the idea had with their own thoughts and beliefs. Some of those interviewed also appreciated the way in which an idea could "integrate" several seemingly disparate insights, feelings and experiences. However, Huczynski admits that these studies were not sufficiently thorough to warrant serious attention and that much more needs to be done in this area (Huczynski, personal communication, January 18, 1994).

In an ethnographic study of managers in a plant in the English Midlands, Watson observed that the buzzwords, fads and flavors-of-the-month spawned by management gurus play a significant part in the "double-control aspect" of the manager's life because

Managers who embrace these notions (whether they be rhetorical devices to persuade people to act in certain ways or are actual practices and techniques) are trying to exert control simultaneously on behalf of the employing organization and over their own lives by using these ideas and actions to *make sense of their own lives and their place in the scheme of things.*

(Watson, 1994: 896)

While the managers in the organization that Watson observed were generally critical of the flavor-of-the month techniques, they felt obliged to pursue them because they were not certain that they would not work. Watson found that, although the managers he worked with appeared to remember little from popular business books, these books did help them to "engage in a brief standing back from their everyday pressures and encourage them to reflect on what they are doing" (1994: 216). Similarly, a survey conducted by Ezzamel et al. (1994), which examined managers' attitudes about recent changes in U.K. management practices, found that managers applied only piecemeal aspects of the gurus' prescriptions to support incremental changes. Their selections were based on an intimate knowledge of the cultural and political conditions of change within their respective organizations. It is in the context of managers attempting to make sense of themselves and their frequently turbulent situations that the gurus have a brief, but potentially powerful, opportunity to question and shape managers' self-concept.

Drawing on the little empirical work that has been done examining the relationship between the guru and his or her manager-followers, I have contended that the management guru is playing an increasingly important role in influencing both the development and the structure of the manager's self-concept (Gergen, 1971; Jackson, 1996a). Drawing on the book *The Saturated Self*, in which Gergen (1991) sketches out some of the profound patterns of social change and their impact on self-definition especially in North America, I have suggested that management gurus are both a product and producer of the saturated self. Gergen's central thesis is that the "technologies of social saturation", such as the automobile, telephone, electronic mail, popular magazines and television, have immersed individuals even more deeply in the social world and exposed them to many more opinions, values and lifestyles than they would have experienced in industrial and pre-industrial societies. This process of "social saturation" is propelling individuals toward a new self-consciousness which, he suggests, is a postmodern consciousness. A critical prelude to this consciousness is the "populating of the self" or "the acquisition of multiple and disparate potentials for being" (Gergen, 1991: 69). As individuals become more exposed to other individuals, they become aware of a much wider range of "possible selves", that is, "the multiple conceptions people harbour of what they might become, would like to become, or are afraid to become"

(1991: 74). He highlights three repercussions of this "multiphrenia syndrome" that have important implications for our understanding of the management guru–manager relationship. First, as managers become aware of the myriad possibilities of who they could be and how good they should be, then self-doubt starts to seep into their everyday consciousness. Second, in their quest to become better at their jobs, managers are rapidly confronted with what Wurman has neatly coined "information anxiety", a state that he argues is produced "by the ever-widening gap between what we understand and what we think we should understand" (1989: 34). Third, Gergen suggests that multiphrenia has precipitated an emerging crisis in the common conception of human understanding, which he describes as "rationality in recession". He argues that, "as the range of our relationships is expanded, the validity of each localized rationality is questionable or absurd from the standpoint of another" (Gergen, 1991: 78). Consequently, individuals' faith in either finding or accepting the existence of one "right" way has become severely undermined, so that they turn instead to celebrity-endorsed "infotainment" that is most visibly manifested in the news media (Mitroff and Bennis, 1989; Postman, 1985; Schickel, 1985). In the management field, this shift has been manifested as managers turning their backs on the efficacy of rational scientific solutions that have been the traditional realm of academe, in favor of the simpler, more motivational solutions that are peddled to great effect by the management gurus. The management gurus have, in the process, become the new "guarantors" of management knowledge for the practicing manager, so that whatever they say should be heard and given serious attention (Burgoyne, 1995a; Jackson, 1994b; Mitroff and Bennis, 1989). This shift has forced the intellectuals to relinquish their traditional role as "legislators" in favor of a newer, somewhat reduced role as "interpreters" (Bauman, 1987). It is to this role that we now turn.

Toward a rhetorical critique

It is clear from the above review that in a relatively short period of time, a considerable amount of progress has been made by academic researchers in developing and advancing explanatory accounts of the management guru and fashion phenomenon. While we have been in "catch-up" mode, my sense is that we are gaining on this phenomenon. What then must be done to insure that we at least draw level with it? From the perspective of a researcher wishing to contribute to this enterprise, the irony is certainly not lost on me that the dilemmas that researchers face are not dissimilar from the dilemmas that managers must find themselves in when deciding what stand to take regarding the adoption or rejection of a new management fashion. Grint has amusingly summarized this dilemma by likening it to the purchase of a pair of flared trousers, as follows:

Should we discard our flared trousers immediately on the grounds that they are no longer legitimate attire and we all want to look trendy and progressive (institutional approach); or because they do not align themselves with the long waves of managerial trousers – that is, they smack of touchy-feely hippies and we are now into a hard-nosed expansionary phase where only pin-stripes will do (structural account); or because the guru doesn't wear them (charismatic account); or because the supervisors are wearing them we need to (re)demonstrate who is in charge (distancing approach); or because, after all, you simply cannot iron them properly and they keep getting caught in the lift doors so that they are completely irrational (rational account)? Or perhaps all five explanations seem equally viable.

(Grint, 1997: 56–57)

Seeing the similarities between the plights faced by both academic researchers and managers in making decisions about selecting the best approach to follow from an ever-increasing array of new and innovative approaches is, I think, an important step forward for us to make. Such has been our enthusiasm for exposing and ridiculing (albeit politely) the manager's susceptibility to gurus and management fashions, that we may have lost sight of our own susceptibilities and weaknesses. As Lilley has poignantly questioned:

are we simply using "our" gurus to critique "theirs"?; and can an accelerating dance upon the stepping stones of new "heroes," (re)instigated by our reading/writing of their texts, prevent us, any more than managers, from a rapid descent into epistemological quicksand?

(Lilley, 1997: 52)

Bearing this warning in mind and heeding Ramsay's (1996) call for a "level-headed" explanation, I would suggest that all four explanatory approaches discussed above have contributed in some measure to our understanding of the management guru and management fashion phenomenon. Clearly, not one of the approaches has distinguished itself as gaining supremacy over the others either in terms of its explanatory power or the degree of enthusiasm and the size of following that it has generated among the academic community. The Rational Approach serves to remind us that management fashions are developed explicitly to improve managerial and organizational performance and that, in some instances, they do contribute, either directly or indirectly, to the company's bottom line. For example, Brickley et al. note that "for all their fad-like behavior, the persistence of management innovations suggests they serve some useful purpose; the benefits of such innovations, at least on average, must exceed the costs" (1997: 38). We need to be mindful, therefore, of the economic implications of management fashions. However, as Abrahamson (1991) has pointed out, an "efficient-choice" perspective provides only limited assistance in addressing the question of when, and by what processes, technically inefficient innovations are diffused or efficient innovations rejected.

The Structuralist Approach, on the other hand, has served to place the management guru and fashion phenomenon in a much broader socio-political and cultural context. The critiques that have been inspired by this approach have, by and large, done a good job of unmasking the internal contradictions and the "real" interests that might be served by management fashions. Ramsay has acknowledged that structural explanations of management fashions make an important contribution in defining external constraint and influence but, "without elaboration, risk reducing the immediate context to a matter of detail or of homogenizing organizational settings, thus formularizing developments with little recognition of the importance of agency or process" (Ramsay, 1996: 162).

The Institutional Approach has given due recognition to the importance of process (although it has downplayed agency), in explaining the management guru and management fashion phenomenon. Writers who have adopted this approach have helpfully identified the role of various agents and their institutional linkages within the management fashion industry and have highlighted the significance of competitive and bandwagon pressures that act upon organizations. Abrahamson, who has given this approach its fullest expression, has highlighted the importance of rhetorics in the promotion and dissemination of new management fashions. However, Kieser (1997) has pointed to several flaws within Abrahamson's theory of management fashions. He notes that

> linking the hypothesis that managers have to adhere to norms of progress with neo-institutional theory smacks of an attempt to create the impression that the explanation of the dynamics of management fashion does not rest on just one single hypothesis but on a highly reputed theory.
>
> (Kieser, 1997: 53)

Moreover, Abrahamson's conception of rhetoric as being something that is applied once the fashion has been produced to "oil the wheels" between the suppliers and consumers is too limiting and serves only to reinforce the conventional scholarly and public wisdom about how the management fashion industry functions.

Abrahamson's explanatory framework is further hindered by his insistence that a management fashion should be considered as an essentially "technical fashion". That is, "a social process that repeatedly redefines technicians' collective perceptions of what constitutes rational progress" (1996b: 117) as distinct from the relatively trivial and cosmetic realm of "aesthetic fashion". By contrast, Kieser argues that rhetoric in its aesthetic form is "the main fabric of management fashions . . . [and] therefore, theories of fashion in aesthetic forms are generally applicable to explanations of management fashions" (1997: 49). Consequently, we need to be as concerned about the aesthetic qualities of management fashions and their ability to gratify our senses and serve our emotional well-being as we are about their technical qualities.

The preoccupation that Abrahamson and others working within this explanatory frame have with broad macrohistorical rhetorical categories limits room for a more finely tuned rhetorical analysis of individual management fashions. While the broader economic and political forces are undoubtedly important in providing the general context for the relative receptivity of a rationally oriented versus a normatively oriented management fashion, we still have to account for the emergence and predominance of just a few particular fashions over many others that are competing for the manager's attention in any given period of time. Academics have tended to aggregate popular management ideas too coarsely. As Huczynski observes, "they address the business publishing explosion as a generalized phenomenon and fail to make any distinctions between the contents of these different books or the backgrounds of their authors" (1993a: 39). Treating popular management ideas as a single, relatively uniform and isolated body of knowledge does little to help our understanding of the effect it has had upon management practice. Similarly, there is a tendency in the literature to treat all management gurus as one and to overgeneralize the ways and means of how they have become constructed. The data that we have to draw on about management gurus tend to be anecdotal, impressionistic and limited. Tom Peters emerges as a justifiably attractive if somewhat well-worn exemplar but we need to find out more about other gurus to fill out our repertoire.

There has been a similar tendency to generalize about the readers or "consumers" of these popular management ideas. On a very basic level no one appears to be sure who reads these books, let alone understands why they read them and what they do differently as a result of reading them. It is implicitly assumed in the literature that managers are the primary readership group. However, there is little explicit evidence to confirm this assumption. If managers are the primary consumers, we need to explore further what kinds of managers (in terms of personal characteristics, level, function, etc.) are particularly interested in these new ideas and why. We should also probe more deeply into the plight of the books. Are they read cover-to-cover and pondered thoroughly? Or, as common wisdom would have it, are they merely flicked through in one momentary sitting? Or are they used as display items to place strategically on coffee tables or on bookshelves to demonstrate that the reader is "up to date" and "in the know"? Or are they confined to briefcases and carried to and from work on the off-chance that the reader might find time to read but never quite manages it?

These criticisms have been echoed by Clark and Salaman (1998a) in their excellent and wide-ranging review of the work that has been done to date to understand the guru's role in the management fashion-setting process. They are particularly critical of the prevailing assumption that the guru–client relationship is a simple one-way affair. In many accounts, they argue, the guru is portrayed as the omnipotent, initiating partner while managers are "conceived largely as passive, docile consumers of gurus' ideas and recommendations, inherently vulnerable to gurus' blandishments, anxiously searching for reassurances and support, looking desperately for new ideas" (1998a: 146). While the guru–manager relationship is one that is predicated on a power differential in terms of knowledge, experience, talent, etc., the guru is also dependent on the manager in order to create and then sustain a mass following of managers. This is a task that is made particularly challenging because, unlike the CEO who can rely on "legal-rational authority" by virtue of his or her position within the organization, the guru's authority in this relationship, working outside of any formal organizational context, is an entirely "charismatic" one that rests, according to Weber, "only on the basis of personal charisma, so long as it is proved; that is, as long as it receives recognition and is able to satisfy the followers or disciples" (1947: 362).

Clark and Salaman propose an alternative, three-faceted approach to better understanding the guru–manager relationship. First, they suggest a more interactive and balanced conception of the relationship, "one where both parties derive benefit from the relationship; where there are no winners and losers but rather a collusion in mutual winning" (1998a: 146). Second, their approach recognizes that the key to the management gurus' influence lies not in their expert knowledge, but in the symbolic quality of their work. Specifically, it is their ability to convey the sense of being knowledge-able or their rhetorical power that is central to their work. Applying this argument to the analysis of management texts, Monin and Monin suggest that a "closer reading of these texts would reveal that reader-response may be based not only on *what* is said but often on *how* it is said . . . rhetorical analysis of [gurus'] texts would lead to more informed assessments of the value of the theory presented" (1998: 2). Similarly, Nohria and Berkley have observed that the new managerialist discourse must be "understood primarily as a form of rhetoric . . . spoken by managerial professionals not to mention professors of management – in ways that are not necessarily coterminous with organizational practice itself" (1994: 125–126). The third element of this approach acknowledges that gurus manage meaning for managers through their use of language. Clark and Salaman conclude:

> It is possible, therefore, that the gurus' success with their clients lies in their capacity, in partnership with the client, to address and manipulate through myths and stories, symbolic issues of great pertinence and

salience to senior managers: managers' own roles and identities within the "new" organization.

(Clark and Salaman, 1998a: 149)

Subsequently, Clark and Salaman (1998b) took these arguments further by conceptualizing management fashions as a form of discourse about organization which constitutes the speakers/performers (gurus) and hearers/audience (managers) through a series of distinct guru narratives. Acknowledging the influence of the recent "narrative turn" in organizational studies (Barry and Elmes, 1997; Boje, 1997; Czarniawska, 1997; O'Connor, 1995), they outline four features of their approach to narrative, which are particularly relevant to their analysis of guru theory. First, they declare an ontological commitment that organizational reality is constituted in the use of language. Second, they argue that "organizational reality is not something which can never be known as something-in-itself; knowledge of organizational reality is only available through the representations of various spokespersons" (1998b: 14–15). Management gurus are particularly significant and influential spokespersons. Third, their approach assumes that gurus influence executives by using a limited number of coherent accounts or narratives. In their study, three such "Ur-narratives" are identified – the organization as community, the organization as market and the organization as adaptive individual. Finally, their approach posits that it is within these narratives that executives seek to "position" themselves and their employees.

In this book I wish to build on the important progress that has been made by such writers as Abrahamson, Kieser and Clark and Salaman in furthering our understanding of management gurus and management fashions. I shall do this by offering detailed rhetorical critiques of three popular fashions that have been instigated by management gurus during the 1990s. These critiques not only provide much-needed empirical material about management gurus and management fashions but also demonstrate an approach that has hitherto not been applied to this phenomenon but has the potential to shed some new light upon it. Before proceeding with these critiques, however, we need to develop our thinking along three interrelated fronts. First, we need a broader and deeper appreciation of the forms and functions of rhetoric in creating the social order. In other words, rhetoric needs to be moved from the margins to the core of our concerns as academic researchers. As Czarniawska-Joerges has observed, while there has been an increasing awareness of rhetoric in the discipline of management and organizational research, there is as yet, "no consolidated effort at rhetorical analysis" (1995: 148).

Second, we should apply sophisticated and proven methods of rhetorical criticism that can provide us with a richer and more complete understanding of the rhetorical content and dynamics of the management fashion-setting process. Along these lines, Monin and Monin have contended that, "a rhetorically aware reader is an empowered reader; and that an organizational theorist is empowered if she recognizes, as she writes and reads, both the root metaphors in the texts of her theory and also the rhetorical skills with which they have been crafted" (1998: 1).

Third, if, as Abrahamson (1996a) has urged, we wish actively to intervene in the management fashion-setting process to make it a more technically useful, collective learning process, we need to become more conscious of the rhetorical qualities of our own work as scholars. In particular, we need to consider how to make our critiques as compelling to our colleagues and to managers as those accounts that have been created by the management gurus and their consultant followers. As Aldag concludes, "we need to pay more attention to *telling* and *selling* our research results and relevance" (1997: 14; italics in original).

The next chapter is devoted to developing these three fronts. There I shall focus my attention upon an established method of rhetorical criticism which, I argue, holds some promise for providing new and important insights into the management guru and management fashion phenomenon and for developing rhetorically compelling critiques of it, for managers and academics alike.

Summary

This chapter has reviewed the substantial and burgeoning literature that has examined various aspects of the management guru and management fashion phenomenon. The review revealed that this phenomenon took off during the 1980s in North America and continues to court the corporate imagination both there and, increasingly, throughout the rest of the world. During the mid-1990s a backlash against the management guru and fashion phenomenon has gathered momentum from both academic and media commentators but it is difficult to assess the scale and long-term effect of this movement. The paradox of a rapidly growing management fashion industry in the face of disappointing material results looks set to be a feature of the business world for some time to come.

The review also revealed a recent, somewhat belated yet nonetheless impressive effort on the part of academic researchers to explain the management guru and management fashion phenomenon. Explanatory accounts were distinguished, on the one hand, by the extent to which they stressed internalist versus externalist forces and, on the other, by the relative emphasis they placed upon logic or emotion. It was concluded that all four approaches (i.e. Rational; Structural; Institutional/Distancing and Charismatic) had, in varying ways, made some contribution to our overall understanding of the phenomenon. In an effort to move forward with this explanatory project, a line of inquiry was drawn out from the most recent literature which, it was argued, might further enrich our theoretical and empirical understanding of the management guru and management fashion phenomenon. This line of inquiry essentially involves systematically probing the relationship and symbolic exchange between the management guru and the manager through the careful rhetorical critique of the narratives underlying individual management fashions.

3 Dramatistic rhetorical criticism

Children, only animals live entirely in the Here and Now. Only nature knows neither memory nor history. But man – let me offer you a definition – is the story-telling animal. Wherever he goes he wants to leave behind not a chaotic wake, not an empty space, but the comforting marker-buoys and trail-signs of stories. He has to go on telling stories. He has to keep making them up. As long as there's a story, it's all right.

(Graham Swift, 1983: 57)

Ideas must be strongly linked[,] must follow one another without interruption. . . . When you have thus formed the chain of ideas in the heads of your citizens, you then will be able to pride yourselves on guiding them and being their masters. A stupid despot may constrain his slaves with iron chains; but a true politician binds them even more strongly by the chain of their own ideas; it is at the stable point of reason that he secures the end of the chain; this link is all the stronger in that we do not know of what it is made and we believe it to be our own work.

(The French reformer J.M. Servan, cited in Foucault, 1977: 102–103)

Introduction

The preceding review of the management guru and management fashion literature led to the conclusion that one potentially profitable line of inquiry for researchers might be to subject individual management fashions to the scrutiny of a sophisticated method of rhetorical criticism. In this chapter I describe a method of rhetorical criticism which I think might be particularly suitable for studying this phenomenon. Fantasy Theme Analysis (FTA) is a peculiarly dramatistic method of rhetorical criticism developed in the 1970s by Ernest Bormann and his colleagues at the "Minnesota School" of communications to understand better how and why certain types of messages excite widespread public attention on sporadic and cyclical bases. The method they developed to do this is founded on a general theory of communication known as Symbolic Convergence Theory (SCT), which attempts to provide an explanatory framework for the analysis of group and mass communication processes. While FTA has become well established within the realm of rhetorical criticism, it has been used only fleetingly within organizational research. It is, however, a method that deserves greater attention as a means to reach a better understanding of not just the management guru and fashion phenomenon, but potentially a number of other management and organizational phenomena.

I have several reasons for suggesting that FTA might be a particularly effective method for analyzing management gurus and management fashions. First, this technique is rooted in a powerful explanatory metaphor – the theater – which, in addition to its noble and distinguished tradition within the social sciences, has already been used to good effect to illuminate and explicate the performative aspects of the management guru–manager relationship (Clark, 1995; Clark and Salaman, 1996, 1998a). Second, this method is embedded in a general and dynamic theoretical framework (i.e. SCT) which can help us understand the linkage between small group and mass-mediated communication processes which are critical in the creation, dissemination and take-up of management fashions. Third, FTA has shown itself to be well attuned to both the aesthetic and technical qualities of rhetoric that I, and others, have argued are critical to understanding the management guru and fashion phenomenon. Fourth, the method combines the capacity for generalization with a finely tuned sensitivity to the unique experiences and insights of the critic. Fifth, FTA has a proven track record of providing theoretical insights into communication phenomena in diverse empirical settings that are analogous to the domain of management fashions. Finally, the method can take into account all of the components associated with management fashions without privileging any one component over another. These components include the gurus who originate management fashions, the consulting firms and business schools that endorse them, the mass media that disseminate them, and the managers and organizations that, ultimately, consume them.

The chapter begins with a discussion of the origins, underlying assumptions and main concepts of SCT and FTA. To give the reader a sense of the reach and depth of this approach, a brief review of its various empirical applications is also presented. This is followed by a review of the critique that has mobilized in reaction to FTA and SCT as well as the response to this by the chief proponents of the theory. Having summarized the case for using Fantasy Theme Analysis, I describe how the method was applied to the present empirical study. I explain why a multiple case study approach was elected for this study and why the three specific cases were chosen. This is followed by a step-by-step description of how the FTA was conducted, including the processes by which the data were collected and analyzed.

The Fantasy Theme method of rhetorical criticism

Origins

Since the 1960s, the Minnesota Group has been preoccupied with the link between small and large group decision-making and communication processes. Symbolic Convergence Theory (SCT) is their attempt at providing an explanation that accounts for the creation, raising and maintenance of group consciousness through communication. The process of symbolic convergence is "symbolic" because "it deals with the human tendency to interpret signs and objects by giving them meaning" (Bormann, 1983: 102). "Convergence" refers to the way "two or more private symbolic worlds incline toward each other, come more closely together, or even overlap during certain processes of communication" (Bormann, 1983: 102).

In addition to trying to better understand group communication processes, the intellectual leader of the Minnesota Group, Ernest Bormann, has a broader ambition in mind with SCT. He views it as one means to help to bridge the wide gap that had opened up during the 1950s and 1960s between two diverse scholarly traditions within the communications field. The "humanistic" and "social science" traditions were separated by different research methods and terminologies with, perhaps ironically given the nature of the field, little communication taking place between them. Bormann distinguishes between the "special" theories of communication that have largely been the preoccupation of the humanists and the "general" theories of communication that have been the major preoccupation of communication scholars with a social sciences inclination (Bormann, 1980). "Special theories" are artistic formulations that specify the nature of conventional forms and usage of communication and provide advice on how to use and criticize such forms. They are therefore bounded by time and culture. "General" theories, by contrast, relate to communication practices that cut across these conventional forms on a recurring basis. Bormann offers the concept of cognitive dissonance as an example of a general theory of communication. He claims that his scientifically oriented SCT combined with his humanistic method of rhetorical criticism, which he christened "Fantasy Theme Analysis" (FTA) may be able to provide a valuable way of unifying the historic divide between the humanistic and social scientific studies of rhetoric and communication.

An important turning point in the work of Bormann and the Minnesota Group came with the publication in 1970 of Robert Bales's book, *Personality and Interpersonal Behavior*. In common with the Minnesota Group, Bales was studying small group interaction under laboratory conditions at Harvard, from which he identified 12 content analysis categories. One of these categories – "shows tension release" – he later changed to "dramatizes". The common element of acts within this category was that they presented potent emotional symbols to the listener, to which she or he may respond without explicit attention or conscious knowledge. Within this category, Bales discovered "group fantasy events" which would "chain out" through the group. When this occurred, the tempo and volume of the conversation would pick up, people became more excited, they would interrupt one another and become more agitated. Bales noted that "a chain reaction of fantasy in the group is set up when one, or some of the participants, presents in his communication symbols which have unconscious meanings for one or some of the other participants" (1970: 138). Drawing upon the Freudian-inspired psychoanalytical literature, Bales suggested that a group fantasy chain was motivated by multiple factors and was a product of the psychological overlap between three symbolic and emotional domains: the "manifest content", which is the situation and persons being talked about, usually "outside the group" (e.g. a news item, a piece of gossip, or a joke); the "here-and now", which is the interacting group with its present members, their relations to each other, the problems of the group and their hidden attitudes; and the "past experience" of the members, particularly their common childhood experience in relation to families in which their personalities were formed. In his studies Bales showed how groups with no previous history would, through time, use group fantasy chains in order to forge a common culture.

Key assumptions and concepts

Ernest Bormann took Bales's concept of group fantasy chain, and from this developed a comprehensive method of rhetorical criticism called Fantasy Theme Analysis. Definitions of the key concepts of this method are provided in Table 3.1 as well as some exemplars that I have drawn from popular management discourse. In his seminal paper, Bormann (1972) argues that dramatizing moments can not only chain within small face-to-face groups but, through the technologies of mass media, to large groups which, in turn, can be chained back into small face-to-face group contexts. A dramatizing message can take the form of a pun or other wordplay, a *double entendre*, a figure of speech, an analogy, an anecdote, an allegory, a fable or a narrative. By way of example, I can recall that during each of my trips back to England I have noted the presence of at least one ubiquitous TV-inspired catchphrase such as "Gizza Job", "Loads-a-Money" and "Sorted" that, once learned, quickly enabled me to demonstrate that I had never really left the old country. Bormann calls the composite dramas that catch large groups of people up in a symbolic reality "rhetorical visions". As people seek to make sense out of their environment and events around them, they come into contact with fantasies that have been chained out from other small groups. If sufficiently compelling, that is if they speak convincingly to the individual's "here-and-now" problems in a dramatic form, these rhetorical visions can be consolidated into a credible interpretation of reality.

Table 3.1 The key concepts of Symbolic Convergence Theory and exemplars from popular management theory

Technical Term	Definition	Exemplar
Fantasy theme	A dramatizing message in which characters enact an incident or a series of incidents other than the here-and-now of the people involved in the communication episode	The Inverted Organizational Pyramid
Symbolic cue	A code word, phrase, slogan, gesture that triggers previously shared fantasies and emotions	Theory Z, The One-Minute Manager, Open-Book Management
Fantasy type	A repeated fantasy theme within a single rhetorical vision and across diverse rhetorical visions	Restoration (Excellence,Reengineering & TQM)
Saga	Oft-repeated telling of the achievement in the life of a person, group, community, organization or nation	Lee Iacocca, Jack Welch, Microsoft, Saturn, Southwest Airlines, Post-War Japan
Rhetorical vision	A composite drama that catches up large groups of people into a common symbolic reality	Excellence, Total Quality Management, Core Competencies
Dramatis personae	The characters depicted in messages that give life to a rhetorical vision	Executives, middle managers, front-line employees, competitors, consultants, customers, etc.
Plotline	A narrative that provides the action for the rhetorical vision	The 14 points of the Deming Management Method
Scene	The location of the action within the rhetorical vision	Corporate North America, The Global Economy
Rhetorical community	Individuals who share a common symbolic ground by participating in a rhetorical vision	American Society for Quality, Constraints Management SIG, APICS, System Thinker Conference Delegates
Sanctioning agent	The individual, person, concept or thing that legitimizes the symbolic reality portrayed by a rhetorical vision	The Management Guru: Peter Drucker, Tom Peters, Kenneth Blanchard

A rhetorical vision is constructed from "fantasy themes", which are the means through which interpretation is accomplished in communication. A fantasy theme is manifested in the form of a word, a phrase or a statement that interprets events in the past, envisions events in the future, or depicts current events that are removed in time and/or space from the actual activities of the group. For example, few would claim that they actually worked in an organization that was shaped like "an inverted pyramid" but most of us can grasp what that might be like and many might wish to work in one. In contrast to normal human experience, fantasy themes are organized and artistic. They have their own internal logic and are aesthetically pleasing. Bormann distinguishes between "*setting themes*", which depict where the action is taking place or the place where the characters act out their roles; "*character themes*", which describe the agents or actors in the drama, ascribe qualities to them, assign motives to them, and portray them as having certain characteristics; and "*action themes*", also called plotlines, which deal with the action of the drama.

Rhetorical visions often compete with one another to explain the same phenomena. From numerous empirical studies, Bormann and his colleagues have observed that rhetorical visions will generally reflect a deep structure that is embedded in one of three "master analogues" – the righteous, social or pragmatic:

> A rhetorical vision based on a righteous master analogue emphasizes the correct way of doing things with its concerns about right and wrong, proper and improper, superior and inferior, moral and immoral, just and unjust. A rhetorical vision with a social master analogue reflects primary human relations, as it keys on friendship, trust, caring, comradeship, compatibility, family ties, brotherhood, sisterhood, and humanness. A vision with a pragmatic master analogue stresses expediency, utility, efficiency, parsimony, simplicity, practicality, cost effectiveness, and minimal involvement.
>
> (Cragan and Shields, 1992: 202)

It was disappointing to discover that Bormann and his colleagues had not elaborated to any significant extent upon this concept of master analogue in their writings other than to refer to them as "archetypal deep structures". They do note a tendency for all of the rhetorical visions they have studied to reflect at least one of these three types of master analogues, but they never delve into a theoretical explanation as to why this might be. They do, however, provide some exemplars of each of them. Looking at American foreign policy in the period immediately after World War II, Bormann et al. identify three amorphous, if transitory, rhetorical visions that emerged to replace the "monolithic rhetoric of the hot war" (1996: 5). Each vision was based on the three different master analogues. The rhetorical vision of the "Cold War" was based on the righteous master analogue as it emphasized the right way of doing things. The "One World" rhetorical vision, by contrast, exemplified a vision that was based on a social master analogue as it was linked to fostering primary human relations on a global scale. The remaining rhetorical vision, "Power Politics", exemplified a vision based on a pragmatic master analogue because it emphasized expediency, practicality, utility and whatever it took to get the job done.

Bormann (1972) indicates that a drama that is close to life for members of a particular rhetorical community constitutes a symbolic reality that can compete or "go to war" with the symbolic reality of others about the same issues. That is, participants in different and competing rhetorical visions interpret the same phenomena in different ways. These warring views reflect the three master analogues. In selecting the three management fashions that were the focus of this study, I deliberately sought out from the many competing management fashions that I was familiar with those that could serve as illustrative or, in Bormann's terms, "paradigm" cases for each of these master analogues (Bormann et al., 1996). The rationale for case selection will be more fully discussed later in this chapter.

Bormann is at pains to insure that his use of the term "fantasy" as a "technical term" is not confused with its general usage connoting something imaginary, like a children's tale or sexual desire, that is not grounded in reality. Fantasy in its technical sense is "the creative and imaginative interpretation of events that fulfils a psychological need" (1985: 5) and serves as "the way communities of people make sense out of their experience and create their social reality" (1983: 107–108). It is in this sense very similar to the Greek root of the term, *"phantastikos"*, which means to be able to present or show to the mind, to make visible. A fantasy theme is, therefore, a way for people to present or show to the group mind a common experience and to invest it with an emotional tone.

The sanctioning agent of the rhetorical vision is a source that justifies its acceptance; it can take the form of an abstract concept such as God, democracy or justice, or it can be an individual who has a particularly charismatic presence. In his study of pre-Civil War America, Bormann discusses the central role that the evangelist played in almost all of the evangelical rhetorical visions (Bormann, 1985). As was observed in the previous chapter, management gurus have come to serve as the equivalent authoritative voice or "guarantor" for management knowledge in contemporary corporate North America (Burgoyne, 1995a: Jackson, 1994b; Mitroff and Bennis, 1989). I would suggest that they have shown themselves to be particularly skilled at crafting rhetorical visions that are compelling to managerial mass audiences. When a rhetorical vision emerges, the participants in the vision come to form a "rhetorical community". They share a common symbolic ground and respond to the message in ways that are in tune with the rhetorical vision. As such, the vision serves to "sustain the members' sense of community, to impel them strongly to action and to provide them with a social reality with heroes, villains, emotions and attitudes" (Bormann, 1972: 398). Some communities are more strongly defined than others and some are more susceptible to new fantasy chains. Based on the rapid turnover of management "panacea" (Gill and Whittle, 1993), the corporate community of North America would seem to be a particularly fertile ground for fantasy chains or fashions which Bormann suggests are "the physical evidence of the symbolic outbursts in which members of the rhetorical community get caught up in fantasies that do not modify their firmly established vision" (1976: 440).

In a later paper, Bormann et al. (1996) laid out a dynamic framework for analyzing the "life-cycle" of rhetorical visions. Using the Cold War as their paradigm case, they identified four continua (creation, development, maturity and decline) at which a number of distinct rhetorical principles operate. Communication that is aimed at consciousness-creating will tend to predominate in the first phase, while consciousness-raising and consciousness-sustaining communication will tend to predominate in the second and third phases respectively. There are some clear and obvious parallels between these continua and the life-cycle stages that have been identified by various researchers of management fashions (Abrahamson, 1996a; Barley and Kunda, 1992; Gill and Whittle, 1993). The particular contribution that Bormann and his colleagues' work could make to that analysis is to encourage researchers to examine the processes by which the management guru, acting as sanctioning agent, changes his or her rhetorical strategy and tactics to adapt to each stage in the management fashion life-cycle. The following review of empirical work that has been inspired by FTA provides some useful pointers as to how this might be accomplished.

Empirical applications of SCT and FTA

Symbolic Convergence Theory (SCT) and its attendant Fantasy Theme Analysis (FTA) method have become well established within the field of communication studies. A bibliography provided by Ernest Bormann (1996) lists 61 periodical articles and 94 theses and dissertations that have utilized this theory and method. Almost all of these studies have focused on North American phenomena. A cursory glance at the bibliography reveals that, while the approach continues to be theoretically refined and actively used in empirical research, it no longer generates either the intensity of intellectual debate in the literature or the volume of empirical studies that was evident in the late 1970s and early 1980s. Cragan and Shields (1995) identify more than 50 studies published between 1972 and 1992 that draw upon SCT to study communication phenomena. They categorize these studies into six communication contexts: political, social movement, organizational, mass, interpersonal and small group, and public relations communication. Because the studies that have been conducted within the social movement, political and organizational communication contexts tend to provide insights that are most transferable to our attempts to understand the growth, diffusion and decline of management fashions, I shall confine my review to these three empirical contexts.

A dominant theme of the research that has addressed the formation of social movements has been the rhetorical power of religious imagery in forging both social and political movements in the United States. In FTA's inceptive paper, Bormann drew upon his research into the preaching of

Puritan ministers in the early years of the Massachusetts Bay Colony to illustrate the utility of his approach. In his analysis, he concluded that, in marked contrast to the day-to-day routine of backbreaking drudgery, the Puritans

> led an internal fantasy life of mighty grandeur and complexity. They participated in a rhetorical vision that saw the migration to the New World as a holy exodus of God's chosen people. The Biblical drama that supported their vision was that of the journey of the Jews from Egypt into Canaan.
>
> (Bormann, 1972: 402)

Bormann identifies two common fantasy themes expressed in the Puritan rhetorical vision that continue to have a powerful and enduring effect on the history of the United States. The first theme depicts the pilgrim making his slow, painful and holy way, beset by many troubles and temptations. It emphasizes the abasement, sacrifice and dedication of the Puritans to the other world. The second theme is that of the Christian soldier fighting God's battles and overcoming all adversaries including an inimical aboriginal population in an effort to establish the true Church. This latter theme Bormann has argued is a significant and recurring fantasy type in the history of American public address, which he dubs "fetching good out of evil". This fantasy type provides a complete and compelling explanation of evil, according to which God afflicts his chosen people with trouble because they are not living up to the covenant that he has struck with them. Bormann is particularly interested in understanding how the rhetorical power of this fantasy type can build a sense of national unity during a time of war. He traces the utility of this fantasy type in building a sense of colonial community in the fight against the French and the Indians and later on in building a sense of community for a new nation in the fight against the British in the War of Independence. Most critically, he points to Lincoln's masterful use of the "fetching good out of evil" fantasy type in his second inaugural address in helping to rebuild and restore a sense of national community in the wake of the destruction of the Civil War.

Bormann has traced the progress of another enduring fantasy type, that of "restoration", from its origins in the Puritan settlements through the early nineteenth-century Disciples of Christ restoration movement led by Alexander Campbell (Hensley, 1975) to Andrew Jackson's bid to restore America's political system to the "real people" and, most recently, to Ronald Reagan's inaugural address which directed the nation to return to its original righteous state. In his speech, Reagan redramatized this fantasy type by using brief encomiums of Washington, Jefferson and Lincoln, who all symbolized "the fantasy of a golden age when a group of founders possessing the wisdom of demi-gods laid down a perfect (or the most perfect to date) system for society" (Bormann, 1982b: 143). Bormann argues that the dramatically charged TV coverage of the return of the American hostages from Iran intertwined with the Reagan inaugural added considerable rhetorical weight to Reagan's conservative message at the subliminal level. In tracing how the threads of premodernist ideas, particularly those with religious underpinnings, persist and endure in modernist discourse, Bormann's work parallels Gergen's tracing of the influence of romanticist discourse in modernist organizational theory (Gergen, 1992) and anticipates the recent emerging interest in premodernism and retro-organizational theory (Burrell, 1997; Cummings, 1999).

The contemporary political arena, particularly from the 1970s onward, has proven to be a particularly fertile territory for FTA. A number of studies have focused their attention upon the heroic personae of political figures. For example, Campbell (1979) has argued that Carter's emphasis on his heroic persona provided his most effective strategy in 1976. Conversely, Bormann (1973) found that a negative fantasy theme that stemmed from the disclosure that Senator Eagleton had previously used electric shock therapy chained out in the media and eventually harmed the heroic personae of both Eagleton and McGovern in their unsuccessful 1972 Presidential campaign. Other studies have analyzed dramatic plotlines in political communication. Goodnight and Poulakos (1981) have explicated "conspiracy" fantasy-type plotlines that chained through the mass media in the coverage of the Watergate scandal. From an entirely different perspective, Porter (1976) analyzed the discourse of the White House transcripts dealing with Watergate and discovered fantasies concerning the belief of Nixon's inner circle that they could control the mass media. This belief is clearly encapsulated in the recurring fantasy type, "the best defense is a good offense".

The studies that have the most obviously direct link with the research problem at hand are in the realm of organizational communication. John Cragan and Donald Shields have been the most actively engaged in research in this area. Their book *Applied Communication Research* (1981) assembles research that has used SCT and FTA to investigate organizational communication and conduct market research. A good example of the former type of research would be Shields's (1981) study, which established concurrent and construct validity for the claim that the firefighters of St. Paul in Minnesota participated in the same heroic fantasies as those in the fire service professional literature. The firefighters' small group communication depicted a heroic self-persona of a courageous, trained professional working in an extremely hazardous scene that competed with a projected-persona which dramatized a loafing, moonlighting, reckless character in the minds of the wider public. More recently, Cragan and Shields (1992) have been particularly concerned with applying SCT to guide strategic planning interventions in a corporate environment. They have worked with a manufacturer of nationally marketed agricultural feeds to try to bring unity of focus to corporate positioning, market segmentation and sales story and advertising creation in the wake of its transition from a public to a privately held company. One of the major findings of the study (apart from the fact that their intervention was fraught with pitfalls) was that, even though new corporate sagas could be identified with relative ease, when they lost their reality-links, it became increasingly difficult for the organization to create new sagas in a timely fashion. When the company was able to gather primary data from the customer and dealer, rather than merely brainstorming and attempting to disseminate a symbolic reality from headquarters, it was able to "link to here and now phenomena so that the new saga would not be a symbol without substance, as was the case with remnants of the earlier sagas recalled by corporate managers" (Cragan and Shields, 1992: 215).

While Cragan and Shields have focused their attention on developing pragmatic, intervention-oriented applications for SCT, a few other researchers have sought to extend Bormann's conceptualization to basic research in organizational and management studies. Two studies are particularly noteworthy in this regard. Kendall (1993) has used SCT to discover and interpret corporate dramas inherent in the language of the "boiler plates" of the annual reports of the 30 companies which comprised the Dow Jones Industrials. "Boiler plates" are the chairman's message that begins each annual report. Kendall's analysis revealed remarkable congruence in the form and style of these boiler plates that reflect strong institutional pressures (Meyer and Rowan, 1977; Powell and DiMaggio, 1991). The U.S. economy of the 1970s provided the dramatic setting, with the company as hero, the government serving as villain, and public interest groups acting as minor players whom she describes as "a thorn in the hero's side" (Kendall, 1993: 589). Kendall discovered that the overarching corporate drama manifested in these reports was one of "pure competition" (1993: 589). Following Bormann's tactic of locating rhetorical resonances in the past, she shows how these rhetorical visions were a vestige of a much larger, economically based drama that, while it had its origins in Adam Smith's *Wealth of Nations* (Smith, 1976), seized the American public imagination after the Civil War. The primary rhetorical function of the boiler plate is to promote unity among corporate shareholders, management and employees. Kendall selected Fantasy Theme Analysis as her critical method because it provided her with a way to examine multiple levels of drama that were being used to unify the corporation and its many constituents in a shared rhetorical vision: as she put it, "this study allows us to break away from the erroneous assumption that corporate dramas only play out economic themes, and instead involve the reader in analyzing the multiple rhetorical visions of corporations within their own contexts" (1993: 573).

The second study is closely analogous to the present study in that it focuses on popular self-help books that give advice to women on achieving success as managers. Koester (1982) conducted an FTA of 28 of these books published between 1970 and 1979. Her analysis revealed one dominant social reality which she dubbed the "Female Manager Vision". This vision emphasized individual action in the male business game, but made gender the determining factor that gave meaning to events. Koester concludes that successful women managers operate as "Machiavellian princesses controlling the impact of their gender in an organizational setting filled with intrigue and innuendo. Success requires a woman to maintain a balance between the negative stereotypes of women, yet retaining femininity" (1982: 165). None of the books advocates any changes to the organization, the legal system or the social structure. It is up to the woman to work, or more correctly, to "act", within the existing male-dominated system. In providing a rationale for selecting FTA to interpret these books, Koester explains that:

> [It] is particularly appropriate because of the writers' consistent utilization of dramas to convey and elaborate their ideas. As authors they are not content simply to present their descriptions of organizational life for women in discursive and abstract language, nor do they simply report suggestions to ease the female manager on the road to success. Instead, they typically dramatize fantasy themes to illustrate their argument. A rhetorical vision, because it depends on drama, has a particular power that argument and evidence do not.
>
> (Koester, 1982: 166)

The preceding review demonstrates that the FTA method of rhetorical criticism has generated a rich, provocative and diverse body of empirical research that has looked at a wide range of communication processes and settings. By reading these empirical studies, one can gain a true appreciation for the value and limitations of this method. It has also become clear to me from this reading that, while the method has not been explicitly applied to the management guru and management fashion phenomenon, it has looked at communication phenomena that have important parallels to it. Before proceeding with the application of this method to the current study, it is important to become aware of the criticisms that have been leveled at the approach so that the appropriate level of care and caution is exercised in its use and claims made. It is to this task that I now turn.

The critique and defence of Symbolic Convergence Theory

In the 25 years or so since its inception, SCT has become an established method of rhetorical criticism that continues to be refined and applied in empirical studies. Most textbooks of rhetorical criticism devote significant space to explanations of SCT and FTA (e.g. Foss, 1989; Griffin, 1997; Hart, 1989) and Bormann has continued actively to publish updates of SCT development and refutations of critics (Bormann, 1982c, 1983, 1985). In 1994, Bormann, Cragan and Shields provided a summative defense of SCT in which they reviewed the collective critique of the theory and how they had responded to it. They bundle the most frequently cited criticisms into one of the following four "negative indictments", to which I have added a fifth.

Indictment 1

SCT's proponents have not clarified the basic presuppositions that undergird the theory. Farrell (1980), Gronbeck (1990) and Mohrmann (1982a, 1982b) have all criticized SCT for overly concentrating on the theory itself at the expense of an exposition of its basic underlying ontological and epistemological assumptions. Bormann, Cragan and Shields reply by spelling out four basic presuppositions of SCT which, they argue, have already been articulated by Bormann (1982c) and, in greater detail, in the book *Communication Theory* (Bormann, 1980). The first presupposition is that a "grounded approach" to theory building can result in a good general communication theory. They argue forcefully that SCT scholars "did not posit fantasy types, inside-cues, rhetorical visions and sagas, and then go out looking for them" but instead, the concepts emerged from their empirical studies over time (Bormann et al., 1994: 263).

Their second presupposition is that an empirically based study of the sharing of imagination could provide a viable account of the rhetorical relationship between the rational and irrational. SCT has evolved as part of a wider movement in communication studies that has endeavored to recover and stress the importance of imaginative language (and the imagination) in nonverbal and verbal transactions but has been forced to face the "barrier of rationality". According to Bormann et al. (1994), SCT has been successful in surmounting this wall because, "the force of fantasy accounts not only for the irrational and non-rational aspects of persuasion but it creates the ground for the rational elements as well" (1994: 265).

The third basic presupposition of SCT is that it encourages a return to the traditions of Classical rhetoric and neo-Aristotelianism in which the audience once again becomes an important part of the rhetorical paradigm. During the 1960s, Black (1965) led an attack on the audience connection because he felt that a concern with the immediate audience for a piece of rhetoric would be an intrusion that would trivialize the analysis. In its concern with the rhetorical community and the process of consciousness-creating, -raising and -sustaining, FTA has done much to bring the audience back into the analytical equation.

The fourth and final presupposition of SCT put forward by Bormann, Cragan and Shields is that it is possible and indeed important to make generalizations based on the results of previous studies. As noted earlier, one of the underlying agendas of the research program of Bormann and his colleagues has been to attempt to provide a framework and language that might unify or at least provide some common ground for the disparate camps within the fragmented field of rhetorical criticism.

Indictment 2

SCT is Freudian-based and therefore applies only to small group communication.
In the May 1982 issue of the *Quarterly Journal of Speech*, Mohrman and
Bormann engaged in an intellectual dogfight verging on open hostility.
A major plank of Mohrman's argument was based on the assumption that,
because Bales (1970), a Freudian, had provided an important starting point
for FTA and SCT, the subsequent rhetorical work had to be essentially
Freudian. It was, therefore, open to all of the criticisms that have been
leveled at the Freudian canon. While acknowledging that he is indebted
to Bales for highlighting the dynamic process of sharing group fantasies,
Bormann flatly denied the Freudian influence, arguing that SCT emphasizes
the rhetorical dimension, which includes the conscious and not the unconscious adaptation by audiences. With the inadvertent exception of "manifest
content" (which has subsequently been dropped from the SCT lexicon),
Freudian terms have studiously not been used in SCT studies.

Mohrman's other major concern is that a Freudian would not attempt to
generalize the sharing of fantasies beyond the small group context because
at each stage, as the drama moves from context to context, it becomes
different not only in degree but also in kind. The critics allege that there is
something uniquely powerful in the chaining of small group fantasy, and
that this is something that does not take place in other communication
settings. In response, Bormann, Cragan and Shields point to the work of
psychohistorians who have extended their studies to historical group
fantasies (e.g. De Mause, 1977). They also refer to Bales's own concern that
Mohrman was being too restrictive in terms of communication settings
when he suggested that Freudians and other psychiatrists had not shown
the usefulness of fantasy sharing in a wide variety of communication
contexts. They affirm that FTA studies have provided a strong non-
Freudian-inspired case for extending SCT from small group communication
to larger group contexts.

Indictment 3

SCT's insights are researcher-dependent and not theory-dependent. Several critics
have suggested that the insights that have been generated through the use
of SCT and FTA studies were perhaps due more to the unique skills and
discernment of the individual researcher than the application of SCT and
its attended methods per se. In reviews of Bormann's *Force of Fantasy*, for
example, Ivie felt that it was "a study that is indebted to the critic's acumen
more than his method" (1987: 102). Similarly, Osborn observed that "it is not
always convincing that the critical insights derive from and depend upon
the theory" (1986: 205). In defence, Bormann, Cragan and Shields suggest
that the perspective and the vocabulary used by the researcher automatically shape the selection of material for study and the interpretation of the

discourse. FTA, they say, "points the scholar to imaginative language, and SCT stresses not a unique reading of myth, metaphor, narrative, or story but provides a clear technical vocabulary for the general analysis of imaginative language and a way to make a coherent analysis of a community's public consciousness" (Bormann et al., 1994: 276). While they acknowledge that individualized literary approaches can occasionally lead to unusual and insightful analyses, they are concerned that these studies do not produce cumulative findings about the nature of communication and human symbol use. They are particularly scornful of the practice among many rhetorical critics of the partial extraction and eclectic mixing of concepts that have been derived from such fashionable authorities as Derrida, Foucault and Barthes.

Indictment 4

SCT is a relabeling of old concepts with trivial jargon that lacks precision and clarity. A number of critics have characterized SCT as jargonistic, ambiguous and somewhat slippery. For example, Osborn has noted the "often cloudy jargon of FTA" (1986: 204) and Gronbeck has stressed "its lack of systematic development of primary vocabulary (especially the theme/type/vision trilogy)" (1990: 324). In response, Bormann et al. (1994) argue that their technical concepts are not merely heuristic or discrete, but in fact, through their research investigations, these concepts have become grounded in rhetoric and increasingly refined so that they have considerably more analytical power than a mere taxonomic structure. In their quest for clarity, they have been guided by Durkheim's argument about the need for social scientists to develop a specialized language so that they can strip away the multiplicity of meanings from words used in everyday language (Durkheim, 1938).

Black has described SCT as a "categorical scheme" that "sometimes has yielded criticism that seems formulatory and predictable" (1980: 335). Similarly, commenting on a collection of SCT studies, Farrell asks the reader to consider the question: "Is there not some danger of a sedimented 'cookie-cutter' mentality developing?" (1982: 96). In this way he is implying that those who use SCT employ it because it is simple and guarantees neat and tidy but superficial results every time. Cragan and Shields acknowledge that, for those who are interested in developing scholarship that is a one-time only introspective intervention between the scholar and communication phenomenon, this view may hold some weight. However, from the perspective of those who are trying to build theories to explain phenomena and provide applied research solutions,

> The better the quality of the cookie cutter (theory), the more assurance we have of imprinting the same design on the dough we call communication, and the more likely we can investigate systematically, generalize

across cases, and replicate findings. What seems to the critics as predictable, formulaic, cookie cutter, and method-as-template is the desired end-state of theory building, as opposed to justification for discouraging words.

(Cragan and Shields, 1995: 193)

While Bormann and his colleagues have done a generally good job of defending and, in some instances, clarifying their theory and method in the face of critical scrutiny, I have identified another indictment that I think may be well worth considering and responding to.

An additional indictment

While SCT presents a developed epistemology, it is ontologically underdeveloped. Bormann has presented us with an essentially "epistemic" rhetoric that suggests that rhetoric actively creates knowledge which, in turn, creates reality and truth (Scott, R.L., 1967). While this "rhetorical perspective" has tended to hold sway among most communication and rhetorical theorists, a number of scholars including Bormann have conveyed a sense of unease about the pitfalls of skepticism and relativism that are associated with this philosophical position, saying, "the question remains about the best philosophical position to account for the relativism and still provide a foundation for scholarship that is based upon what is the case" (Bormann et al., 1994: 284). Bormann (1980) has attempted, with limited success, to develop an empirical and logical philosophical analysis that can sort out this issue by following Gregory Bateson's (1973) lead and applying Bertrand Russell's theory of types. Using Russell's schema, Bormann suggests that natural phenomena occur at Level I, the lowest level of philosophical analysis. By contrast, human communication occurs at Level II and is theorized by FTA and SCT at Levels III and IV of philosophical analysis respectively.

Chesebro (1988) has located in Kenneth Burke's later writings an intriguing possibility for bridging the philosophical gap graphically illustrated by the Bormann–Mohrmann exchange: through Burke's "ontological-epistemic dialectic". For Burke, "a dialectical relationship – an epistemic and ontic interaction – defines and determines the functions of rhetoric, fostering creative human responses to environments but also responding to the nature of environments" (Chesebro, 1988: 176). Given Burke and Bormann's mutual investment in and passion for the dramatistic metaphor, it seems reasonable to see if some of Burke's work might help to enrich further SCT and FTA. One of the obvious contributions that Burke could make toward enriching SCT and FTA is in explicating some of the human motives from which language derives its rhetorical potency. According to Bormann, each rhetorical vision contains as part of its substance the motive that will impel the participants. He explains, "motives do not exist to be expressed in communication but arise in the expression itself and come to be embedded in the drama of the fantasy themes that generated and served to sustain them" (Bormann, 1972: 406). Beyond this, he is not as clear or as expansive as we might have liked in defining and identifying what these motives might be.

In his extensive canon, Burke identifies a number of critical human motives that can be exploited by rhetoric. For the purposes of this study, I want to highlight three of these motives – Identification, Hierarchy and Transcendence – as I believe them to be particularly pertinent to our understanding of the management fashion-setting process, especially when we focus on the management guru–manager relationship that lies at the heart of it. Burke considered Identification to be the key differentiator between his new rhetoric and the old rhetoric, with its emphasis upon persuasion and the implicit deliberation by which rhetoric was designed and brought about by the rhetor (Corbett, 1990). According to Burke (1962), human beings communicate in order to eliminate the "division" or "alienation" or "disassociation" that arises from being inevitably isolated and divided from one another as a result of their separate physical bodies. In our communication, we form selves or identities through various properties or "substances", including physical objects, occupations, friends, activities, beliefs and values. As we ally ourselves with these properties or substances, we share substance with whatever or whomever we associate and, in the process, become "consubstantial" or "identified" with it or them (Cheney, 1983). With identification comes the possibility of persuasion for, as Burke argues, "you persuade a man only insofar as you can talk his language by speech, gesture, tonality, order, image, attitude, idea, identifying your ways with his" (Foss et al., 1985: 158). For Burke, then, "rhetoric occurs when individuals examine their identities to determine who they are and how they fit into groups with others who share those identities" (Heath, 1986: 202).

Another key motive within Burke's rhetorical system is "hierarchy". Burke suggests that people are "goaded by hierarchy" to do more and have more. Hierarchy is fundamentally and inevitably entrenched in all human activity. In their quest for more money, more knowledge, more beauty, humans become gluttons for the "rhetoric of perfection" (Burke, 1962). Rhetoric is filled with overstatements because it so often focuses on the end-points of the hierarchy, inspiring us with the highest highs and frightening us with the lowest lows. The general principle is that persuasion profits directly from the "hierarchical energy" contained within an audience.

In addition to hierarchy, Burke identifies a "transcendental" motive which stems from humans' need to feel that they are doing something important with their lives, that they are rising above the ordinary. In meeting these needs, rhetoric acts as a "secular prayer" which can have tremendous motivational power over individuals. Hart has neatly summarized and distinguished the motivational potency of hierarchy and transcendence as conceptualized by Burke:

> If hierarchy gives rhetoric a quantitative dimension (how much, how often, how high), transcendence gives it a qualitative dimension (how good, how grand, how noble). Hierarchy argues that people can get more; transcendence argues that they can become better. Hierarchy suggests how people can improve; transcendence tells them why they should.
>
> (Hart, 1989: 351)

Kenneth Burke's elaborate, inventive and frequently perplexing system of rhetoric is appealing because of its concern with the rhetor–audience relationship and its desire to look beyond a text to try to understand how that relationship serves the audience's needs and expectations. A distinguishing feature of Burke's system is that the self can act as the audience for rhetoric, in the manner of Mead's "I" addressing its "Me" (Burke, 1962). It is these concerns that make Burke a manifestly "psychological" critic (Hart, 1989). Burke finds rhetoric in places that are well beyond the traditional concern of rhetoricians in such novel realms as sales promotion, courtship, social etiquette, education, hysteria and witchcraft. Wherever he looks he continually asserts through his pentadic structure of act, agent, agency, purpose and scene, the importance of all of the various elements of the dramatic context of discourse, showing that any piece of discourse must be judged against the situational and cultural contexts in which it was produced and in which it is being interpreted (Horner, 1990). Burke defines rhetoric as "the use of words by human agents to form attitudes or to induce actions in other human agents" (1962: 565). It is "rooted in an essential function of language itself, a function that is wholly realistic, and is continually born anew; the use of language as a symbolic means of inducing co-operation in beings that by nature respond to symbols" (1962: 567).

Burke believes that drama is present whenever people congregate but that the essential drama of a situation is not revealed until rhetoric exploits it. Rhetoric not only provides a name for that situation but also presents a creative strategy for dealing with it or for solving problems inherent in that situation. Rhetoric helps the rhetor maneuver through life, directs the operations of life and provides ways of feeling more at home in the chaos of the modern world. A piece of rhetorical work provides assistance to the rhetor and the audience by providing them with a vocabulary of thoughts, actions, emotions and attitudes for codifying and thus interpreting the situation (Burke, 1931). The job of the rhetorical critic is, therefore, to inspect the discourse of the rhetorical work to locate its model of motivation and to explain the rhetor's dramatic actions parsimoniously (Hart, 1989).

In his review of group communication theories, Poole (1990) has identified SCT as one of the most useful because it is grounded in a powerful metaphor (i.e. dramatism) and is situated in a "theory–method complex " that is an interdependent whole in which the method shapes the theory and vice versa. Moreover, Griffin has applauded Bormann's efforts to create a "joint venture between the arts and sciences that encourages rhetoricians and empiricists to work in harmony" (Griffin, 1997: 43). Within this theory–method complex, FTA allows the critic to examine systematically, yet sensitively, the unique as well as the common rhetorical features of each management fashion. The method enables the critic to strike an important balance between the individual perspective that the researcher brings to the critique by virtue of her or his background and experience with these management fashions and the need to learn from and share with other critics who have pursued this method with different experiences in different empirical contexts. As Black has observed in his landmark essay on rhetorical criticism,

> because only the critic is the instrument of criticism, the critic's relationship to other instruments will profoundly affect the value of critical inquiry. And in criticism, every instrument has to be assimilated by the critic, to have become an integral part of the critic's mode of perception.
>
> (Black, 1965: xii)

Golden, Berquist and Coleman observe that "a special insight which Bormann brings to his analyses is his contention that meaning and motives are not embedded in the minds of people alone but are also found in the message itself" (Golden et al., 1976: 432). In privileging the message over these other components, Bormann has found an effective way to transcend the question about which point the critic should enter into his or her analysis. With regards to the study of management gurus and fashions, should we be most concerned about the guru, or about the content of the management fashion itself, or about the manager who follows the fashion, or the community within which the guru formed his or her ideas? According to Bormann, we need to look to the rhetoric alone for its understanding. The second half of this chapter will explain how the critic located the rhetoric in this study of management gurus and management fashions.

Research design

Case study selection

In this study I examine three separate case studies, each of which focuses on a particular management fashion as a rhetorical vision that has been created by a single or pair of management gurus. The case studies provide both a deep description of the discourse related to management fashions and the beginnings of an explanatory framework, informed by SCT, within

which to understand better the management fashion and guru phenomenon. In this respect, the case studies will be used "as a small step toward
grand generalization" (Stake, 1993: 238) by uncovering "the interplay of
significant factors that is characteristic of the phenomenon" (Merriam, 1995:
108).

Yin has presented a composite definition of "case study" which suggests
that it is an "empirical inquiry that investigates a contemporary phenomenon within its real-life context; when the boundaries between phenomenon
and context are not clearly evident; and in which multiple sources of
evidence are used" (1989: 23). It is a particularly appropriate research
strategy when researchers are trying to ask "how" or "why" questions
about a contemporary set of events over which they have little or no control.
Given its all-pervasive and contemporaneous nature, the management guru
and fashion phenomenon clearly fits these criteria.

The three management fashions selected in this study have provided
competing explanations and prescriptions for managerial and organizational success and have generated considerable followings during the 1990s
particularly in North America. All three have questioned established
managerial identities and organizational forms and each has provided
compelling alternative models. Each rhetorical vision is at a mature or
"consciousness-sustaining" stage in its evolution (Bormann et al., 1996).
Because interest has peaked in them, the challenge currently facing the
management guru is to sustain and prolong interest in them. The three case
studies were selected not because they attempt to be exhaustive but because
they highlight three quite different rhetorical strategies by which the gurus
have established themselves. Specifically, they provide useful exemplars
of each of the three master analogues identified by Bormann and his
colleagues.

The first case study examines the rhetorical vision of Michael Hammer
and James Champy's reengineering movement, which is undergirded
by an essentially pragmatic analogue that tells managers, "you have to
do this because it is your *only* choice". The second case study looks at
the effectiveness movement led by Stephen Covey, which is based on
a righteous master analogue that could be neatly encapsulated in the
phrase "you should do this because it is the *right* thing to do". The final case
study examines the social master analogue of the learning organization
popularized by Peter Senge that can be summarized as "think about doing
this because it is a *good* thing to do".

While it is difficult, and perhaps impossible, to gauge the true scale and
sphere of influence of a particular management fashion, indirect indicators
of influence can be used as surrogates. In Figure 3.1, I have plotted the
frequency with which each of the management gurus studied was cited in
the full texts of UMI's ProQuest Direct on-line information service
(http://www.umi.com/proquest). The graph clearly shows the rapid and
parallel rise of Michael Hammer, James Champy, Stephen Covey and Peter

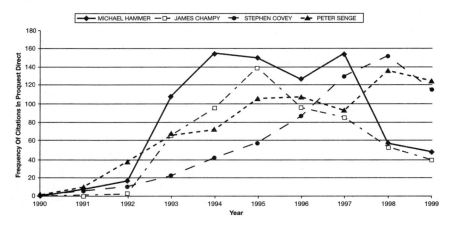

Figure 3.1 The rise of four prominent management gurus during the 1990s

Senge from relative obscurity in 1990 to widespread recognition by the mid-1990s. Since that period, interest in them has waxed and waned at quite different rates. Stephen Covey and Peter Senge have apparently sustained attention longer than the other three gurus (though a recent downward trajectory is clearly discernible), while interest in James Champy has fallen off quite rapidly. Michael Hammer enjoyed a late revival in 1997 before experiencing a decline in media attention. In the empirical case studies that follow we shall explore some of the reasons behind these varying fortunes.

Data collection

In accordance with Bormann's strongly asserted view that a single text is insufficient to conduct a proper fantasy theme critique (1972), the data sources used in each of the case studies here are multitextual. They encompass a wide range of media including not only the books, videos, cassette tapes and articles that have been produced by the guru but also the media accounts of them that have appeared in the mainstream and business press. Because I am primarily interested in analyzing the collective "message" that the guru has been responsible for generating either directly or indirectly, my focus was not exclusively confined to the original texts written by the gurus. Apart from the fact that many of these texts are, in fact, ghost-written (Crainer, 1998b), it is the active dissemination of the message in the realm of popular managerial discourse that is critical to analyze because it is here that the managerial audience is exposed to these ideas. Similarly, it is not assumed that managers will slavishly read every word of the original texts. My discussions with a number of management book readers from Canada, New Zealand and the U.K. suggest that, despite their best intentions, they invariably find time to read only the introductory chapter and browse through the remainder of the book, relying more on media accounts to summarize the key ideas.

I have drawn on both "rhetorical acts" performed by the management gurus in the form of live and satellite videoconferences and numerous "rhetorical artifacts" – texts by and about the management gurus and the rhetorical visions that they have helped to foster (Foss, 1989). This range of sources allows for the tracking of fantasy themes across discourse situations, which Bormann says is essential for genuine thematizing to take place (Hart, 1989). Reliance on media accounts also reflects my conviction that, as management gurus are socially constructed through many media (Berger and Luckmann, 1966; Chen and Meindl, 1991), they are best understood by endeavoring to build a composite picture from texts produced by the gurus themselves as well as from media accounts of them. These data sources for this study are summarized in Table 3.2.

The gurus' presentations varied in length (from three hours to a full day) and format (one was live and the remainder were delivered "live" via satellite). Most of the presentations featured the guru lecturing at length with some time left at the end of the presentation devoted to audience questions. In observing the presentations, I was able to gain a good appreciation of the performative aspects of each guru's rhetorical message. My role as the local organizer of these presentations on behalf of the University of Calgary also afforded me a good opportunity to interact with various members of the audience to gain a sense of how they were responding to the guru's message. Through this interaction and subsequent analysis of the presentation's evaluation forms that were completed by

Table 3.2 The types and number of data sources utilized in the study

	"Reengineering" Michael Hammer & James Champy	"Effectiveness" Stephen Covey	"The Learning Organization" Peter Senge
Number of live presentations/satellite videoconference performances	3	3	3
Number of books authored by the management guru	4	3	2
Number of articles authored by the management guru	15	47	12
Number of articles about the management guru and the management fashion	112	41	54

audience members, I derived a grounded, albeit anecdotal, appreciation of what parts of the message the audience members found particularly stimulating and worthy of comment.

The media accounts were obtained directly from UMI's ProQuest Direct on-line bibliographic service. This service provides search and retrieval access to summaries and complete articles from over 5,000 business and business-oriented publications and is particularly suitable for researching organizational communication phenomena (Rubin et al., 1993). The articles were identified by using either the gurus' name or the symbolic cue (i.e. "reengineering", "seven habits" and "learning organization") as the search criteria. Articles were included if they were either authored by the guru or made mention of his name in the body of the article. The business media comprise journalistic products such as newspapers, magazines, trade journals, television programs and radio broadcast segments that are designed to be consumed primarily by the business community. As texts, the products of the business media provide a potentially rich and insightful data source because of the passive and active roles they play in the social construction of everyday management knowledge. The media, in order to be successful, strive to reflect the principal concerns and preoccupations of their readership. As such, in this passive role, they provide an unobtrusive window onto the everyday lifeworld of the business community (Webb et al., 1966). On the other hand, the business media also work actively to shape the agenda of the everyday business lifeworld by making decisions about what accounts they present and how they shape these accounts. As such, the business media are a critical element in the management guru industry. They are instrumental in first identifying gurus to the broader business public, in actively promoting them and, most critically, by virtue of their privileged status, in legitimating the management gurus to the consumer population of practicing managers who read them.

Data analysis

Before describing step by step the method used to analyze the data, it is useful to distinguish Fantasy Theme Analysis from Content Analysis. While both methods take the written word as their starting point and both examine written texts for insights into the subject at hand, FTA differs in three significant ways. First, FTA is an explicitly subjective technique. As was indicated earlier in a previous chapter, it "owns up to the fact that the value of what critics find in a text depends on who they are, what they know and how they use their knowledge to identify and interpret dramas" (Kendall, 1993: 577). Second, FTA takes a systemic as opposed to a systematic viewpoint to data analysis. Because the critic is concerned with the whole of the rhetoric within which the drama unfolds, "rather than systematically deconstructing a text by counting words, phrases and structures, the dramatistic critic attempts to discern dramas that compose an overall rhetorical vision, experiencing the text to arrive at an interpretation of the system in its entirety" (Kendall, 1993: 577). Finally, unlike the quantitatively based content analysis, FTA is a qualitative research method. Van Maanen defines qualitative methods as "an array of interpretative techniques which seek to describe, decode, translate and otherwise come to terms with the meaning, not the frequency, of certain more or less naturally occurring phenomena in the social world" (1983: 9). In this study I have, as Burgoyne has advised, "counted the countable" (Cassell and Symon, 1995: 4), such as considering book sales and citation frequencies. I have not, however, attempted to impose restrictive a priori classifications on either the collection or the analysis of the data. I have been more concerned with emergent themes and idiographic descriptions.

Cresswell acknowledges that qualitative research is a form of social and human research that does not have firm guidelines or specific procedures and is evolving and changing constantly. It therefore "complicates telling others how one plans to conduct a study and how others might judge when the study is done" (Cresswell, 1998: 17). True to form, Bormann and his immediate colleagues do not spell out in any detail the nuts and bolts of conducting Fantasy Theme Analysis. However, Foss (1989) has helpfully identified and described five steps in conducting fantasy theme criticism. These are

1   finding evidence of the sharing of fantasy themes or a rhetorical vision;
2   coding the rhetorical artifacts for setting, character and action themes;
3   constructing the rhetorical vision(s) on the basis of the fantasy themes;
4   naming the motive for the visions identified; and
5   assessing the group's rhetorical vision.

This framework guided the conduct of the present study.

In searching out evidence of the sharing of the rhetorical vision within a rhetorical community, I sifted through the various newspaper, professional and trade journal articles, noting the use of symbolic cues such as catch-phrases and slogans that had been coined by the management guru and had now fallen into regular currency. For example, Stephen Covey's phrase "putting first things first" cropped up in a wide range of articles and is one that I have heard colleagues and students allude to on numerous occasions in the course of everyday conversation. As Foss observes, "when people have shared a fantasy theme, they have charged that theme with meanings and emotions that can be set off by an agreed-upon cryptic symbolic cue" (1989: 294).

Having confirmed that a particular rhetorical vision was widely shared, I then coded the rhetorical artifacts in order to isolate the recurrent fantasy themes within that vision. This involved a careful reading of the artifact, sentence by sentence, to pick out references to settings, characters and actions that might form the basis for major fantasy themes. Setting, character and action themes were colour-coded to make it easier to distinguish between them. In reading the texts, I was mindful of Hodder's concern that "different types of text have to be understood in the contexts of production and meaning" (1993: 394). For this reason I was primarily concerned with what these different texts said about the manager's role, behaviors and identity within the organization. Using the coding procedures developed by Glaser and Strauss (1967) and refined by Miles and Huberman (1994), I was able to generate a set of initial codes from reading and rereading the texts through a process of "simultaneous collection and analysis of data" (Merriam, 1995: 116). The coding continued until I reached a point of "saturation" at which "no additional data are being found" and I could "develop properties of a category" (Glaser and Strauss, 1967: 61).

I moved on to the third step, which involved looking for patterns from which I could isolate major from minor themes. Those that appeared most frequently and seemed to subsume a number of lesser themes were identified as the major fantasy themes that became the subject of the analysis. These were given labels, often derived from the guru's own text, which I thought would best convey the essence of the individual theme to the reader. So, for example, when it became clear that the agrarian motif and, specifically, a nostalgic view of rural life, continually cropped up in Covey's writing, his presentations and his interviews, I thought that the label "Back to the Farm" could most potently communicate this theme to the reader. The theme's labels, of course, are by no means the end of the story. It is in the elaboration of this theme under the label that its rhetorical potency can be understood. The rhetorical vision was then constructed by linking the setting themes that I had identified with the characters depicted in those settings as well as with the actions those characters were shown to be performing. Having laid out the rhetorical vision, I began to explore the motives for the participants in the rhetorical vision, drawing on Burke's schema of motives (Burke, 1962; Hart, 1989).

The final stage involved an evaluation of the management fashion with reference to the rhetorical visions that have been offered by competing management fashions. In making this assessment, I asked the following questions, suggested by Foss (1989):

- How well did the rhetoric deal with the problem of creating and celebrating a sense of community?
- Did the rhetoric help generate a group and individual self-image that was strong, confident and resilient?
- How did the rhetoric aid or hinder the community in its adaptation to its environment?
- How did the rhetoric deal with the problem of creating a social reality that provides a norm for community behavior in terms of the level of violence, exploitation, dominance and injustice?

Each of the case studies presented in this study in Chapters 4, 5 and 6 follows a similar but by no means identical format. This variance reflects both the distinctiveness of each rhetorical vision plus an improved facility and comfort with this approach as each case study was conducted. The case commences with an examination of the person and persona of the sanctioning agent for the rhetorical vision. The guru's background and formative experiences are summarized and the various rhetorical strategies that he has developed to articulate, disseminate and legitimate his rhetorical vision are highlighted. This is followed by an examination of the rhetorical community that has developed around the rhetorical vision. This provides the reader with a sense of the types of individuals and groups who have been the most vocal in their endorsement of the vision and of the particular aspects of the vision that the followers have most heavily emphasized. The rhetorical vision of the management fashion is then presented by providing a description of each of the fantasy themes identified in the analysis. This description lays out the key properties of the theme, provides illuminating quotations from the data, and ascribes the underlying motive that gives the theme its rhetorical potency. Following Merriam's observation that "there is not a standard format for reporting case study research" but the "overall intent of the case study undoubtedly shapes the larger structure of the written narrative" (cited in Cresswell, 1998: 186), each case closes with a different line of inquiry that the FTA triggered for the author. As Foss observes, "once a rhetorical vision has been identified, the critic is free to evaluate it according to whatever social and theoretical goals interest the critic and are suggested by the artifacts" (1989: 297).

Summary

A connection between the dramatistic method of rhetorical criticism outlined in this chapter and the celebrated showmanship and theatricality of the management gurus' performances does not require a large leap of the imagination. Further reflection has revealed, however, that Symbolic Convergence Theory and its attendant method, Fantasy Theme Analysis, possess an analytical value that is well beyond this immediate and intuitive appeal. First, the dramatistic method of rhetorical criticism provides a useful theoretical framework for analyzing the symbolic exchange between the manager and management guru that was identified in Chapter 2 as being a critical analytical element for current research efforts. Second, the method's preoccupation with scripts, roles and settings provides a powerful window for the researcher to observe the process of identity construction for both the guru and his or her followers. Third, the dramatistic method provides a framework for interpreting a wide range of situations, events and texts, while allowing for the unique qualities of each account to emerge. As Mangham and Overington observe, "it provides possibilities for demystifying the conditions of organizational life, as these are directly or indirectly experienced, while it resists being turned into a literal myth" (1987: 2). Fourth, its preoccupation with the persuasive properties of language or rhetoric means that the dramatistic method of rhetorical criticism is ideally suited to an analysis of actors who derive their authority charismatically.

In this chapter I have also described the rationale for the present study and details of the research design that guided the empirical portion of the book. A case study approach was chosen because it is well suited to the complex, contemporary and relatively under-theorized nature of the management guru and management fashion phenomenon. Three case studies were selected in an effort to help the research effort move toward generalization and to illustrate ideal types of the three master analogues that Bormann and his colleagues have found to underpin all of the rhetorical visions that they have studied. The cases – reengineering, effectiveness and the learning organization – encompass management fashions that have captured the corporate imagination of North America in a substantial way during the 1990s. Data collected for these case studies were drawn from a wide array of media sources including the guru's products (i.e. live and taped presentations, books and articles) and the media's accounts of the guru and the management fashion that he was proposing. The data were analyzed using a five-step process. It is to the first of the management guru and management fashion case studies that we now turn.

4 Michael Hammer, James Champy and the Reengineering Movement

American managers are adept at moving in unfamiliar territory. It's why reengineering happened here before it took root in Europe or Japan. We're good at remaking everything in business – the product, the processes and everything around us. Now we as managers have to remake ourselves.
(James Champy interview, *Insights Quarterly*, 1994: 21)

Suck it up. . . . Live with it. . . . Get used to it. In other words, no whining. It may not be pretty but it has to be done. It's better than being bored.
(Michael Hammer cited in Church, 1999: B23)

Introduction

The empirical section of this book begins with an analysis of the work of James Champy and Michael Hammer, the leading luminaries of the reengineering movement and two of the most influential management gurus in recent years. The reengineering movement has had a massive and far-reaching impact on the way work is done in organizations throughout the world. While the attention it has garnered reached its peak in the mid-1990s, projects continue to be launched in the name of reengineering on a daily basis in all sectors of the economy and spheres of business. In its wake reengineering has, by virtue of its close association with downsizing and the accompanying loss of jobs, generated considerable controversy. Consequently, it is perhaps the most publicly debated and hotly contested management fashion to have emerged in the last 30 years.

The chapter begins with a discussion of the origins of the reengineering movement and the role that Michael Hammer and James Champy have played in its creation, promotion and dissemination. This is followed by a description of Hammer and Champy's rhetorical vision of reengineering, which I argue is underpinned by an essentially "pragmatic" master analogue. The vision derives its rhetorical power by stressing the practical reasons for engaging in reengineering and emphasizing its appeal to common sense. Reengineering is not necessarily a good thing to do. Nor is it necessarily the right thing to do. But it is the *only* thing that managers can do in the face of a business environment that is so wrought with risk and uncertainty. As Fincham asserts in his critique, "like magic, re-engineering is part of a self-perpetuating total discourse that excludes alternatives and neutralizes dissent" (1996: 15).

In the second part of the chapter I identify and describe three main fantasy themes that I argue act as the building-blocks of Hammer and Champy's rhetorical vision of reengineering. All three are character themes that endeavor to shape and influence the self-concept of the manager (Gergen, 1971, 1991). The third and final part of the chapter shows how a dramatistic analysis recasts the reengineering movement as a 'performance' that is enacted in two different analytical realms. The first realm encompasses the broad arena of managerial discourse. It focuses on how Hammer and Champy successfully persuaded managers to become interested in reengineering and, ultimately, pursue a reengineering project within their own organization. The second realm encompasses reengineering as a drama as it is 'played out' within the organization. The chapter closes by describing several empirical studies that have revealed a significant and problematic disjuncture between the rhetorical vision of reengineering and how individuals within organizations have, in fact, experienced it.

The reengineering movement

The rise and fall of reengineering

In the mid-1990s, reengineering or Business Process Reengineering (BPR) eclipsed Total Quality Management (TQM) as the most widely recognized, if not practiced, organizational improvement initiative (Burdett, 1994). Despite its popularity, considerable confusion remains about its content and character so that "the concept remains surprisingly ill-defined" (Jones, M., 1994: 358) and "there is not even an agreed name for this ill-defined idea" (Edwards and Peppard, 1994: 252). For the purposes of this study, I shall be referring to it as reengineering.

Knights and McCabe (1998a) distinguish between two main variants of reengineering. On the one hand, there are the "dream-like exhortations" of Hammer and Champy, who define it as "the fundamental rethinking and radical design of business processes to achieve dramatic improvements in critical, contemporary measures of performance, such as cost, quality, service and speed" (Hammer and Champy, 1993: 32). On the other hand there is the "hard-headed, pragmatic but nonetheless somewhat mechanistic incitements" of Davenport's "process innovation", which "encompasses the envisioning of new work strategies, the actual process design activity, and the implementation of change in all its complex technological, human, and organizational dimensions" (Davenport, 1993: 2).

Grint (1994) has identified several features that are common to all conceptions of reengineering. These include the switch from functional departments to process teams; the shift from simple to multi-tasked work; a reversal of power relations from superordinate to subordinate; the empowerment of employees; changes in employees' focus away from a hierarchical concern with one's superior toward customers; changes in management's behavior from that of supervising to coaching; and the flattening of hierarchies. Knights and McCabe (1998a) argue that the essence of reengineering is its emphasis upon a process-based, rather than a functional, approach to the organization of work which is facilitated by the increased and intensive use of information technology. While Hammer and Champy have cast it as a novel approach, several commentators have firmly identified reengineering with the traditions of Taylorism, arguing that it is merely a form of warmed-up Scientific Management (e.g. Cummings, 1999; Grint and Willcocks, 1995; Taylor, 1995).

A telephone survey conducted in 1994 by Mercer Management Consulting of 180 U.S. and 100 European companies found that 75 percent of these companies had engaged in "significant" reengineering efforts in the last three years and the results had either "met or exceeded" their expectations in 80 percent of these cases (Kinni, 1994). Studies conducted by CSC Index in early 1994 (Champy, 1995) and Pitney Bowes Management Services in late 1994 (Verespej, 1995) respectively found that 69 percent of 497 companies surveyed and 83 percent of 100 companies surveyed had already engaged in one or more reengineering projects. It is not surprising, therefore, to learn that the reengineering movement spawned a significant consulting boom that was estimated by one market research firm to be worth more than $7 billion in reengineering projects during 1994 (Hammer and Stanton, 1995). Andersen Consulting has taken the lion's share of the consulting spoils and, in the process, was able to quadruple its worldwide revenues in five years to $4.2 billion in 1995 (*Economist*, 1996b).

Drawing on the results from a multi-year survey of the usage and satisfaction levels with organizational improvement tools that was conducted by Bain & Company, Rigby notes that

> Reengineering's five-year survey scores reveal the vagaries of a tool's results over time. In 1993 and 1994, reengineering was the rage. Early adopters gave it impressive ratings, and its usage climbed from 67 percent to 71 percent. But in 1995 reengineering's satisfaction scores plummeted. Early users started to complain about unexpected long-term side effects such as declining morale, loss of innovation, erosion of trust, and weakened teamwork.
>
> (Rigby, 1998: 162)

The survey, which included 4,137 responses and 224 personal interviews with senior managers in 15 countries, revealed that the use of reengineering peaked at 78 percent in 1995 and declined to 64 percent in 1997 as satisfaction levels fell to the lowest of all organizational improvement tools identified. Similarly, Holland and Kumar (1995) found that between 60 and 87 percent of reengineering projects had ended unsuccessfully.

The business media have also played a major role in promoting this movement to the broad business constituency. This is poignantly illustrated in the number of citations of the terms "reengineering" or "re-engineering" that were traced in the ProQuest Direct database either in the abstract/citation or within the full text of the article. Prior to 1990, the term was cited in a total of 80 articles. Figure 4.1 plots the dramatic rise in the use of the term in business and academic periodicals from 1993 onwards. The usage of the term appears to have peaked in 1998 with a total of 8,571 citations and has been followed by an equally dramatic fall-off in usage that has continued into the first half of 2000.

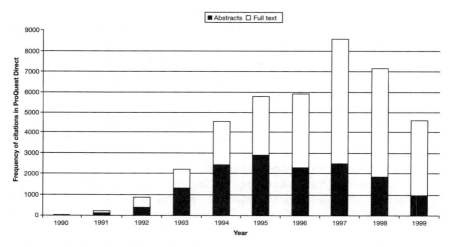

Figure 4.1   The reengineering decade of the 1990s

The falling in and out of favor of the reengineering movement with the media can be alternatively portrayed in a selection of headlines that appeared in popular business journals between 1993 and 1996 as follows:

PHASE ONE: THE UNIVERSAL ELIXIR
"The Age of Reengineering", *Across the Board*, June 1993
"Reengineering, the Hot New Management Tool", *Fortune*, August, 1993
"The Reengineering Rage", Industry Week, February, 1994
"Reengineering Europe", *Economist*, February, 1994

PHASE TWO: THE DOUBTS CREEP IN
"Reengineering is *not* Hocus Pocus", *Across the Board*, September 1994
"Hammer Defends Re-engineering", *Economist*, November 1994
"Reengineering: What Happened?", *Business Week*, January 1995
"Reengineering: A Light that Failed?", *Across the Board*, March, 1995

PHASE THREE: WHAT'S NEXT?
"The Antidote for Reengineering", *Industry Week*, April 1996
"Business Process Re-engineering RIP", *People Management*, May 1996
"Re-examining Reengineering: Down to Microsurgery",
Chemical Week, June 1996
"Reengineering Recycled", *Business Week*, August 1996

Michael Hammer and James Champy's leadership role

While many have been involved in the reengineering movement, Michael Hammer and, to a slightly lesser extent, James Champy, have played a pivotal role in distilling and disseminating the principles of the approach to a mass business audience. As a managing partner from Andersen Consulting remarked, "God Bless Michael Hammer – because he really popularised and legitimated the concept" (Thackray, 1993: 40). Hammer, who has copyrighted the reengineering term, is not reticent about taking the credit for being the "father" of the movement. He acknowledges that "I don't have to be the mother, the sister and the great-uncle as well . . . there's room for a lot of people to make contributions" (Maglitta, 1994: 85). The foundation for the movement was prepared in Michael Hammer's stinging polemic titled 'Reengineering Work: Don't Automate, Obliterate' that appeared in the *Harvard Business Review* in 1990 (Hammer, 1990). This article stimulated considerable reaction and primed the business community for a more substantial work, *Reengineering the Corporation*, which was published in 1993 and went on to sell two million copies worldwide in 15 different languages in under two years (Hammer and Champy, 1993). For this book, Hammer teamed up with James Champy, who, at the time, was chairman of CSC Index Inc., a consulting firm based in Cambridge, Massachusetts, specializing in implementing reengineering projects.

Hammer and Champy have capitalized on their popularity in two different ways. Michael Hammer has a particular flair for performance. His "barking, Rottweiler delivery" (Kennedy, 1994b) keeps the audience on its toes in a way that is eerily reminiscent of the actor Richard Dreyfuss in the movie *The Apprenticeship of Duddy Kravitz* (dir. Kotcheff, 1974). His larger-than-life presence and outlandish remarks have made him something of a media darling and scourge in the mould of Tom Peters. In 1992, *Business Week* named him as one of the "four pre-eminent management thinkers of the 1990s" (Byrne, 1992). He was also named by *Time* in 1996 as one of America's 25 "most influential individuals" (*Time*, 1996). Hammer was formerly a professor of Computer Science at the Massachusetts Institute of Technology. He left the academy in 1990 to form Hammer & Company, a "management education and research firm that focuses on cutting edge issues in operations, organizations, and technology utilization" (www.hammerandco.com). Based in Cambridge, Massachusetts, the company offers a variety of public seminars, conferences and videos in various countries around the world. Michael Hammer personally delivers seminars to between 5,000–10,000 executives annually and gives numerous keynote speeches (Church, 1999). Through its Phoenix program, Hammer & Company also serves a blue-chip consortium of 27 "leading-edge companies committed to the process revolution". In addition, Hammer has set up a number of spin-off companies that focus on reengineering projects in niche industries. For example, recognizing the obvious opportunities that the healthcare field presents for reengineering, Hammer has formed Praxis, a consulting company that specializes in studying the flow of work in healthcare (Grayson, 1997).

Adopting a relatively lower public profile, Champy comes across as being a considerably kinder, gentler and generally more humane individual than does his pugnacious partner. He is a clear and thoughtful presenter who has polished his calm and understated style to persuasive effect. Through direct consulting work with reengineering projects, he was able during the reengineering boom to expand the revenues of his practice significantly, from $30 million in 1988 to $150 million in 1993 (McConville, 1994). A lawyer, who also holds a Master of Science in Engineering from MIT, Champy founded his management consulting company in 1969. This was to be later absorbed by the multinational giant Computer Sciences Corporation and renamed CSC Index. Champy has subsequently left CSC Index and holds directorships with SYSTOR (an IT service provider for the financial services industry based in Zurich) and Perot Systems Corporation, where he is also chairman of its consulting practice. He continues to write a number of newspaper columns that are syndicated by Tribune Media. From this platform, he has been able to maintain his profile and keep the reengineering movement on the public agenda.

Given these different styles and strategies, it is perhaps not surprising that Hammer and Champy elected not to co-author the inevitable sequel to *Reengineering the Corporation* which, adapting a metaphor from the not-too-distant world of popular music, presented them with the "difficult second album syndrome". First out of the chute was James Champy with his book, *Reengineering Management*, which was published in early 1995. It was quickly followed by Hammer's book, *The Reengineering Revolution: A Handbook*, co-authored with Steven Stanton (Hammer and Stanton, 1995). Both books were pitched as responses to the criticisms that had started to build up against the reengineering movement. However, the authors chose to take two different tacks in their defense.

Champy decided to lead his assault on senior managers whom, he argued, had been primarily responsible for the failure of many reengineering efforts. He opens the book with the following comment:

> This partial revolution is not the one that I intended. If I've learned anything in the last 18 months, it is that the revolution we started has

gone, at best, only halfway. I have also learned that half a revolution is not better than none. It may, in fact, be worse.

(Champy, 1995: 3)

Champy suggests that the "other half" of the reengineering revolution should focus on reengineering the management function. Drawing on the testimony of 150 managers, he urges that management processes must be reengineered so that managers will now focus upon mobilizing, enabling, defining, measuring and communicating in order to achieve a business culture that enables a continuous process of reengineering. Champy's most recent book, *The Arc of Ambition*, which he co-authored with Nitin Nohria, continues his concern with the leadership question but this time he promotes a much more sympathetic picture of organizational leaders (Champy and Nohria, 2000). From the potpourri of contemporary and historical figures that are presented in the book, the authors argue that the critical quotient of organizational success is not how well business processes are designed, but the scale of the ambition of its leaders.

Hammer, on the other hand, argues that the reason why so many reengineering efforts failed was not because reengineering itself was wrong, but that organizations had not properly followed the procedures that he obligingly lays out in his no-nonsense, softcover "handbook". While he acknowledges the significant reengineering failures, he points out that these "reflect a fundamental fact of reengineering: it is very, very difficult to do" (Hammer and Stanton, 1995: xiv). The handbook is offered to the reader to give them the benefit of "the experiences of a great many companies without having to endure those experiences yourselves" (1995: xv).

Perhaps anticipating that interest in the reengineering movement was beginning to wane and that the backlash was now in full swing, Hammer followed up the handbook with the predictably titled *Beyond Reengineering* (Hammer, 1996). He opens the book in full capitulation mode, by stating that "this book is not about reengineering; it is about its aftermath, and its abiding legacy" (1996: xi). Billing the book as a "first draft of a business guide for the twenty-first century", Hammer argues that the business systems that were specifically targeted for reengineering (e.g. new product development, order fulfillment and customer management) should "become the permanent armature on which work is hung, not just the focus of one-shot improvements" (Stewart, 1996: 197). Twenty-first century organizations should in his mind, therefore, no longer be centered around function but on "process", that is, a "complete end-to-end set of activities that together create value for a customer" (1996: xii). Perhaps endeavoring to present a kindlier, gentler outlook on the world, Hammer confesses that, "I have come to realize that I was wrong, that the radical character of reengineering, however important and exciting, is not its most significant aspect. The key word in the definition of reengineering is 'process'" (1996: xii). The process-centered organization is characterized by responsibility, autonomy, risk, and uncertainty. It may not be a gentle environment, but it is a very human one. Gone are the artificial rigidities of the conventional corporation. In its place is a world full of messiness, challenges, and disappointments, that characterize the real world of real human beings.

(Hammer, 1996: 14)

Reengineering has "done the world of good" because it has enabled executives to see through the surface structure of their organizations and to home in on their fundamental purpose: delivering value to customers in a way that creates profits for shareholders (Hammer and Stanton, 1999).

While the reengineering movement reached its zenith in the mid-1990s, Michael Hammer has recently pointed to a "second wave" of popularity for the concept that has been prompted by the rising use of the Internet. He argues that, by linking companies together, Internet technologies can create savings and improve productivity by coordinating efforts across corporate boundaries in a process which he dubs "intercorporate reengineering" (Hammer, 1999). The net result, according to Hammer, is that "whole industries start working like one company [and] the barriers between customer and supplier, between companies, start to fall" (Church, 1999: B23). Following suit, Champy has recently argued that the reengineering movement is far from over. He states, "the hard work still lies ahead. Why? Principally, because we have yet to experience the full effect that the ubiquity of information technology will have on the way we operate" (Champy, 1998a: 26). The next phase of the reengineering war will be fought in the sales and marketing theater as organizations battle for electronic customers in the name of e-commerce. The traditional salesforce will likely sustain the heaviest casualties (Champy, 1999).

There is also evidence that reengineering is still very much on the agenda of a number of professions. For example, reengineering was selected as one of the "top ten technologies" that would affect Certified Public Accountants in the year 2000 (*Accountancy*, 1999). Reengineering also continues to be a major force for healthcare management (Grayson, 1997), human resources (Wilkerson, 1997), internal auditing (Chapman, 1998), purchasing (Morgan, 1997) and sales (Prince, 1998). Fincham (1999) has also noted that BPR has evolved from being a management fashion that was largely the brainchild of Hammer and Champy to becoming an integral component of the consultant's armoury of change management techniques.

The rhetorical vision of reengineering

Overview

What was it about Hammer and Champy's vision of reengineeering that inspired such rapid and massive interest and, subsequently, widespread take-up by Corporate America? The FTA that I conducted of their rhetorical vision revealed three very strong and interrelated character themes that build progressively upon one another. These are summarized in Table 4.1 along with metaphors that most strongly illuminated the theme. A Burkean motive is ascribed to each theme. While the gurus allude to various settings, no one theme emerged as being important to the rhetorical power of the reengineering vision. Similarly, no major action themes came to the fore during the analysis.

All three character themes speak directly to individual managers' sense of themselves – who they are and what they should be doing as managers. As Stewart has observed, Hammer and Champy are "superb at describing what's in it – and not in it – for people" (1996: 198). The first character theme, which I describe as "Preservation of Self", reflects the gurus' powerful use of fear as motivation for managers to reexamine their roles. They skillfully grab the manager's attention by placing him or her squarely at the center of the drama. By describing the ultimately untenable fate of managers who are just like them, they encourage the manager to *identify* closely with the characters they are describing. The second theme, "Redemption of Self", stresses to managers that all is not lost as they have the ability to change themselves. Should they choose not just to support but actively to pursue a reengineering project within their own organization, they have the means to *transcend* their current precarious situation. The third theme, "Representation of Self", captures the new roles that the gurus suggest managers must play in the new "reengineered" organizational reality. It lays out a clear path to help managers to progress and to continue to make their way upwards, through a transformed hierarchy. There is still a way to advance oneself more effectively within this new kind of organization.

Table 4.1 Key fantasy themes within the rhetorical vision of the reengineering movement

Fantasy theme	Type	Metaphors	Motive
Preservation of Self	Character Theme	The Death Zone Marching into Battle Painful Therapy	Identification
Redemption of Self	Character Theme	Test of Faith Adam Smith Sixties Revolutionary	Transcendence
Representation of Self	Character Theme Leader	Process Owner Coach	Hierarchy

Character theme 1: Preservation of Self

Using fear to grab people's attention is one of the world's oldest and most persuasive strategies. It is a device that has been used to powerful effect by tele-evangelists and many prominent management gurus, most notably Tom Peters. Michael Hammer and James Champy demonstrated that they had learned well from their predecessors. They use fear on three levels. First, fear is used to convince managers that they have no option but to reengineer. The tenor of their argument is simply yet powerfully stated at the top of the cover of their first book in the solemn pronouncement by Peter Drucker, the elder statesman of management gurus, that "Reengineering is new, and it must be done". Hammer reinforced this argument in his seminars with the chilling observation that, "the choice is survival: it's between redundancies of 50 percent or 100 percent" (Kennedy, 1994b: 14). In particular, they singled out middle management, ironically perhaps, their prime readership group, as the prime target for downsizing, or the "death zone" of reengineering (Hammer and Stanton, 1995: 35). Along these lines, Hammer typically remarked, "the true losers turn out to be those folks in the middle, because we need far fewer of them. And what they need to do is very different from what they're accustomed to, and many of them are hopelessly unqualified" (*Wall Street Journal*, 1995: B1). The most frequent estimate that they gave for the number of middle management positions that would be removed by reengineering was a very eye-catching 75 percent. In view of the fact that they have the most to lose in terms of authority, status, rewards and, more fundamentally, their jobs, Hammer warns that, "the instinctual reaction of most middle managers is to attempt to forestall or freeze any reengineering effort" (1995: 35).

Second, Hammer and Champy also suggested that fear was the major reason why reengineering was either ignored or sabotaged by senior managers. For example, Hammer claimed that, "a lot of people embark on reengineering but don't go anywhere because of failures of intellect or courage". Resorting to his favorite military metaphor, he taunted his readers with the observation that, "companies that unfurl the banner and march into battle without collapsing job titles, changing the compensation policy and instilling new attitudes and values get lost in the swamp" (1995: 30).

Third, Hammer and Champy suggested that managers themselves should use fear as an important element in their plans to implement reengineering within their organizations. Hammer, for example, stated that, "you must play on the two basic emotions: fear and greed. You must frighten them by demonstrating the serious shortcomings of the current processes, spelling out how drastically these defective processes are hurting the organization" (1995: 52). More philosophically, Champy observes

> The history lesson produces a good scare – that past success does not guarantee future success – but there's nothing wrong with that. For one

thing, capitalism is a system that quite literally *works* on fear. For another thing, the only way to persuade many folks to undertake painful therapy like reengineering, followed by a permanent state of mobilization, is to persuade them that the alternative will be more painful.

(Champy, 1995: 49)

However, Champy eventually softened his hard line to reengineering. When pressed in an interview about the parting of the ways with Hammer, Champy mentioned that Hammer should be more careful about his use of violent images, concluding that,

> this language of violence is now acting against the corporate interest because employees are already in such a condition of fear. Deep, deep fear. Managers, too. This has to change if reengineering is to realize its full potential.
>
> (*Across the Board*, 1995: 31)

Character theme 2: Redemption of Self

The reengineering movement posed an interesting paradox for middle managers. On the one hand, it quite clearly posed a serious threat to their very existence within the organization. On the other hand, if they dug in against it, they would lose even their remote chance of survival within the organization. As Hammer rather matter-of-factly observed:

> These downsized middle managers will have two options. A great many of them will go back to doing "real work", because for most middle managers I know it was excellence at real work that got them on the middle management track in the first place.
>
> (Cited in Hogarty, 1993: 52)

While few middle managers would, in all honesty, share the same relish, their chances for rehabilitation were relatively good. According to Champy, "we estimate that 20 percent will be unable to make the transition. I think those people will be lost – they are not going to find other middle management jobs" (Hogarty, 1993: 52).

Against this gloomy backdrop, Hammer and Champy set about laying out the path to salvation for middle managers to insure they survive the transition and remain a vibrant part of the "permanent mobilization". To do this they used four very powerful persuasive techniques. First, they empathized with their readers, demonstrating that they knew what it's like to be in their position and offering hope that there is a way out of it. For example, in his introductory chapter, Champy states:

> This book is not about operational processes. It is about managing, written for managers, and (it may be reassuring to note) by a manager. It is about us, about changing our managerial work, the way we think, organize, inspire, deploy, enable, measure, and reward the value-adding operational work. It is about changing managerial work itself.
>
> (Champy, 1995: 3)

A second technique was to provide the readers with numerous role models or "heroes" of reengineering who have shown that they can make the transition. A frequently cited case is the "test of faith" for a manager who had created self-managed work teams in a supermarket chain warehouse. He was confronted with the challenge of letting the team members decide on their own whether or not they would send a new shipment after working hours to replace one that had been damaged in a truck accident. This manager was held up as being someone who "has felt the whole nine yards of fear that reengineering often brings to managers . . . the fear of letting go, the fear of losing control, the fear of misplaced trust, of betrayal, the fear of losing popularity (or of not being 'tough'), and always, of course, the fear of failure" (Champy, 1995: 24). A great deal of both of their texts were given over to descriptions of case studies like this one – 70 pages in *Reengineering Management* and 126 pages in *The Reengineering Revolution*.

The third persuasive technique was to appeal to the manager's patriotism. Reengineering was seen as being an essentially American process that fits well with the culture of the country and, as such, is considerably easier to implement there. In the opening chapter of their first book, Hammer and Champy state that

> Reengineering capitalizes on the same characteristics that have traditionally made Americans such great business innovators: individualism, self-reliance, a willingness to accept risk, and a propensity for change. Business reengineering, unlike management philosophies that would have "us" become more like "them", doesn't try to change the behavior of American workers and managers. Instead, it takes advantage of American talents and unleashes American ingenuity.
>
> (Hammer and Champy, 1993: 3)

Similarly, Champy argues that

> Americans are good at moving on into a changing, contingent, turbulent, adverse, and largely unpredictable universe. That's the universe we're used to, and we're good at meeting the challenge, (re)making, (re)discovering, (re)presenting – in a word, reengineering – everything, including ourselves.
>
> (Champy, 1995: 33)

The argument proceeds that, in view of its privileged situation, America has an obligation to spread the word about reengineering to the four corners of the world. However, Hammer and Champy frequently mentioned that they have encountered real resistance to the technique in Europe, especially in Germany and France, but praise the faster-growing East Asian and Latin American countries for making "a better fist of reengineering" (*Economist*, 1994c: 64).

The final technique that Hammer and Champy have used to particularly dramatic effect is to stress the historical significance of the reengineering movement. Their argument was that reengineering by no means constitutes another fad or buzzword like so many that have passed through before. This time it is for real and they, as managers, have a very important part to play in making history. A recurrent theme that Hammer and Champy liked to play on was that they are, in fact, reversing the Industrial Revolution and undoing the work of Adam Smith's *Wealth of Nations* (Campbell and Skinner, 1976). Typical of the scale and scope (and audacity) of their vision was the statement that, "just as the Industrial Revolution drew peasants into the urban factories and created the new social classes of workers and managers, so will the Reengineering Revolution profoundly rearrange the way people conceive of themselves, their work, their place in society" (Hammer and Stanton, 1995: 321). Champy took this revolutionary theme one step further by arguing that

> We are in the grip of the second managerial revolution, one that's very different from the first. The first was about a transfer of power. This one is about an access of freedom. Slowly, or suddenly, corporate managers all over the world are learning that free enterprise these days really is free.
>
> (Champy, 1995: 204)

Their work was an uncanny evocation of the counter-culture movement of the 1960s. It was chock-full of the language of revolution, urging managers to liberate themselves and become as radical as they possibly can. As Champy says, "radical change through radical goal definition holds out a secret satisfaction to the manager who pulls it off. If you can learn to do what other managers in your industry thought to be impossible, you will not only thrive, you will literally redefine the industry" (1995: 122).

Character theme 3: Representation of Self

In a lecture titled 'Beyond Reengineering' that was beamed via satellite throughout North America in May 1995, Michael Hammer told his audience that one of the critical elements of a "sniff test" to determine whether genuine reengineering work was actually being done within an organization, was whether or not the people in that organization had been "reinvented". He elaborated by saying that reengineered organizations required "new folks", not necessarily from outside the organization but existing employees who had developed new skills, new perspectives and new attitudes. For those employees who think this is impossible, he quoted W. Edwards Deming's popular saying, "If you can't change the people, change the people". The hierarchically based organization structure that now predominates must, through reengineering, be "smashed" according to Hammer, so that there will be no more "workers" and "managers". Instead, the new team-based organization would be staffed by "professionals" and "entrepreneurs". Those managers that remain will cease to act as supervisors but will instead become "coaches". Similarly, the role of the executive will change from one of being a "scorekeeper" to a true "leader". With typically revolutionary zeal, reengineering was conceived by Hammer and Champy as a way of fast-tracking the democratization of American corporations that had been progressing for some time. As Champy observed, "America's great achievement in the last fifty years or so – and reengineering's achievement more recently – has been to open up managerial status, rewards, and responsibilities to everyone" (1995: 163). This kind of statement had a profound significance for the manager's self-concept. Those middle managers who were neither let go nor reassigned as "professionals" had a choice of several options for the future. In an interview about the future of jobs, Hammer predicted,

> When we get through with reengineering, the few managerial jobs that will remain will have three flavors – none of which has much of anything to do with a traditional manager. One I call a process owner. It's really a work engineer, who's concerned about how to go about filling work orders, designing products. The second is a coach – teaching, developing people. The third kind is the leader, who primarily motivates – creates an environment where people get it done. Hardly any existing managers have the ability to do any of those things, or the inclination.
>
> (*Wall Street Journal*, 1995: B1)

Hammer and Champy have used this casting technique before, but for a more specialized audience. In an earlier collaboration in which they exhorted information system (IS) organizations radically to change their skill mix and management methods, they identified three emerging roles for IS professionals which included "Witch Doctors", who are independent thinkers and leaders in the efforts to revitalize the business; "Magicians", who actually build the new types of systems; and "Wizards", who are characterized by genuine technical expertise and a wide-ranging toolkit (Hammer and Champy, 1989). This earlier article, which appeared in a relatively obscure journal, provided a kind of a dress rehearsal for the main performance which was to take place four years later.

The performance of reengineering

Rethinking reengineering

In an inquiry into the popularity of the reengineering movement, Grint rightfully concludes that few of the principles contained within the reengineering movement are actually innovations, let alone radical innovations. Instead, he suggests that we look for an "externalist account" of the movement's popularity which addresses the ways in which "the purveyors of reengineering manage, in and through their accounts, to construct a series of sympathetic 'resonances' or 'compatibilities'" (Grint, 1994: 179). Grint identifies three such resonances: cultural and symbolic; economic and spatial; and political and temporal. While Grint's analysis does an admirable job of situating the reengineering movement in a macrohistorical context, this chapter has examined the appeal or "resonances" of the reengineering movement from the perspective of the individual manager as a consumer of management ideas. I am, therefore, suggesting that an "internalist account" of the popularity of reengineering is, in fact, still valid, if we examine the process from a rhetorical standpoint and not purely the inherent rationality of its ideas.

My encounter with the reengineering movement stemmed from two imperatives. First, as a manager, I and several of my colleagues were intrigued by the potential that the concept had for getting our own organization out of its immediate financial difficulties and breaking down some of the institutional barriers that had impeded our progress to date. Since implementing a reengineering project, the Faculty of Continuing Education at the University of Calgary was able to reverse three years of successive financial deficits with two years of generating healthy surpluses (Taylor and Jackson, 1996). The sense of excitement, risk and adventure that accompanies reengineering is a tempting combination for individuals like myself, who tend to be frustrated with inaction and want to make something happen immediately within their organization. Case has pointed to the "masculine idealism" that is self-consciously embodied in reengineering and which invites men to "indulge wilfully their desire to obliterate – to blast through unrepentant obstacles" (1995: 17). Grint and Case speculate that the "violent managerial rhetoric" of reengineering is itself "part of a backlash against the construction of some forms of gender equality; a throwback to the time when 'men were men'" (1998: 573). What is critical to reengineering's appeal, therefore, is not that it is a call to action, but that it is a call to a particular kind of action – dramatic action. Restating Hammer and Champy's definition, reengineering is "the fundamental rethinking and radical redesign of business processes to achieve *dramatic* improvements in critical measures of performance, such as cost, quality, service and speed" (1993: 33, my italics).

The second imperative for analyzing the reengineering movement derived from my role as a researcher. From this more distant and critical vantage point, I gained an admittedly grudging appreciation for how the gurus weave dramatic qualities into their work. Of all of the contemporary management gurus, Hammer and Champy, in particular, have demonstrated an acute sensibility toward the rhetorical power that dramatizing their organizational change strategies holds for their audience (Boje et al., 1997). In this respect, we can look at reengineering essentially as a performance that takes place in two distinct realms: in the broad arena of general management discourse and as a drama that unfolds within the organization.

The guru as rhetorical performer

In the first realm, which might somewhat melodramatically be described as the realm of "seduction", the management guru performs through a variety of media in order to capture the manager's attention and then persuades him or her that reengineering is the appropriate course of action to take within his or her organization. If managing is essentially a performance, as Mangham (1990) has so eloquently argued, then being a management guru demands a performance par excellence if it is to convince an audience of performers.

The account presented in this chapter shows how Hammer and Champy appealed directly to the manager's self-concept and took that self-concept through three acts of a drama – "Preservation of Self", "Redemption of Self" and "Representation of Self". This is not a particularly novel approach. It has an impressive track-record as a rhetorical strategy. For example, in his study of the communication practices of a number of pre-Civil War evangelical religious movements in the United States, Bormann identifies three remarkably similar stages in consciousness-raising communication episodes. In the first stage, referred to by nineteenth-century evangelicals as "breaking up the old foundations", converts feel a combination of revulsion and attraction as

> Among the more important targets for attack are their definitions of self, the fantasies in which they create their own self-consciousness. Being social creatures people tend to define themselves in terms of group consciousness in which they participate, so the attacks on self-definition are often attacks on the core fantasies of old visions.
>
> (Bormann, 1985: 13–14)

At the second stage, "pouring the truth", the evangelist encourages the neophyte to share the positive fantasies that form the core of the new consciousness. Once the individual experiences conversion, which is usually portrayed as a sharp and sudden experience, he or she is expected to demonstrate commitment publicly by taking action.

Bormann's study reveals the central role that the evangelist has played in almost all evangelical rhetorical visions. There are some intriguing parallels between the new rhetorical style that was brought to the New World by the likes of Whitefield, which emphasized drama, passion and power, and the kind of oratory that has been exemplified by Michael Hammer. This religious parallel has not gone unnoticed by the business press. For example, *Fortune* magazine described Hammer as "reengineering's John the Baptist, a tub-thumping preacher who doesn't perform miracles himself but, through speeches and writings, prepares the way for consultants and companies that do" (Stewart, 1993). The parallel is made all the more intriguing when we note that this kind of speaking, which measured its success purely in terms of the numbers of souls that were saved, eventually superseded the puritanical preaching style that, in common with today's contemporary academic scene, strove to find a balance between intellect and emotion and found the evangelical style to be crude, unlearned and repulsive (Bormann, 1985).

Bormann has described a rhetorical tradition that is one of the most strongly rooted in North America as being "protestant", "popular", "pragmatic" (i.e. it emphasizes everyday practicality) and "romantic" (i.e. where content is subordinated by form). A recurring theme of all of the rhetorical visions to have emerged from within this tradition is one of "restoration", of returning an essentially good society to its former glory. As Bormann observes, "many American reformers began their journey forward into a better society by moving backwards towards the true foundations, by a restoration of the original dream of the founding fathers" (1985: 17). Contemporary reformers like Hammer and Champy have obviously not lost sight of the rhetorical potency of an appeal to the past.

Critics of reengineering have observed that the restoration theme is integral to its persuasive appeal. Grint has described it as a "radical return to tradition" (1994: 197) which is "an essentially mechanistic, almost seventeenth century view of how organizations function and can be changed" (Grint and Willcocks, 1995: 86). Grey and Mitev characterize it as an attempt to go "back to the future" (1995: 7), which, despite its promise of a return to a glorious pre-bureaucratic past, "(as its name suggests) remains firmly embedded within the 'engineering' tradition of management thinking" (1995: 8). Grint and Case (1998) suggest that reengineering can be read as a form of "inverse colonization" in which U.S. managerial discourse assimilated and revolted against the growing domination of Japanese thinking and practice. This argument is given further weight in an article by Champy, in which he credits America's preeminence over Japan as being the result of three things: an embrace of new information technologies; the redesign of business processes, resulting in fewer people producing more output; and a willingness to make big, painful decisions involving change (1998b). The primacy of American business is further underlined in his assertion that "the idea of radical change caught on in the U.S. faster than in any other parts of the world probably because of our tradition of not standing on tradition" (Champy, 1998a: 26).

The guru as organizational playwright

The second realm of performance – "consummation" – takes place when reengineering is brought into the organization and actively implemented. The theatrical metaphor, which can be briefly represented with the phrases "life as theater" and "theater as life", has proven to be a remarkably insightful and durable one for social theorists. Lyman and Scott (1975), for example, show how the metaphor has been used by Freud, George Herbert Mead and Erving Goffman. In a series of stimulating works, Mangham and Overington have introduced this metaphor to good effect into their studies and intervention work with organizations, finding that it "provides possibilities for demystifying the conditions of organizational life, as these are directly or indirectly experienced, while it resists being turned into a literal myth" (1987: 25).

When an organization decides to introduce such a wide-ranging organizational improvement initiative as reengineering, it has chosen to participate in a highly theatricalized, organizational drama in that it has been comprehensively scripted. It is this scripted quality, after all, that is a major element in the appeal of an improvement initiative that is imported by the organization and has been tried and trusted. Hare and Blumberg (1988) have suggested that any performance starts out with an idea about a situation and the action that may unfold from it. The idea may be a single image or it may be as fully developed as the detailed script of a play, with parts for each member of the cast and stage directions to guide the performance. Many of the ideas that management gurus put forward to managers come in a prescriptive form. That is, they describe your problem, tell you what to do, how to do it, who should do it, when and where. In this regard the management guru acts as "playwright" to the organization that chooses to participate in his or her "play" (Mangham, 1978).

Applying the theatrical analogy to a performance of reengineering, Hammer and Champy and lesser guru figures have acted as the playwrights. The "producers" of the drama (i.e. those who sponsor the reengineering process) are the organization's senior executive group. The "director" of the process is, in Hammer and Stanton's terminology, a "reengineering czar" whose role is "to insure that all these efforts are co-ordinated, facilitated, and supported" (Hammer and Stanton, 1995: 13). In the "on-stage" area, Hare and Blumberg identify a "protagonist" to whom we could equate the "process owner" and whom Hammer and Stanton define as "a senior individual designated by the leader to have end-to-end responsibility for the process and its performance" (1995: 13). The protagonist assembles a team or "chorus" to support him or herself. He or she may also bring in from outside the organization some "auxiliary players" or consultants to whom Hammer devotes a whole chapter. In this chapter he assiduously distinguishes between his role and the role of the consultant, saying "we're not in the consulting business – although one of us used to be – and have no allegiance to any consulting firm" (Hammer and Stanton, 1995: 68).

Earlier in the chapter, I suggested that Michael Hammer and James Champy had cast the beleaguered middle manager to play the all-important "antagonist" in the drama: that is, someone with a measure of influence within the organization as it stands who is unwilling to accept reengineering as it threatens his or her present privileged status. Through dramatism, Burke (1968) has identified the "scapegoat principle" as a perennially vital motive. In the antagonist role, middle managers prove to be a worthy choice of scapegoats that have to be sacrificed in the name of reengineering. While middle managers are a major component of the audience for management gurus, they prove to be an excellent choice because the title "middle manager" is not something with which they identify strongly. They would prefer to be seen either as "senior" or "front-line" managers in their organization. The "middle managers" that Hammer and Champy refer to are the "other" middle managers who have ignored the guru and have not changed their ways. As such, they will face their day of reckoning when reengineering commences.

Once the protagonists in the reengineering drama begin to see their role reduced to one of a "bit part", or worse, a "has been", they may be willing to take on the antagonist's role to insure they are still an important member of the company. However, this role reversal is something that should not be taken for granted. As Wilmott observes,

> BPR goes beyond declaring war upon supervisory and middle levels of management to attack head-on the very functional structures that have traditionally provided an identity and a career path for the managers that have formed an integral part of the collective worker. For this reason, among others, BPR is likely to encounter difficulties of implementation even where employees overtly espouse its objectives. It is not just that the "process" thinking advocated by BPR is often foreign to those who are being required to apply it. It also poses an immediate or deferred threat to job security and conditions of work.
>
> (Wilmott, 1994: 44)

Harrington et al. (1998) highlight two logical inconsistencies that they argue run through the reengineering vision and hang on securing commitment and promoting empowerment. The problem of securing commitment from employees to reengineering projects has been characterized as the "Catch-22"of reengineering (Tomasko, 1996) and has been rather succinctly posed by Wilmott (1995) in the question "Will the turkeys vote for Christmas?" Reengineering requires the active participation of employees who have intimate knowledge of the existing processes in order to guarantee its success. However, knowing that past experience strongly intimates that they may well be out of work at the end of the reengineering project, why would anyone actively support the project, let alone resist the temptation to derail it? As Grey and Mitev observe, "resistance to change should be understood not as an irrational, psychological attachment to the 'old days' but a rational response to the brutal and . . . futile managerialism of BPR" (1995: 12). Expanding on this, Beugré (1998) has suggested that reengineering frequently fails because it is fundamentally unjust. It asks employees to put their own jobs on the line. She shows how reengineering violates "organizational justice" at four levels: distributive, procedural, interactional and systemic.

Another central tenet of reengineering is that employees should be empowered so that managerial decisions are made at lower levels of the organization where information is richer and the impact of the decision more immediate. However, reengineering is an approach that Hammer and Champy have stressed needs to be imposed from above so that, although hierarchical layers of management may be removed, hierarchical principles are, in practice, actually reinforced. In an interview Hammer states, "to put it bluntly, it's not consensual. Radical change is always led from the top, but a leader doesn't just tell people that they must do it. A leader makes people recognize why they must do it" (*Performance*, 1995: 26). Argyris has, however, noted that, "although the rhetoric of reengineering is consistent with empowerment, in reality it is anything but . . . it has not produced the number of highly motivated employees needed to insure consistently high-performing organizations" (1998: 98). Similarly, Jaffe and Scott have observed from their studies of a dozen large reengineering engagements "a common disjunction between the assumptions the organizations make about change and the nature of the changes they want. They approach change using the mind-sets and techniques of the command-and-control workplace, and it does not work" (1998: 251).

In discussing the unique quality of drama compared to other art forms, Fowler notes that, while the playwright is the instigator in the organizational drama, "performances even of the same production will vary, sometimes radically, from night to night, and the variation will primarily depend on the different audiences, and the actors' response to them" (1987: 53). Knights and McCabe (1998b) have suggested that critics of reengineering may have become too focused on the script of reengineering at the expense of its actual performance. They observe that "while providing a welcome counter to guru evangelism, attention needs to be given to the particular circumstances of the development of BPR and, in particular, the 'experiences' of those who are involved in its practical implementation and adaptation" (Knights and McCabe, 1998b: 165). Their detailed case study of two back offices of a U.K. clearing bank reveals that reengineering led to more of the intensive work experience predicted by its critics than the satisfying experience promised by the advocates of reengineering. The employees, however, were not the powerless dupes that many critics have tended to portray them as. The employees in this case study "were able to retain control over some areas of the work whether by management design or default, and this provided an important channel through which staff stress levels were contained if not diminished" (1998b: 186). In his ethnographic study of the installation of a computerized student system within a U.K. university, Case (1999) noted that, with its call to wipe the slate clean, BPR offered a form of "cathartic absolution" of the collective guilt that had accumulated as a result of the installation team's chronic mismanagement of information technology.

Clemons has observed from his experience as a consultant that, despite the dramatic performance improvement promises made by the "high priests of reengineering . . . many, even most, reengineering efforts ultimately fail" (1995: 62). Pointing out that reengineering is an inherently risky endeavor, he states that the two greatest risks associated with reengineering are "functionality risk" and "political risk". Functionality risk is created either by making the wrong changes to systems and processes or by making inadequate changes that do not accommodate changes in the competitive environment. Political risk is engendered when the organization will not complete the project "either because of serious internal resistance to the proposed changes or because of a more gradual loss of will to continue the project" (Clemons, 1995: 63).

The "functionality risk" is powerfully described by Sennett (1998) in his critical essay on the consequences of new capitalism. He argues that reengineering is an irreversible and highly chaotic process, concluding that, "while disruption may not be justifiable in terms of productivity, the short-term returns to stockholders provide a strong incentive to the powers of chaos disguised by that seemingly reassured term 'reengineering'" (1998: 51). Two case studies of reengineering projects provide strong support for this argument. They reveal that the substantive and frequently damaging change reengineering wreaks on organizations that embark upon it sets it apart from other consultant-driven organizational improvement programs (Blair et al., 1998; Leverment et al., 1998).

The "political risks" associated with reengineering are clearly portrayed in Knights and McCabe's bank case study. Based on their analysis, they take to task the claim made by the gurus and their supporters that reengineering could be decontextualized and decoupled from organizational politics and that it can be managed instantaneously and unproblematically. They argue instead that BPR "is likely to be constituted by and through political relations, and that BPR in turn will reconstitute organizational forms and norms in a highly political fashion" (Knights and McCabe, 1998a: 761). They also argue that managers cannot ameliorate or even overcome employee resistance to reengineering projects merely by providing more and improved communication and information provision which several authors have suggested is required for success (Mariotti, 1998; Wall and McKinley, 1998). Politics, in their mind, is an essential component of the fabric of organizational life, which inevitably makes the outcomes of reengineering projects uncertain and contested.

My own experience working on a reengineering project within the university faculty I was associated with at the time bears witness to how politicized reengineering projects can be (Taylor and Jackson, 1996). The technical complexities associated with analyzing and streamlining business processes proved to be minor compared to the political processes that were required in order to move the project forward. My colleague and I totally underestimated the hostility that the project would generate from our colleagues and various staff members. In fact, on several occasions we questioned our decision to initiate the project in light of the negative effect it had upon morale within the faculty and, more pointedly, our new low standing within the faculty! Four years on, relations were still strained despite the fact that the faculty is widely acknowledged to be operating considerably more efficiently and effectively than it was previously.

When the performance of a play fails to live up to the advance billing, the playwright, in a classic rhetorical ploy, is quick to place the blame firmly in the camp of the actors and the audience. This is a tactic that Hammer and Champy have readily utilized with regard to the reengineering movement. For example, Hammer says: "It is terrible that some people are hurt in the process. But to be blunt, that's not my fault – it's the fault of the people who got those companies into their problems in the first place" (*Performance*, 1995: 28). Showing typically more restraint, Champy notes that

> some managers, misled by wishful thinking, believe that merely repeating the key words in *Reengineering the Corporation* is enough to bring the transformation, like the newsboy in the comic strip who yelled "Shazaam"! And became powerful Captain Marvel. . . . Reengineering prescribes actions, not words, and difficult, long-term actions at that, not just one-shot expedients like downsizing or outsourcing. Reengineering involves a voyage that will last years, possibly our entire management lifetime.
>
> (Champy, 1995: 6)

Conversely, the actors and audience can blame the script and proceed to find another playwright. It is apparent that, in the latter half of the 1990s, many managers have taken this route, having become disillusioned with the reengineering movement and the gurus who forged it (Blackburn, 1996; Lowrekovich, 1996). The increasing doubts about reengineering are reflected in the question posed by *Business Week* in its cover story "Has Outsourcing Gone Too Far?" (Byrne, 1996). All this has left Davies to reflect that

> It would be easy, but facile, to have fun at the expense of a man so short on humility. And Hammer deserves no less. But there is a bigger mystery here. Why do business gurus feel the need to make such

absurdly extravagant claims to attract attention? Why can they not explain simply that they have developed a technique, or a way of thinking, that may allow some businesses to accelerate their rate of productivity growth? Why, in other words, do they have such obvious contempt for the managers they hope to influence?

(Davies, 1997: 45)

In light of this observation, there is a certain delicious irony that Hammer, himself, has argued that "open-minded humility, and a recognition that we have to reinvent ourselves for the customer, will be the difference between those who survive and thrive in the twenty-first century and those who become footnotes in history" (Hammer, 1997: 6).

Summary

In this chapter I have described how Michael Hammer and James Champy have forged a rhetorical vision of reengineering that speaks directly to, and shapes the manager's self-concept. The vision is undergirded by a pragmatic master analogue, which argues that reengineering must be done because there is essentially no other choice, it is a simple matter of personal survival. This argument is given rhetorical weight by three fantasy themes that focus on the character of the manager and build logically on one another to build a compelling drama. 'The Preservation of Self' character theme threatens head-on the manager's self-concept by questioning his or her very existence within the organization. The second theme, 'the Redemption of Self' shows managers a way out of their plight by extolling the merits and inevitability of reengineering and encouraging them not only to support but actively to promote it within their organizations. The final theme, 'the Representation of Self', provides the managers with new roles and role models that, the gurus argue, they should be playing in order to survive but also fully to realize their selves within the newly reengineered organization.

This chapter has argued that the rhetorical power of reengineering is derived more from its dramatic qualities than its innovative or instrumental qualities. That is, its ability to capture the manager's attention and stir him or her into dramatic action. This vision is a compelling one because it speaks to the here-and-now problems facing many managers and it resonates with a rhetorical tradition of "restoration" that is strongly rooted in American society. Moreover, it provides the manager with a comprehensive script that has been written by authoritative dramaturgs and a familiar cast of characters with whom he or she can act, in a leading role of course, to create a historically significant organizational drama. Performing reengineering in practice has, however, proven to be neither as compelling nor as simple as was implied. Managers have encountered considerable problems and obstacles in translating the rhetorical vision into a day-to-day reality. The play has, alas, not always been the thing.

5 Stephen Covey and the effectiveness movement

Speaking is a kind of lonely world. But I belong to a business . . . and I love it. It's a tremendous mission. Anyone who gets close to it also gets drawn in because it's so consuming.

(Stephen Covey interviewed in the *Financial Post* [Bouw, 1998: C4])

Why, I ask Elaine, are you here? "I really like his message," she says. "It's the basic truths. It gets you back to the Ten Commandments." Next to her, Sharyn agrees with me that a lot of Covey's message is common sense, "But you tend to forget it". "Plus", she says, "there's an aura about him". "He must know what he's talking about if so many people keep going to him."

(Two seminar participants interviewed in *Sales and Marketing Management* [Butler, 1997: 21])

Introduction

The subject of this chapter is Stephen Covey, arguably North America's preeminent management guru who has been instrumental in forging a management fashion which focuses on personal rather than organizational responsibility, accountability and effectiveness. The chapter begins with a discussion of the distinguishing features of Stephen Covey's management guru persona and the movement or rhetorical community that he has helped to foster. While there are clear similarities between the management fashion that Covey has spawned and preceding and competing improvement programs, there are also some important differences vis-à-vis how this movement has been rhetorically constructed, the manner in which it has been organized, and the ideological roots from which it draws its inspiration.

In the body of this chapter, three main fantasy themes are identified as the building-blocks of the rhetorical vision of effectiveness that Covey has skillfully constructed through a number of media. This vision is under-girded by a righteous master analogue (Cragan and Shields, 1992). The fundamental argument put forward by Covey in favor of following his vision is that it is based on a few timeless principles that, because they are unequivocally and inviolably right, cannot be ignored. The chapter concludes by exploring the contribution that Stephen Covey's Mormon background may have had upon the success of the ostensibly secular effectiveness movement. Both Mormonism in general, and Covey's secular work in particular, resonate powerfully with the existential and spiritual needs of many individuals in the late modern age.

The seven highly effective habits of Stephen Covey

Stephen Covey began his professional life with a 25-year stint at Brigham Young University, initially as an administrator before becoming a professor of Organization Behaviour. Even at this proto-guru stage, Covey commanded large audiences, with his classes reputedly attracting between 600 and 1,000 students (Smith, 1994). In 1984 he left academe to found the Covey Leadership Center (CLC), the mission of which was to

> Serve the worldwide community by empowering people and organizations `to significantly increase their performance capability in order to achieve worthwhile purposes through understanding and living principle-centered leadership. In carrying out this mission, we continually strive to practice what we teach.
>
> (http://www.imall.covey)

The CLC clearly took its mission to heart. Within ten years, it had grown from two to 750 employees, and was generating annual revenues of $90 million, a feat that made it the 404th fastest-growing company on the Inc. 500 list in 1994 (*Inc.*, 1994). Today, the CLC, now known as the Franklin Covey Company, has a 10,000-plus client list, which includes 82 of the Fortune 100 and over two-thirds of the Fortune 500 companies (Wolfe, 1998).

The foundational text for the effectiveness movement, Covey's *The Seven Habits of Highly Effective People*, was first published in 1989. It has sold over 12 million copies, been translated into 28 languages and has spent over 270 weeks on the *New York Times* bestseller list (Chambers, 1997). According to Covey, this book emerged from a combination of his consulting work with IBM's Executive Development Program and his doctoral research which examined the "success literature" that had been published in the United States since 1776. In his research, Covey found that in the first 150 years, this literature, best exemplified by Benjamin Franklin's autobiography, argued that the foundation of success was the "character ethic" which included "integrity, humility, fidelity, temperance, courage, justice, patience, industry, simplicity, modesty and The Golden Rule" (1989: 18). In the last 50 years, however, Covey noted that the basic view of success had shifted from the character ethic to the "personality ethic" which emphasized "quick-fix", "outside-in" solutions through human and public relations techniques and a positive mental attitude.

Covey's book is pitched as an attempt to return to the character ethic, which is based on the fundamental idea that "there are principles that govern human effectiveness – natural laws in the human dimension that are just as real, just as unchanging and unarguably 'there' as laws such as gravity are in the physical dimension" (Covey, 1989: 32). Covey locates seven "habits" which lie at the intersection of knowledge, skills and desire. These habits are "effective" because they are based on principles that are timeless and universal. Table 5.1 lists the seven habits and briefly defines each of them. Covey advocates that they should become the basis of a person's character, "creating an empowering center of correct maps from which an individual can effectively solve problems, maximize opportunities, and continually learn and integrate other principles in an upward spiral of growth" (1989: 52).

Covey followed up the *Seven Habits* with two books that, while they have not generated the same level of sales, have been effective in keeping Covey's profile high. Most significantly, they helped to consolidate the remarkable interest that had been shown by the corporate sector in the *Seven Habits*. These books employ Covey's approach to revitalize two of the major preoccupations of the executive and management development market – leadership and time management. The first book, *Principle-Centered Leadership* (Covey, 1990b), was a loose collection of essays written primarily for an executive audience to demonstrate how Covey's work could be brought into the corporation to bring about organizational change. In 1994 Covey co-authored *First Things First*, a book that presented a new "fourth-generation" of time management based on the "importance paradigm" which stressed "knowing and doing what's important rather than simply responding to what's urgent" (Covey et al., 1994: 32).

In common with other management gurus, Covey combines a keen marketing sense with a seemingly innate gift for self-promotion. However, he has done a number of things that distinguish him from his peers. First, he has been able successfully to straddle both the business and the personal growth markets which, while they have significant overlap in terms of audience and content, have traditionally been treated as quite separate markets by publishers. Originally, the *Seven Habits* was positioned as a self-help book. However, it, and its more explicitly business-focused successors, have now become business book staples. With the publication of *The Seven Habits of Highly Effective Families* (Covey, 1997), which draws heavily on his own family for its inspiration, Covey has further bolstered his standing as a guru with a message that transcends all spheres of human endeavor (Ferguson, 1997).

Second, Covey, a devout Mormon, has been able unashamedly to adapt his essentially spiritual message to a corporate world that has traditionally

Table 5.1 Stephen Covey's seven habits of highly effective people

Habit	Principles	Brief synopsis
1. Be proactive	Personal Vision	Between stimulus and response lies the power to respond. Proactivity implies that you are responsible for what happens in your life.
2. Begin with the end in mind	Personal Leadership	Imagine your funeral and listen to what you would like the eulogy to say about you. Use this frame of reference to make all day-to-day decisions, and work toward your most meaningful goals.
3. Put first things first	Personal Management	Keep your mission in mind, understand what's important as well as urgent and maintain balance between what you produce today and your ability to produce in the future.
4. Think win/win	Interpersonal Leadership	Agreements or solutions among people can be mutually beneficial if all parties cooperate and begin with a belief in the "third alternative".
5. Seek first to understand, then to be understood	Empathic Communication	You'll be more effective in your relationships with people if you sincerely try to understand them fully before you try to make them understand your point of view.
6. Synergize	Creative Cooperation	The whole is greater than the sum of the parts. Value differences because it is often the clash between them that leads to creative solutions.
7. Sharpen the saw	Balanced Self-Renewal	Four dimensions: *Physical* (exercise, nutrition, and stress management); *Spiritual* (value clarification and commitment, study and meditation); *Mental* (reading, visualization, planning, and writing); *Social/emotional* (service, empathy, synergy, and intrinsic security).

Source: Adapted from Covey (1989)

preferred to keep its gurus strictly secular and to leave spirituality behind at home (Fort, 1997). As a reviewer in the *Wall Street Journal* remarked, "his work is busy with buzzwords, charts and grids, Mr. Covey has a knack of dressing up spiritual principles in pinstripes to suit a business audience"

(Shellenbarger, 1995: 13). Wooldridge and Kennedy have similarly observed, "Covey has a genius for mixing three great American themes – religion, self-help and management. The implication is that if you subscribe to his ideas, you get the whole American dream in one go" (1996: 56). This is a theme that I think is Covey's critical distinguishing feature and is one that I will return to in some depth in the final section of the chapter.

Third, in addition to targeting a very wide potential market, Covey has created a significantly broader array of products than his predecessors, who have tended to focus on speaking engagements, books and tapes. Covey maintains a hectic speaking schedule for which he charges over $75,000 per day or between $30,000 to $40,000 for a satellite conference (*Across the Board*, 1999). In addition, Franklin Covey's on-line catalogue reveals a seemingly exhaustive array of products and programs, including workshops, audio and video cassettes, organizers, calculator/rulers, desk calendars and watches that enable you to "start each day with an excerpt from the *Seven Habits*" (http://www.franklincovey.com). As one commentator observes, "the Covey teachings are pyramidal: buy the book, crave a one-day lecture, attend for a day, desire a three-day seminar" (Wells, 1995:14). Covey's market reach is broad; his company organizes workshops in over 300 cities in North America and 40 countries worldwide (Wolfe, 1998). When questioned if he considers himself to be a salesman, Covey replies: "In one sense, yes. My presentations are attempting to influence behavior. But I have a total disdain for talking products. I never mention my book when I speak to a group" (Lawlor, 1996: 71).

Fourth, the organization that Covey has created around him is considerably larger and more centralized than the ones that other gurus have created. CLC maintains a substantial network of consultants, which has enabled Stephen Covey to maintain effective control of a considerable amount of the consulting activity that is generated in the wake of his book sales and speaking engagements. In North America alone, there are over 5,100 individuals who have paid the $1,995 fee for certification by CLC (Gubernick, 1995). This control has been further strengthened by Covey's continued ability to position himself as central to the movement he has spawned. In the case of the Excellence, TQM and reengineering movements, there was a sense that the gurus, although undoubtedly important, were not as big as the movements they helped to spawn. It was, therefore, acceptable for executives to go to one of the "Big Five" consulting firms or even to a local independent consulting firm to get their brand of reengineering or TQM. By contrast, the effectiveness movement is still very much seen as Covey's movement. Facsimiles thereof would be seen as entirely insufficient. With the merger in 1997 of CLC with Franklin Quest, a rival day-timer company led by Hyrum Smith, a fellow Mormon, Covey has further extended the reach of his products and his share of the personal and professional growth market. The publicly held Franklin Covey Co. employs 4,000 and operates more than 120 retail stores throughout the world (*Calgary*

Herald, 1998). Two years into the merger, several embarrassing cracks started to appear. Operating earnings had plummeted, substantial layoffs were required, and Covey and Smith had been forced to assume non-executive vice-chairman roles to make way for a turnaround specialist who has been appointed chairman (Grover, 1999). Stories of internal bickering between Covey and Smith factions within the organization in addition to well-publicized arguments about sales compensation cast doubt about the wisdom of turning CLC into a public company (Marchetti, 1999).

A final distinguishing feature of Covey is that he has proven himself to be remarkably adept at reinforcing his credibility by associating with other management gurus and major public figures. The monthly magazine *Executive Excellence*, published by Covey's non-profit Institute for Principle-Centered Leadership, typically features a keynote article by Covey and numerous short articles by other management gurus such as Kenneth Blanchard, Peter Senge and Warren Bennis as well as prominent CEOs. This guru's digest graphically demonstrates the "quality" of the company that Covey keeps. In September 1996, Covey joined fellow gurus Tom Peters and Peter Senge in true "three tenors" fashion, for the first "Worldwide Lesson in Leadership Series" that was beamed via satellite to over 221,000 individuals in 40 different countries (Mahoney, 1997). This conference was followed up by three half-day sessions featuring Covey solo. CLC has also collaborated with Microsoft, a pacesetting guru company, to incorporate the Seven Habits into its *Microsoft Schedule+* software (Smith, 1995a). On the wider public stage, Covey has been positioned in the media, along with fellow motivational speakers Anthony Robbins and Marianne Williamson, as an adviser to both Bill Clinton and Newt Gingrich (Quinn, 1995). Covey's media prowess has been recognized by *Time* magazine, which included him in its 1996 list of the "25 Most Influential Americans" along with other such luminaries as Jerry Seinfeld, Oprah Winfrey and fellow management guru Michael Hammer. According to *Time*, "being influential" is "the reward for successful salesmanship, the validation of personal passion, the visible sign of individual merit. It is power without coercion, celebrity with substance" (1996: 15).

Defining the rhetorical community of the effectiveness movement

Ascertaining the scale and scope of the rhetorical community that Stephen Covey has helped to create would be an extremely difficult, if not an impossible, exercise. While many have purchased the books, listened to the tapes and attended the seminars, it would be unwise to equate this high degree of market penetration with widespread acceptance of and commitment to Covey's rhetorical vision. In truth, we would probably see a full spectrum of commitment ranging from cynical disgust through to casual interest to manic devotion. In looking at the relationship between stars and their audiences, Tudor (1974) has identified four levels of involvement: emotional affinity, self-identification, imitation and projection. My own interactions with Covey followers suggest that most of them would probably fall into the first and weakest category, in which "the audience feels a loose attachment to a particular protagonist deriving jointly from the star, the narrative and the individual personality of the audience member" (Tudor, 1974: 80). Some of Covey's followers, however, may also experience some "self-identification", whereby they place themselves in the same situation and persona of Covey, and this identification may spill over into a certain amount of imitation and, occasionally, "projection" in which part of their identity is lived through this persona.

Evidence of the kind of intensity that Covey can foster in his audience can be found in comments made by participants who attended a one-day seminar delivered in Calgary via satellite. In responding to a question in the evaluation regarding what they most liked about the seminar, one participant said "the opportunity to hear from Covey in the flesh and see his commitment and believability to [*sic*] the material he presents". Another participant mentioned, "Having Stephen Covey here, bigger than life" while another answered, "All Stephen Covey *himself*". Business media accounts of Covey are chock-full of these kinds of testimonials which, in turn, further serve to widen the boundaries of and to strengthen his rhetorical community. For example, *Business Week* quotes a manager with the U.S. Federal Aviation Administration and self-described "Covey disciple" who brought 15 employees with him to a Covey seminar: "Covey is able to identify and put a handle on so many of the things I've thought and felt" (Bongiorno, 1993: 52). In *Fortune* magazine, the president of Ritz-Carlton credits Covey's organization-wide training program with his company's dramatically low turnover rate because "people feel they are part of the organization. People have a purpose going to work" (Smith, 1995b: 126). *Inc.* (1995) magazine also ran an article that featured three different success stories of companies whose managers had attended Covey's seminars and where sales had risen dramatically shortly thereafter. In a subsequent volume, *Inc.* profiled three individuals whose lives had been radically changed by following Covey. In the article, an operations manager at an industrial laundry remarks "reading Covey and writing a mission statement – making my goals and deciding what was important to me – really made me see things differently in my life. My life has changed" (Whitford, 1996: 77).

Trade journals regularly feature articles extolling the virtues of Covey's work to a wide range of professions including risk managers (*National Underwriter*, 1995), bankers (*Bank Marketing*, 1988), meeting planners (*Successful Meetings*, 1993), and security managers (*Security Management*, 1992). The latter was especially intriguing with its completely unironic account of how Covey's principles had been incorporated by rangers working at Texas Fiesta, a brand new family-oriented theme park set in an abandoned rock quarry sponsored, in part, by Opryland USA Inc. Covey's work has also proven to be particularly popular among the training and organizational development community. In a survey conducted by *Training* magazine, *The Seven Habits* garnered the most votes (9 percent of respondents) as the book that had been most helpful to them in their jobs (1992). Among the MBA students across seven U.S. business schools who were surveyed by publishers Booz, Allen, & Hamilton, 6 percent picked *The Seven Habits* as the book that had most influenced their lives (*Director*, 1997). Only the Bible was picked by more students (12 percent). Finally, Stephen Covey was selected as sixth of the 25 "power brokers" who are the "most influential in getting product sold in today's marketplace" by *Sales and Marketing Management* (Conlon, 1996).

The rhetorical vision of the effectiveness movement

Thus far, I have described how Stephen Covey has developed, articulated and organized his rhetorical vision of effectiveness and have shown some evidence of the sharing of that vision by an extensive, if loosely organized, rhetorical community from a wide range of sectors within North America. The chapter will now turn to a discussion of the three fantasy themes that emerged from the analysis of the rhetorical acts and artifacts. Covey's rhetorical vision is based on a combination of strong setting, action and character themes that are summarized in Table 5.2.

Bormann provides little in the way of guidance in selecting names for fantasy themes. Past analyzes have found inspiration in both the rhetor's and others' language to name fantasy themes. For the purposes of this study, I chose to use Covey's own phrases to represent the action and

Table 5.2 Key fantasy themes within the rhetorical vision of the effectiveness movement

Fantasy theme	Type	Metaphors	Motive
Back to the Farm	Setting Theme	Law of the Farm; The Golden Goose; Transforming the Swamp; Fishing the Stream	Identification
Working from the "Inside-Out"	Action Theme	Ladder Against the Wrong Wall; The Emotional Bank Account	Hierarchy
Finding "True North"	Character Theme	Compass, Clock, Map; The Living Tree; Charles Dickens; Victor Frankl	Transcendence

character themes as they best captured the essence of their subject matter. In elaborating each theme, the recurrent symbolic cues employed by Covey to illuminate and add rhetorical weight to his vision are identified. Finally, for each theme, one of Burke's motives is ascribed as the basis for the fundamental human appeal that this theme has for the audience.

Setting theme: "Back to the Farm"

Early on in the seminar I attended, Covey asked how many of the audience had "crammed" while they were at school. Having established almost universal assent, Covey then went into confessional mode explaining that he had crammed as an undergraduate but found that this strategy failed miserably when he got into graduate work and paid for years of cramming by winding up in hospital with ulcerated colitis. The somber lesson he divines from this experience is that

> Cramming doesn't work in a natural system, like a farm. That's the fundamental difference between a social and a natural system. A social system is based on values; a natural system is based on principles. In the short term, cramming may appear to work in a social system. You can work for the "quick fixes" and techniques with apparent success. But, in the long run, the Law of the Farm governs in all arenas of life.
>
> (Covey et al., 1994: 55)

Covey suggests that we can learn a lot from agriculture because "we can easily see and agree that natural laws and principles govern the work and determine the harvest" (1994: 54). He reinforced this point in his seminar with an idyllic short video film of a potato farmer earnestly discussing his respect for "unforgiving Mother Nature", which drew nods of recognition from some members of the audience. Covey suggests that, in social and corporate cultures, because natural processes are less obvious, the "law of the school", based on quick fixes and cheating the system, predominates in the short term but, in the long term, the "law of the farm" predominates.

In situating his rhetorical vision firmly in a premodern agricultural context, Covey has built a setting theme that provides a compelling basis for universal identification among his audience, many of whom, while now firmly based in the modern corporate culture, fondly recall their distant roots in an honorable, if by and large mythical, agricultural past. In common with the reengineering rhetorical vision described in the previous chapter, Covey's "law of the farm" theme draws on the "restoration" fantasy type for its rhetorical potency. It encourages the audience to help America create the good society by returning it to its former glory.

Throughout his presentation, Covey frequently refers to the "law of the farm", as a seemingly all-encompassing universal explanation for all that is wrong with contemporary society without ever attempting to elaborate in any great detail. The rhetorical potency of his argument is reinforced by a number of stock metaphors rooted in an agricultural heritage. Perhaps the most notable (in light of the fact that Covey grew up on an egg farm!), is his use of Aesop's fable of the goose and the golden egg (Covey, 1989: 52–54). The goose, according to Covey, represents the "performance capability" (PC) of an organization, while the egg represents the "production" (P) of desired results. He suggests that the wise executive should learn from Aesop's farmer that he or she needs to detect and correct any "P/PC imbalances" before it is too late. In typically heavy-handed fashion, this metaphor is symbolically reinforced with the presentation of golden eggs to successful Covey training program participants.

Another powerful fantasy that Covey presents, which has real resonance with the pioneering days of the expanding frontier, is the transformation of an individual or an organizational "swamp culture" based on adversarialism, legalism, protectionism and politics into a "garden oasis culture" which is created by the application of "natural laws" and "principles" (Covey, 1990b: 278–287). Similarly, Covey quite skillfully exploits to sound rhetorical effect, the parallels he sees between fishing and managing. Covey presents senior executives, and those aspiring to be, with a drama that positions them as proactive anglers who have constantly to read and adapt to the "stream" of business trends and "currents of cultural megatrends". It is a fantasy which many senior executives with their penchant for getting away from it all would have great difficulty resisting. The rhetorical effect is effectively sealed when Covey cleverly intersects this fantasy with the well-worn but surprisingly resilient axiom that has become a Covey motif: "Give a man fish and you feed him for a day; teach him how to fish and you feed him for a lifetime."

Action theme: "Working from the Inside-Out"

Covey distinguishes between his "inside-out" approach to personal effectiveness and the prevalent approaches that are "outside-in", in that they look for problems and solutions "out there". His approach begins with the self, in particular, "the most inside part of self – your paradigms, your character, and your motives" (1990a: 3). In Covey's schema, the "Seven Habits" are positioned along a "maturity continuum" that moves the individual progressively from "dependence" to "independence" to "interdependence". The first three habits deal with self-mastery and are designed to enable the individual to move from a state of dependence to a state of independence which Covey calls the "paradigm of the $I - I$ can do it; I am responsible; I am self-reliant; I can choose" (1989: 49). Two aspects are particularly remarkable about Covey's approach to self-mastery. First, he encourages his followers to be "proactive" by focusing their efforts within their "Circle of Influence" and not their "Circle of Concern" as "the nature of their energy is positive, enlarging and magnifying, causing their

Circle of Influence to increase" (1989: 83). Second, Covey cautions his followers not to assume that they are in control as "this mindset leads to arrogance – the sort of pride that comes before the fall". Instead he advocates "humility" which means saying, "I am not in control; principles ultimately govern in control" (1996: 17). In this way, Covey establishes clear boundaries and prescribed limits to the process of self-actualization; such a move is significantly at odds with the main thrust of humanism but well in line with his religious beliefs.

Within the organization, the inside-out approach works at four progressively higher levels at which different principles operate. At the "personal" level, the principle of "trustworthiness" prevails. Trustworthiness is based on the executive's character and competence. With trustworthiness, the executive can establish "trust" at the second, "interpersonal" level. The next level is the "managerial level", at which the principle of "empowerment" operates. Finally, at the "organizational level", the executive can create "alignment" by ensuring that all structures reinforce the empowerment principle. Covey argues that the reason so many organizational change efforts have failed is because executives have ignored the fact that they cannot secure their "public victories" before they secure their "private victories":

> Until individual managers have done inside-out work, they won't solve the fundamental problems of the organization, nor will they empower others, even though they might use the language of empowerment. Their personality and character will manifest itself eventually. We must work on character and competence to solve structural and systematic problems.
>
> (Covey, 1990a: 4)

The "Public Victory" for executives is achieved through Habits 4, 5 and 6, which take the individual from a state of independence to a higher level of interdependence. This level is dominated by what Covey dubs the paradigm of "we – *we* can do it; *we* can cooperate; *we* can combine our talents and abilities and create something greater together" (1989: 49). This stage is another feature that Covey feels distinguishes his work. According to Covey, other approaches dwell entirely on helping people become independent but these approaches ultimately fail because they encourage "running way" from a problem that is, in fact, internally – not externally – rooted.

The central organizing metaphor within the paradigm of interdependence is the "emotional bank account".

> In the area of human relationships, unlike normal bank accounts, we must make daily deposits to maintain the balance and to build equity. Deposits are made through courtesy, honesty, and keeping

commitments. Withdrawals are made through discourtesy, disrespect, threats and over-reactions.

(Covey, 1988: 3)

He urges executives, whom he recognizes as being astute financially but generally not emotionally, to make "daily deposits" into their employees' emotional bank accounts by doing such things as "remembering the little things", "sincerely apologizing" and not "bad-mouthing" them in their absence. In this way they can build up sufficient reserves of trust that can be drawn upon when they need to without becoming "overdrawn". This essentially transactional approach to human relationships is blended skillfully into the well-worn and hackneyed human relations concepts of "win–win" and "synergy" which, like an old pair of slippers, provide the audience with a feeling of comfort and security based on years of familiarity.

In developing this schema, Covey has elaborated a conceptual framework that actively plays upon and addresses the hierarchical motive highlighted within Burke's rhetorical system. Covey himself recognizes the inherent hierarchical appeal of his schema with the promise that "inside-out is a continuing process of renewal, an upward spiral of growth that leads to progressively higher forms of responsible independence and effective interdependence" (1990a: 4). This motif is visually reinforced with his "ladder against the wall" metaphor which captures the essence of hierarchical progress but is used by Covey to caution his followers to insure that they aren't pursuing the wrong goals. The audience is presented with a clear sense of where they are now, where they need to be, and how to get there. In Bormann's terminology, Covey has created a powerful action theme that is rooted in the desire of individuals to try to obtain something that they don't currently have but should have.

In this vein, the "Seven Habits" could be seen as a personal drama written in three "acts" and seven "scenes", which provides the central protagonist (e.g. the individual manager) with a carefully scripted plotline that, against all odds, will guide him or her safely to a personal Holy Grail. In Act 1, the individual is cast out into the wilderness to struggle with personal demons, forge his or her character base, and gain clarity about whom he or she is and what he or she wants to achieve. Having successfully negotiated this trial, the individual is then ready to return to "civilization" to work through the three scenes of Act 2 with a comprehensive cast of characters from his or her family, community, church and workplace. In the final Act, subtitled "Sharpening the Saw", the protagonists can bask in the glory of their "private" and "public" victories, reap the rewards of their "harvest", yet take care by continuing to practice the habit of renewal and continuous improvement not to slip down the spiral from this higher plane.

With his "inside-out approach", Covey has successfully exploited a niche that has been left vacant by other management gurus who have tended to focus their attention on providing grandiose, organization-wide improvement programs. From the perspective of executives who are looking to sponsor programs that show that they are "doing something constructive about their employees", Covey's program is attractive for a number of reasons. First, the onus for change is placed firmly upon the employee and not the organization. Employees are encouraged to focus on themselves and their immediate work teams and to ignore the wider structural conditions over which they have no control. Second, within Covey's framework, the individual employee is urged to deflect the blame for things that are happening around him or her – such as downsizing, reorganization and reengineering – away from the senior executives onto him- or herself. In the process, Covey has presented a more subtle and an infinitely more palatable alternative to another contender in the "personal accountability" vanguard codified in a book called *The Oz Principle*. Through a shamefully brutal reconstruction of *The Wizard of Oz*, the book promises a "step-by-step plan to overcome corporate America's obsession with the 'blame game' and achieve new levels of performance and competitiveness" (Connors et al., 1994). Third, many find Covey's program attractive because, while promising fundamental change, it is a comprehensive recipe for conservatism. As an English professor in *Fortune* magazine dryly observes,

> One of the ways that you know that you are dealing with an idea that is bound to become a huge success in America is to get an assurance that it is not going to be about a substantive difference in society. It's the American dream of life as barn raising.
>
> (Smith, 1994: 126)

From the perspective of the individual employees, the Covey program presents, on the surface at least, some clear attractions. First, the Covey program gives them ample opportunity to pursue, on the company's time and money, one of America's fastest-growing leisure pursuits, that is, the exploration of self and identity. It has been estimated that in 1998, self-improvement books alone generated $581 million in sales in North America (Gordon, 1999). Second, Covey doesn't just talk about work, but also about their situations at home, with their marriages and families and, again, these are discussed on the company time and money. Third, Covey's program is designed for all employees within the organization regardless of rank or function. While the executive may have the opportunity to attend the Covey Leadership Week at Robert Redford's verdant Sundance Resort in Utah, and regular employees may have to settle for the video facilitated in-house program, everyone can take comfort in the knowledge that they will all receive essentially the same message. Indeed, the whole program depends on the universal involvement of the organization to insure that everyone is properly aligned with Covey's principles. Finally, Covey presents employees with a visible and concrete means by which they can "transcend" the daily grind of stress, overwork and insecurity and finally have the opportunity to "put first things, first", all with the blessing and magnanimous support of their organization.

Character theme: "Finding 'True North'"

In the final chapter of *First Things First*, invitingly titled the "Peace of the Results", Covey and his co-writers sketch out a list of the characteristics of "principle-centered people" that would invite the envy of all but the beatified (Covey et al., 1994). These range from having richer, more rewarding relationships with other people to producing extraordinary results to developing their own healthy psychological immune system. To add rhetorical weight to this seductive picture, Covey's texts contain numerous stories of individuals who were having difficulties and were generally unsatisfied with their lives until they became more principle-centered. For example, in the one-day seminar I attended, Covey showed a video depicting an obviously distressed and impecunious Charles Dickens wandering aimlessly around London until he realizes, in a typically Hollywood-inspired moment, that he can make a difference to the misery all around him by promptly writing *A Christmas Carol*. Another frequently used exemplar is Victor Frankl, the Austrian psychologist who survived the death camps of Nazi Germany because he had a sense of future vision that included the mission that he had yet to perform. Throughout the text, Covey and his colleagues dovetail numerous commentaries on their own experiences with the principles they are discussing, showing that they too had weak moments which they resolved by following the "Habits".

This process of finding direction after being lost in the wilderness is captured metaphorically in Covey's frequent reference to the "compass". According to Covey, the dominant metaphor of our lives is still the "clock", as it symbolizes our preoccupation with speed and efficiency. Instead, we should be focused on our effectiveness, which comes from a sense of direction, purpose and balance. Our values can offer only limited help to us as, like "maps", they are only subjective attempts to represent the territory. When the territory is constantly changing, as it is in today's highly competitive world, any map soon becomes obsolete. Covey suggests that what we need to find our way is to locate our own internal "moral compass":

> A compass has a true north that is objective and external, which reflects natural laws or principles, as opposed to values that are subjective and internal. Because the compass represents the eternal verities of life, we must develop our value system with deep respect for "true north" principles.
>
> (Covey, 1990b: 94)

One of the critical "true north" principles is the need to find a balance between all of the roles we play in our lives. Covey criticizes the "personality ethic" literature for suggesting that we find "success" in some roles by putting on a different personality. This creates fragmentation and duplicity as "whatever we are we bring to every role in our life" (Covey et al., 1994: 122). Instead, Covey suggests that we need to replace our "scarcity chronos mentality" with an "abundance mentality" that thinks "win–win" with all of the roles and sees them as part of a highly integrated whole. Covey's argument is, once again, seemingly sealed with yet another organic metaphor. This time it is a "tree" in which the individual's roles or "branches" grow naturally out of the "common trunk" of our personal mission and "common roots" which are the principles that give sustenance and life. Covey also provides a touching vignette of an executive who becomes a better "husband" by taking his wife out to lunch in the same way he honors the business relationships that matter to him. In a classically smooth and untroubled conceptual leap, Covey suggests that the same principles that apply to individuals also apply to organizations and even nation states, especially the United States. In typically stirring style, he promises that

> With moral compassing, we can beat Japan. My view is that the Japanese subordinate the individual to the group to the extent that they don't tap into the creative and resourceful capacities of people – one indication being that they have had only four Nobel Prize-winners compared with 186 in the U.S.
>
> (Covey, 1990b: 99)

In establishing the quest to find "true north" by rising above the day-to-day preoccupations and frustrations, Covey directly addresses the transcendental motive identified by Burke. Relating back to Hart's (1989) distinction, the "moral compass" and its related imagery adds a qualitative dimension to Covey's argument which provides individuals and organizations with a sense of higher purpose by answering the all-important "why?" question. In promoting the "principle-centered" life, Covey adopts a classic rhetorical ploy of setting up and destroying a number of alternative foci upon which individuals could base their lives. Systematically, he dismisses becoming work- or money-centered, possession- or pleasure-centered, friend- or enemy-centered, church- or family-centered, and self- or spouse-centered. Moreover, he rejects the compromising appeal of a "combination-centered" life because "it offers no consistent sense of direction, no persistent wisdom, no steady power supply or sense of personal, intrinsic worth and identity" (1988: 5). He writes:

> My experience leads me to believe that when a person centers his life on correct principles, he becomes more balanced, unified, organized,

anchored, rooted. He finds a foundation and cornerstone of all his activities, relationships, and decisions. Such a person will have a sense of stewardship about everything in his life, including money, possessions, relationships, his family, his body, and so forth. He recognizes the need to use them for good purposes and, as a steward, to be accountable for their use.

(Covey, 1988: 5–6)

With descriptions such as these, Covey creates a fantasy theme that is based on the character of the protagonists within his rhetorical vision. He presents his followers with an ideal person, someone whom we can admire and try to measure up to. These characters include famous historical figures as well as ordinary, middle-class American folk like the readers themselves. Covey, therefore, supplies us with not only a script of what we need to do to become more effective but also numerous positive and negative role models, including himself, from which we can take our cues and base our own lives. He has taken this winning formula to its next logical step in his most recent book, *Living the Seven Habits* (Covey, 1999). This book consists almost entirely of stories from his readers who reveal how the habits have changed their lives. The Franklin Covey web site invites individuals to "share your own story" for possible inclusion in a future volume of *Living the Seven Habits* (http:/www.franklin.covey/communities/share.html). Reflecting on this strategy, Seglin observes that "Covey has used a brilliant method to prolong the life of his franchise: he lets his readers do it for him" (1999: 97).

Using strong characters to reinforce the rhetorical power of a vision is not, however, a strategy without pitfalls, particularly when one uses oneself as the exemplar. Referring to the text of one of Covey's personal accounts of an episode in which he was faced with the task of persuading his reluctant son to clean up the yard, Argyris (2000) identifies a troubling inconsistency between the theory that Covey espouses and the one he actually uses. Instead of confronting his son, Argyris notes that Covey suppresses his own negative feelings about his son's behavior and, most significantly, covers up the fact that he is doing so. The problem this poses in Argyris's mind is that "although Covey advises people to act authentically, he himself does not do so" (Argyris cited in Shapiro, 2000: 178). While Covey's emphasis upon such qualities as personal responsibility, authenticity, trust and genuine caring are morally attractive to Argyris, he is concerned that Covey's theory of personal leadership is fundamentally flawed. Moreover, the causal claims of the theory are structured in ways that cannot be tested in real life.

Managing spiritual movements in a secular age

Stephen Covey's Mormon heritage

Stephen Covey is an active member of the Church of Jesus Christ of Latter-Day Saints (LDS), the official church of the Mormon faith. He served his two-year mission in England, has been a regional representative and bishop of the church and, as president of the Irish Mission, was credited with making remarkable inroads into a territory that had been traditionally inimical to Mormonism. Whenever he makes a presentation for a business audience in a city, he regularly offers to speak at the local LDS church or temple. While Covey does nothing to hide his Mormon roots, he recoils at the suggestion that his management training work is a recycled and secularized version of Mormonism. For example, in an interview with *Fortune*, he responded to such a suggestion with the following comment: "I say nothing that is unique to my own religion. You'd hit a volcano there. I don't want to go the next step and get into a person's relationship with God" (Smith, 1994: 119). Micklethwait and Wooldridge write, "Covey's own Mormonism has been lifelong and unflinching", but they add, "he bridles at the thought that his ideas are particularly American, let alone Mormon" (1996: 349–350).

By contrast, Covey is willing to acknowledge, if not actively promote, the spiritual quality of his message. In reacting to an interviewer's suggestion that characterized his approach to management development as "almost spiritual", Covey responded that this would be true if the term were being applied in its "universal sense". He added, "I would think these principles are principles that lie deep in the consciousness of everybody, so if you want to define that as spiritual then I would agree" (*Training*, 1992: 42). When pressed on this issue, Covey will talk about his extensive study of other religions as well as his experiences with individuals from a number of different faiths. He frequently quotes Gandhi to add weight to his polytheist argument. What emerges is an essentially pragmatic stance to a potentially thorny theological problem. The general thrust of his position is that it is okay either to follow or not to follow a particular God, but you ignore at your peril the self-evident, universal and non-discriminatory principles that Covey identifies. Ultimately, these principles emanate from some source and Covey is not ambivalent in his own mind what that source might be. In the Epilogue of *First Things First*, Covey and his co-authors close with the following statement:

> Above all, we feel a sense of reverence for God, whom we believe to be the source of both principles and conscience. It's our own conviction that it is the spark of divinity within each of us that draws us toward principle-centered lives of service and contribution. But we also recognize – and reverence – the diversity of belief manifest in our own

organization and throughout the world by people of conscience and contribution.

(Covey et al., 1994: 305)

Before the *Seven Habits* brought Covey to the attention of a mass audience, he had already authored a number of books intended primarily for Mormon readers, including *Spiritual Roots of Human Relations, Marriage and Family Insights* and *The Divine Center*. Much of the latter book (Covey, 1982) appears in secularized form in a number of Covey's articles and books written later for a mainstream audience. Perhaps the most blatant example of adaptation comes in a diagram that displays a ring of potential "centers" upon which to base one's life. In the Mormon version, the diagram depicts the "Divine Center" as the correct center, whereas in the secular version, this is replaced by "Principles". A Calgary-based LDS bookseller told me that, since Covey's success, he has sold a considerable number of Covey's Mormon books to non-Mormon or gentile clientele interested in finding out more.

Covey is not the only management guru to have emerged from the Mormon faith. Hyrum Smith, author of the *The 10 Successful Laws of Time and Life Management* (Smith, 1994) and creator of the "Franklin Day Planner", has developed a time management system that was a close competitor of Covey's system until the Covey Leadership Center and Smith's Franklin Quest merged in 1997 (*Workforce*, 1997). Margaret Wheatley, also a former professor at Brigham Young University and author of the bestseller *Leadership and the New Science*, has established a consulting practice in Provo, Utah, which is "committed to self-organizing processes that involve the whole system of an organization in planning its desired form and function" (1992: 166). Historically a relatively poor area of America, Utah has recently emerged as a Mecca for progressive, high-tech companies and as a hub for numerous new management consultancy firms promising an alternative vision of organizational transformation to their blue-chip customers.

Comparing the effectiveness movement with Mormonism

While Mormonism is a religious movement with a considerably longer history, it shares a number of intriguing features with the effectiveness movement led by Stephen Covey. Both movements are explicitly expansionary and driven to grow well beyond their American origins. Stark (1994) has calculated that between 1980 and 1990 the worldwide population of Mormons increased by 67 percent to 7,762,000 to make it one of the world's fastest-growing religions. Most of this growth came from conversions that took place outside of the United States, with the fastest growth recorded in Latin America, the West Indies and Asia. Similarly, the Covey Leadership Center has experienced spectacular growth in a relatively short period of time on a global scale. Covey is quoted in *The Economist* as saying that "he will be disappointed if the business is not ten times bigger in ten years" (1996a: 74).

The growth in both movements has been fueled by extremely well-organized, proselytizing strategies. With its non-professionalized lay hierarchy, the Mormon faith provides ample opportunity for individuals from all walks of life to develop the rhetorical prowess and oratorical skill for which Covey, with his distinctively hushed and calm delivery, is widely celebrated. In his most popular Mormon text, *Spiritual Roots of Human Relations*, Covey (1993) shares his "ten principles of effective missionary work", the first of which is to encourage aspiring missionaries to act as "gospel teachers" not "gospel salesmen". At the one-day seminar that I attended, Covey demonstrated the effectiveness of this approach. At regular intervals during his presentation, he asked each member of the groups sitting around the small tables to take a turn at "teaching" the others the main points that he had covered. My group took their task very seriously, doing their utmost to recall exactly what Covey had said. He also urged us to "teach", within 48 hours of the seminar, at least two others who had been misfortunate enough to miss the seminar. Interestingly, when guiding the audience, Covey did not suggest that the small groups discuss the validity of what he was saying. When I attempted to introduce this element into our discussion, I was politely reminded by the group that that was not what we had been asked to do.

There are also some similarities in the way in which Mormonism and the effectiveness movement are organized, with both exhibiting strong centralizing and hierarchical tendencies. The church of the LDS is headed by a president who is considered by his followers to be a living prophet and is authorized to proclaim God's will through direct revelation. Immediately below him is a small group of men known as General Authorities, who are believed to be divinely chosen and inspired of God. The greatest rhetorical exposure of Mormon General Authorities is provided through the General Conference, held biennially in Salt Lake City. The president's address at these conferences is the single most important source for rulings on key social issues and guidance about where the church is heading in the future. Similarly, the Covey Leadership Center remains very much a "prophet-centered" organization. Covey leaves most of the running of the business to his "inner circle", which includes three of his nine children, one of whom has assumed control of the operations of the CLC (Smith, 1995b). However, he and his "words" are central to the organization's success and continued mobilization.

Alan Wolfe has found some strong similarities in the ways that Stephen Covey and Joseph Smith, the religious founder of the Mormon faith, have promoted their ideas. Both, in his mind, are practitioners who offered "a doctrine for the pragmatic, no-nonsense kind of person who practiced a kind of white magic on the material world, demanding that it yield its secrets for the cause of human betterment" (Wolfe, 1998: 29). In persuading followers to pursue their respective visions, both Covey and Smith divined what their followers wanted and offered it to them through a relationship between leader and audience characterized by Brooke in *The Refiner's Fire* as "interactive performance or theatre" (Brooke, 1996) Most critical to their success, however, has been their ability to persuade people that things that are perfectly obvious, even completely known to them, can nonetheless be revealed to them. In this regard, the secrets that they reveal are "this-worldly" rather than "other-worldly", bound up in a "weightless spirituality" that provides all of the benefits of a religion without having to suffer through the denial, sacrifice and endurance that religious asceticism demands. Wolfe argues that, by offering a non-judgmental religion linked to a hierarchical and authoritarian structure, Smith and Covey have created a religion that is incapable of judging its supreme leader. Following the "Seven Habits", he suggests, produces "obedient automatons" who will willingly absorb Covey's habits unconsciously but not question their fundamental intellectual basis. Wolfe concludes, therefore, that, "in Covey's system, you gain control over your life by giving up control over your destiny" (1998: 32).

Harold Bloom has identified Mormons, along with Southern Baptists, as the quintessential representatives of what he labels the "American Religion" in that they see themselves as not being created because they are coexistent with God, they are Gnostic or experiential in focus and they revere freedom. However, Bloom points out that

> Freedom for an American . . . means two things: being free of the Creation, and being free of the presence of other humans. The Mormons rejoice in the first freedom, while fleeing the solitude of the second . . . [Mormons see themselves as] each progressing from human to divine on the basis of hard work and obedience to the laws of the universe, which turn out to be the maxim of the Latter-Day Saints Church. Organization, replacing Creation, becomes a sacred idea, and every good Mormon indeed remains an organization man or woman.
>
> (Bloom, 1992: 114–116)

Hansen (1981) describes how Mormonism underwent a dramatic paradigm shift at the turn of this century. Prior to the admission of Utah into the United States in 1896, the Utah Saints had been profoundly isolationist, communitarian and anti-American in outlook. They engendered tremendous suspicion and hostility from a mainstream America that, having vanquished slavery, was committed to eradicating the surviving "twin" of the "relics of barbarism" – polygamy. In a remarkably short period the Mormons were able to turn about-face, both ideologically and politically, to become one of the foremost champions of America and its capitalist glory. As Hansen remarks,

While building their anti-modern kingdom of God, [they] developed those modern habits of initiative and self-discipline that helped dig the grave of the kingdom and ushered in a new breed of Mormon thoroughly at home in the corporate economy of America, and its corollaries, political pluralism and the bourgeois family.

(Hansen, 1981: 206)

Today Mormons are actively encouraged to channel their work ethic and conformist outlook toward occupying the senior ranks of corporations. Through Mormon-run high-tech companies like Word Perfect, Novell and Dayna Corporation as well as the LDS church's own formidable business arms, Zion Securities and Zion's Co-operation and Mercantile Institution, they have been able to make an impressive mark upon the corporate land-scape of America and beyond (de Pillis, 1991). Traditionally, the separation between religion, state and commerce has been an important and enduring touchstone of American society. In the past, Covey's Mormon roots may have significantly hindered him from taking his message to a wider audience. By contrast in the contemporary setting, Covey's Mormon-influenced message is given added credence by a mass audience that may still harbor some vague lingering suspicions about Mormonism but recognizes the unqualified success and celebrated loyalty and work ethic of the movement's followers.

Mormonism moves to the mainline

Secularization is one of the central yet most widely disputed concepts in the sociology of religion. Originating in the writings of Compte and further elaborated by Marx, Durkheim and Weber, the "secularization thesis" suggests that secularization is a process that is strongly linked to indus-trialization and urban life and leads to the rise of rationalism and the declining influence and gradual disappearance of religion in modern society. According to Berger (1967), the single most important consequence of secularization is the creation of a pluralistic situation where, in times past, religious monopolies were the rule. A pluralistic situation undermines the taken-for-granted character of religious traditions and results in religious institutions becoming subject to the logic of market economics. Consequently, religious organizations tend to become increasingly bureau-cratized, results-oriented and more sensitive to the problems of public relations.

In their analysis of the changing official rhetoric of Mormon leaders, Shepherd and Shepherd (1984) show how the LDS church has been able not only to survive but also to thrive at a time when membership in its mainstream Protestant rivals has fallen dramatically. The emergence of modern Mormonism has been accompanied by a relative increase in the rhetoric of family unity and personal morality. At the same time, in the rhetoric of the leaders, public emphasis on supernatural beliefs and uniquely Mormon doctrines has declined. This rhetorical maneuver is particularly remarkable in light of Mormonism's reputation for scriptural literalism and adherence to prophetic dogma. Stark (1994) suggests that the more conservative religious bodies have tended to profit from secularization because they attract individuals seeking to "take flight from modernity" and have become disillusioned by the excessive accommodation of the more liberal denominations. In the case of Mormonism, the prospect of becoming a "mainline religion" has become an issue that is hotly debated among Mormon scholars. It has opened up an the age-old dilemma of reconciling the desire on the part of many Mormons to become accepted by the wider society while maintaining the distinctive identity which is the faith's primary socio-psychological attraction (Mauss, 1994).

Thomas Luckmann attacks the proponents of the "secularization thesis" for mistakenly equating declining church membership and attendance with an increasingly irreligious society. He argues that, while church-oriented religion has undoubtedly declined in the face of modernity, it has been replaced by a new form of religion which he calls "invisible religion". This new form of religion is an inevitable product of the post-industrial society, where religion becomes an increasingly private affair that can be experienced individualistically and expressed in isolation. The "invisible religion" is mediated socially not through the traditional "primary institutions" of churches, sects and cults but through a wide array of "secondary institutions" which

> Expressly cater to the "private" needs of "autonomous" consumers. These institutions attempt to articulate the themes arising in the "private sphere" and retransmit the packaged results to potential customers. Syndicated advice columns, "inspirational" literature ranging from tracts on Positive Thinking to *Playboy* magazine, *Reader's Digest* versions of popular psychology, the lyrics of popular hits, and so forth, articulate what are, in effect, elements of models of "ultimate" significance. The models are, of course, non-obligatory and must compete on what is, basically, an open market. The manufacture, the packaging and the sale of models of "ultimate significance" are, therefore, determined by consumer preference, and the manufacturer must remain sensitive to the needs and requirements of "autonomous" individuals and their existence in the "private sphere".
>
> (Luckmann, 1967: 104)

Following Luckmann's line of argument, I would suggest that, through the effectiveness movement, Covey has been able to create an "invisible religion" of his own. We have seen from the preceding rhetorical critique that he has shown himself to be extremely sensitive to the needs and requirements of "autonomous" individuals and that he has cast his ideas well within their "private sphere". He has created an ostensibly secular and rational rhetorical vision that speaks to, and appeals to, the spiritual needs of a wide range of individuals, many of whom have removed themselves from the traditional primary institutions of religion. This vision has been constructed through the creative and well-organized use of such secondary institutions as the general and business media, publishers and Covey's own consulting organization. The authority for this vision is derived neither from a deity nor from divine doctrine nor sacred law, but from the charismatic leadership that Covey has exhibited to powerful effect. Importantly, the models are non-obligatory. Within Covey's rhetorical community, the consumer is given full sovereignty. He or she is free to move in and out of the "cafeteria", selecting the attractive elements of the vision and adding them to the highly individualized pastiche of spiritual, religious and quasi-religious beliefs and tenets that form the basis for defining self and identity in late modernity (Creedon, 1998; Heelas, 1996). In the elaboration of his rhetorical vision, Covey has been able to adapt some of the doctrine of an essentially premodern theology and disseminate these ideas in a seemingly new model of "ultimate significance" to a much wider (and largely unsuspecting) audience than even his most zealous forebears would have ever dreamt possible.

Summary

In this chapter I have described the content, style and processes by which Stephen Covey has created an enormous following within North America and throughout the world for his vision of personal and professional effectiveness. Covey has distinguished himself from other gurus and consultants by his highly centralized and hierarchical organizational modus operandi and by the scale and ambition of the marketing apparatus he has assembled. He has successfully bridged the business and personal growth markets by disseminating a pragmatic, seemingly universal, relativist message that promises something for everybody but fundamentally does little to change the status quo. By placing the responsibility firmly on the shoulders of the individual, Covey has absolved corporations, government and other institutions of their responsibilities and obligations. While Covey is clearly no master of the English language, the rhetorical vision he has skillfully articulated comprising three compelling fantasy themes – "Back to the Farm", "Working from the Inside-Out" and "Finding True North" – provides a powerful, dramatizing message for individuals struggling to define and assert themselves through activities which may, to them, seem increasingly purposeless and over which they feel increasingly powerless. The absolutist conviction that Covey invests in his "Seven Habits" provides his vision with the impressive moral authority that can be derived from an analogue that is fundamentally righteous. Other visions may come and go, but Covey's vision will endure because it is timeless, universal and unassailably "right". Followers are free to look at and even pursue alternatives but Covey conveys to his audience worldly insight and unwavering confidence in the fact that they will eventually see the light and return. Backed by the righteous analogue, Covey's rhetorical skill has placed him at the vanguard of the growing hybridization of managerial, political and religious rhetoric in popular business discourse (Conlin, 1999).

6 Peter Senge and the learning organization

> We are taking a stand for a vision, for creating a type of organization we would truly like to work within and which can thrive in a world of increasing interdependency and change. It is not what the vision is, but what the vision does that matters.
>
> (Kofman and Senge, 1993: 16)

> The fundamental purpose of any organization is not to make a profit. A social mission is the essence of a successful business; doing something that makes a difference to somebody. Organizations need to begin thinking of leaders as designers, stewards, and teachers, and not as the key decision-makers. Business is about making a better world. Everyone needs to live their lives in the service of their highest aspirations.
>
> (Senge, 1995a: 18)

Introduction

The third and final management guru and fashion case will be examined in this chapter. The subject is Peter Senge, a professor at the Massachusetts Institute of Technology who, with the publication of his book *The Fifth Discipline* in 1990, emerged from the relative obscurity of academia to full-blown guru status in a very short time. Since the publication of this and two subsequent books, *The Fifth Discipline Fieldbook* (Senge et al., 1994) and *The Dance of Change* (Senge et al., 1999), he has continued to be prominently featured in the business media and is widely cited in practitioner publications and the academic literature. The symbolic cue for the rhetorical vision that he has helped to construct is the "learning organization". While Senge was by no means the first author to coin this term, he has been primarily instrumental in popularizing it to the point that it has become a staple of everyday business discourse.

The chapter is organized into five parts. In the first part I briefly review the evolution of the idea of the learning organization, with particular attention paid to how other writers have contributed to the development of this concept. The second part of the chapter examines the processes by which the rhetorical vision of the learning organization has been assembled, organized and disseminated by Peter Senge and his colleagues. I highlight the characteristics that distinguish Peter Senge from other management gurus and suggest why these characteristics have helped to make the learning organization vision such a compelling one for corporate North America and beyond. In the third part of the chapter, the rhetorical community that has developed around the learning organization is described with specific reference to two sub-communities that have shown themselves to be most strongly associated with it: senior executives and human resource development/training professionals.

The rhetorical vision of the learning organization is described and analyzed in the fourth part. In contrast to the two preceding rhetorical visions that have been examined in Chapters 5 and 6, Senge's vision is undergirded by an essentially "social" master analogue. That is, it emphasizes the primacy of human relations, focusing on trust, caring, comradeship and humanity (Cragan and Shields, 1995). In this vision, the individual can realize his or her full self only through social interaction with other individuals who are working toward a common cause. In this respect, Senge offers a collectivist vision that stands in stark contrast to the individualistic visions developed by Hammer and Champy and Covey. I will describe five interrelated fantasy themes that run through the rhetorical vision of the learning organization and identify the more common metaphors that Senge uses to illuminate each theme. In the final part of the chapter, I examine the critique that has developed on several fronts to the learning organization concept and discuss how Senge and his colleagues have responded to this critique in order to sustain their rhetorical vision.

Forerunners and variants of the learning organization vision

While the term "learning organization" has in the last decade become a widely used and, as many would argue, abused term in the business lexicon, it is by no means a new concept. Garratt suggests that, although the desire to create organizations that can consciously cope with change by learning continuously can be traced back to antiquity, "all the necessary conditions to create both the intellectual and practical basis of a learning organization were in place by 1947" (1995: 25). Specifically, he points to the creation of the intelligence unit by Sir Geoffrey Vickers at the newly nationalized National Coal Board (NCB) which contained the radical triumvirate of thinkers, Reg Revans, Fritz Schumacher and Jacob Bronowski. Garratt identifies Revans as being a particularly influential figure in the evolution of the learning organization concept. Drawing on his experience in fostering learning within the NCB, Revans (1980) likened the organization to an organism that has to increase its capacity to learn if it is to function successfully in an environment characterized by continual change. Transplanting a formula from ecology, he noted that in order to survive, an organization, like an organism, must be able to learn at a rate that equals or exceeds the changes that are occuring in its environment.

Pedler et al. (1997) have similarly acknowledged the contribution of Reg Revans, whom they value both for his distrust of experts and his passionate commitment to promoting the learning of the individual-within-the-company. They also point to the contribution made by six other writers in shaping the idea of the learning organization, organizational learning and their own construct, "The Learning Company". In terms of intellectual contributions, they single out the work of Argyris and Schon (1978) in translating Gregory Bateson's ground-breaking three "levels of learning" into the organizational setting with their concepts of "single-loop", "double-loop" and "deutero-learning". They also credit Roger Harrison (1995) for his insights in highlighting the positive role that "defensive behaviors" and "organizational healing" can play in creating a learning organization as well as the work of Nancy Dixon (1994) in trying to put ideas of organizational learning into practice. In terms of promoting the concept to a broader audience, they recognize the contribution of Peters and Waterman's book, *In Search of Excellence,* in paving the way for mass acceptance of the learning organization by stressing the importance of adaptability and responsiveness and stating that "the excellent companies are learning organizations" (Peters and Waterman, 1982: 110). Similarly, W.E. Deming's widely accepted 14 principles of quality are credited with laying the foundation for widespread acceptance of the idea of the learning organization (1986). These contributions notwithstanding, it is Peter Senge's bestselling book, *The Fifth Discipline* (1990b), which has, in their minds, "been largely responsible for bringing the learning organization into the mainstream of business thinking" (Pedler et al., 1997: 196).

In the last ten years, a number of competing visions of what a learning organization should look like and how to get to it have gained varying degrees of acceptance within academic and practitioner communities. The word "competing" is used quite loosely in this instance because most of the writers in this area are at pains to acknowledge the related work of others and to stress the need for a collective effort to move toward their overarching goal. The most significant visions of the learning organization are presented in Table 6.1 along with a brief definition. Not all of these writers have chosen to label their vision specifically as a "learning organization" but there is considerable overlap between them in what they are trying to articulate and promote. For example, Pedler et al. (1991) prefer to use the term "learning company" rather than "learning organization" because it is less mechanical and focuses on the idea of any group of people being "in company" with others as they seek to explore collectively how best people may live and work together. They have produced a model of the learning company which depicts four interlocking circles of Policy, Operations, Ideas and Action and have isolated 11 features which, they argue, characterize a learning company. These have formed the basis for

Table 6.1 Defining the learning organization and its variants

Author(s)	Symbolic cue	Definition
Senge (1990b)	The Learning Organization	Organizations where people continually expand their capacity to create the results they truly desire, where new and expansive patterns of thinking are nurtured, where collective aspiration is set free, and where people are continually learning how to learn together. (p. 3)
Pedler, Burgoyne & Boydell (1991)	The Learning Company	A learning company is an organization that facilitates the learning of all its members and consciously transforms itself and its context. (p. 3)
Nonaka (1991)	The Knowledge-Creating Company	When markets shift, technologies proliferate, competitors multiply, and products become obsolete almost overnight, successful companies are those that consistently create new knowledge, disseminate it widely throughout the organization, and quickly embody it in new technologies and products. (p. 96)
Garvin (1993)	The Learning Organization	An organization skilled at creating, acquiring, and transferring knowledge, and at modifying its behavior to reflect new knowledge and insights. (p. 80)
Watkins & Marsick (1994)	The Learning Organization	The learning organization is one that learns continuously and transforms itself. (p. 8)
Kilmann (1996)	The Learning Organization	A learning organization describes, controls and improves the processes by which knowledge is created, acquired, distributed, interpreted, stored, retrieved, and used for the purpose of achieving long-term organizational success. (p. 208)
De Geus (1997)	The Living Company	Living companies have a personality that allows them to evolve harmoniously. They know who they are, understand how they fit in the world, value new ideas and new people, and husband their money in a way that allows them govern their future. (p. 52)

diagnostic instruments that are used to look at company-wide learning processes under the umbrella of the Learning Company Project, which works with a number of prominent companies in the United Kingdom and other countries but has yet to make major inroads into North America.

It is clear from this brief review that, when it was first articulated in the early 1990s, Peter Senge's vision of the learning organization was neither novel nor original. Moreover, he was by no means the only writer working on the development of the concept. In fact he was in extremely good company along with numerous high-profile academics and consultants on both sides of the Atlantic. Knowing this raises the question of what it was about Senge's vision that enabled it to catch on and be assimilated in such a substantial way, attracting so much attention over such a short period of time. Was it the manner in which he constructed his particular vision? Or was it more to do with the way in which he went about communicating this vision? Or was it more a function of how he and his colleagues organized themselves? These three questions will be the primary concern for the remainder of this chapter.

Organizing the learning organization vision

Background

Raised in Los Angeles as the son of a Kodak salesman, Peter Senge pursued undergraduate studies in Engineering at Stanford, during which time he developed a strong interest in population growth and environmental degradation (Dumaine, 1994a). This interest led him to the Massachusetts Institute of Technology (MIT), where he completed an M.Sc. in Systems Modeling and a Ph.D. in Management before becoming a member of the faculty at MIT's Sloan School of Management. The turning point for Peter Senge came with the publication in 1990 of his book, *The Fifth Discipline: The Art and Practice of the Learning Organization*. The book was published by Doubleday under the Currency imprint, which specializes in books that set out to find meaning in the workplace. In explaining the reasons for targeting this new segment of the business book market, Harriet Rubin, Doubleday's influential executive editor, observes, "Meaning is hot, and it's getting hotter. This is the age of enchantment, and people are looking for an antidote to the masochism of work" (Dumaine, 1994b: 197). Senge has acknowledged the importance of Rubin's role in getting the book to market, particularly in introducing him to Art Kleiner, a former contributing editor to the *Whole Earth Catalogue* and *Garbage Magazine*, who coached Senge and urged him to express the essential message of the book in just one sentence.

In keeping with Currency's efforts to stake out a new territory for business books, the book was strikingly packaged with a solemn matt black dustjacket with a muted gold "V" emblazoned on the front cover, signaling the primacy of the "fifth discipline" – systems thinking. At the top of the cover were the prophetic words from *Fortune* magazine: "Forget your old, tired ideas about leadership. The most successful corporation of the 1990s will be something called a learning organization" (Dumaine, 1989: 48). Intriguingly, neither the article from which this quotation was taken, nor a subsequent article devoted to learning organizations that appeared a year later (Kiechel, 1990), makes any reference to Peter Senge. It is a testament to the impact of *The*

Fifth Discipline that almost every article regarding learning organizations that I have come across since its publication makes some reference to Peter Senge. Indeed, it would appear to the casual reader of the business media that the learning organization has become inseparable from Peter Senge.

Senge defines learning organizations as "organizations where people continually expand their capacity to create the results they truly desire, where new and expansive patterns of thinking are nurtured, where collective aspiration is set free, and where people are continually learning how to learn together" (1990b: 3). In the book, Senge identifies the following five "learning disciplines", or lifelong programs of study and practice, upon which the learning organization is based: Personal Mastery; Mental Models; Shared Vision; Team Learning; and Systems Thinking. Each of these is briefly described in Table 6.2. The fifth discipline privileged in the book's title is that of Systems Thinking, which Senge argues is the most important because it integrates the disciplines, fusing them into a coherent body of theory and practice. Intriguingly, he ascribes this discipline a kind of "mother hen" role to the other disciplines by suggesting that "it keeps them from being separate gimmicks or the latest organizational fads" (1990b: 12).

Senge's next book, *The Fifth Disciple Fieldbook* (Senge et al., 1994), was written with four other authors who have worked with him over a long period. These were Charlotte Roberts, a principal at Innovation Associates who had co-led numerous "Leadership and Mastery" seminars with Senge;

Table 6.2 The five disciplines of Peter Senge's learning organization

Discipline	Definition
Personal Mastery	Learning to expand our personal capacity to create the results we most desire, and creating an organizational environment which encourages all its members to develop themselves toward the goals and purposes they choose.
Mental Models	Reflecting upon, continually clarifying, and improving our internal pictures of the world, and seeing how they shape our actions and desires.
Shared Vision	Building a sense of commitment in a group, by developing shared images of the future we seek to create, and the principles and guiding practices by which we hope to get there.
Team Learning	Transforming conversational and collective thinking skills, so that groups of people can reliably develop intelligence and ability greater than the sum of individual members' talents.
Systems Thinking	A way of thinking about, and language for describing and understanding, the forces and interrelationships that shape the behaviors of systems. This discipline helps us to see how to change systems more effectively, and to act more in tune with the larger processes of the natural and economic world.

Source: Senge et al. (1994, pp. 6–7)

Rick Ross, an organizational consultant based in San Diego, California; Bryan Smith, president of Innovation Associates of Canada, who played the role of "team diplomat" according to Senge; and Art Kleiner, who, with this book, now received equal billing with Senge. At the beginning of the book, Senge explains that it was written in response to the widespread question provoked by its predecessor: "This is great . . . but what do we do Monday morning?" (Senge et al., 1994: 5). Positioned as the first in an ongoing series, the book contained 172 pieces of writing by 67 authors. In contrast to the restrained presentation of *The Fifth Discipline*, Doubleday Currency bypassed the conventional hard-cover package, presenting a bright red, blue and yellow-covered paperback that was studiously devoid of solemn pronouncements and brimful of practical how-to advice.

Guru of the new

In 1992 Peter Senge was singled out in a *Business Week* cover story as one of a highly influential group of management's "new gurus", alongside Michael Hammer, Edward Lawler III, David Nadler, C.K. Prahalad, and George Stalk Jr. The article's author, John Byrne, argued that this group differed from the previous generation of management gurus such as Peter Drucker, Kenneth Blanchard and Tom Peters in several important ways. First, their message was considerably more revolutionary in tone, urging managers to think in radically different ways and to overhaul their operations dramatically. Second, this group was convinced that management should stop organizing itself around functions such as marketing and manufacturing, as had traditionally been the case, and begin to focus on processes, such as order fulfillment and distribution. Third, Byrne observes that this new group of gurus "cast unusually wide conceptual nets, basing their ideas on theories and experiences borrowed from the non-business world" (1992: 42). This shift beyond the sphere of management theory signals a turn toward intellectual liberalism and a new willingness on the part of managers who, having been steeped in a management education, are more receptive to the insights and theories developed in other disciplines in a bid to find new and innovative solutions to their pressing business problems. Finally, many of these new gurus played down the significance of strong heroic leadership and the strong corporate cultures that were championed by the likes of Tom Peters and Kenneth Blanchard in favor of an approach that encourages managers to get out of the way and let the employees assume fluid leadership roles according to their skills and situations.

Peter Senge certainly shares the distinguishing characteristics of the "new gurus" identified by Byrne but he has also demonstrated qualities and developed a message that sets him apart from this illustrious group. In watching Senge speak to a large audience, the first thing that strikes one is the ordinary, unassuming, boy-next-door persona he projects through his soft-spoken, high-pitched voice and casual dress. Senge's comparatively muted persona stands in striking contrast to the strident, larger-than-life figures of Hammer and Covey. While most management gurus tend to distance themselves from the rarified concerns of the academic milieu, Senge is unapologetic about his intellectual predisposition, making his professorial image a critical component of his persona, even though he is still only a senior lecturer at MIT. He also makes an effort to maintain his academic profile. For example, Senge actively participated in a number of sessions at the 1999 Academy of Management Meeting in Chicago.

Senge's anti-guru image is further reinforced by the reverence that he conveys in his speaking and writing for the contributions that his mentors have made to his thinking. In responding to questions about the origins of the learning organization concept, Senge states that "the idea of approaching them as disciplines was mine, but the theories themselves are the work of some leading thinkers. My contribution was to put the pieces together in a way that people can understand" (Galaghan, 1991: 39). In particular, he singles out Jay Forrester, his doctoral adviser at MIT, for his work on systems theory; quantum physicist, David Bohm, for his contribution to dialogue and team learning; Chris Argyris and Donald Schon, for their group dynamics research; Robert Fritz, the musician and composer, for the discipline of personal mastery; and Charlie Kiefer, from Innovation Associates, for the theories of shared vision. Senge has admitted that the book was supposed to have been a collaborative venture with these and other writers but "one by one the others dropped out and I found myself standing alone on the playing field. It was a matter of going ahead alone or quitting" (Galaghan, 1991: 39).

A collaborative approach to organizing

Senge distinguishes himself with his markedly collaborative and collegial approach to his work. In contrast to Michael Hammer and Stephen Covey, who are unquestionably the dominant figures in their respective movements, Senge appears to be quite comfortable in letting his associates take their share of the limelight, hence, his willingness to co-author the *Fieldbook* with so many colleagues. As he reflects in the materials that accompanied the "1996 Worldwide Series in Leadership" videoconference,

> Alone I would have never been able to realize the vision. Fortunately, a group of longtime collaborators shared the vision of the *Fieldbook*. It was delightful to watch how we quickly became a coherent team, with each of us bringing his or her distinctive sensibility to the project.

Senge's collaborative approach was also graphically demonstrated at a videoconference that I was involved in delivering to a local business audience. The videoconference purported to feature Peter Senge, but Senge happily gave most of the airtime to his partner Rick Ross and the guest learning organization practitioners – a high school principal and a newspaper publisher. Interestingly, a number of attendees at the video-conference complained of feeling somewhat short-changed by Senge's subsidiary role. A colleague of mine has made a wry parallel between Senge's organizational approach and the "disciple" model adopted by Jesus, while another has likened it to George Sand's "salon" of eminent artists and thinkers.

Whereas Covey, Hammer and Peters are all closely associated with one organization that bears their name (Franklin Covey, The Tom Peters Group and Hammer & Company respectively), Peter Senge appears to prefer to be loosely linked with numerous organizations. Senge is a faculty member and was, until recently, director of the Center for Organizational Learning at MIT's Sloan School of Management. The purpose of the Center was to "discover, develop and integrate multiple theories and practices of leading, learning and working together" (http://learning.mit.edu). Founded in 1990, the Center had 18 blue-chip corporate sponsors, including AT&T, Ford, Motorola and Federal Express, who each contributed a minimum of $80,000 per year (with some contributing over $1 million per year) to create learning organization "pilot programs" with members of the Center's MIT faculty. Membership entitled organizations to participate in a five-day course, biannual meetings, seminars, advanced courses, dialogue courses and to access collaborative networking arrangements with researchers and other sponsors. According to Senge, "the Center is designed to spread ideas and to create a few successful models of the learning organization that can't be ignored" (Dumaine, 1994a: 148). Moreover, the Center was designed as a conscious experiment in building a learning organization that can act as a model itself to clients interested in putting the disciplines into practice. Reflecting on his association with the Center as a visiting scholar in 1993/94, Robert Fulmer observes with undisguised relish:

> I was impressed by the extent to which staff members at the Center attempted to practice the principles associated with the "five disciplines". Regular staff meetings utilized the dialogue process. Support staff, as well as researchers, are highly conversant with the tools of systems dynamics and practice systems thinking. There is a general agreement as to the vision of how the learning center can make a difference in the world. This is not simply a grandiose statement. People at the learning center are committed to a vision of organizational life as better than most of them have known in any other setting. Each person at the Center seems committed to improving his/her "personal mastery".
>
> (Fulmer, 1995: 12–13)

In addition to his work at the Center for Organizational Learning, Senge was a founding partner of the management consulting and training firm, Innovation Associates Inc., which has enabled him to reach a much broader corporate audience. Senge participates in several other influential communication vehicles that are dedicated to fostering and broadening the rhetorical community of the learning organization. He is a frequent contributor to a monthly newsletter, *The Systems Thinker*, which "provides managers with the systems thinking knowledge and tools they need to meet the challenges of a rapidly changing business environment". Pegasus Communications, the newsletter's publisher, also organize an annual "Systems Thinker" conference which headlines Senge, showcases his associates and attracts thousands of individuals from around the world. They also produce an extensive glossy cataloge of "organizational learning resources", which include tapes, videos, software and books designed to "create and sustain a responsible and harmonious global learning community" (http://www.pegasuscom.com). Senge was also an active participant in The Learning Circle, one of numerous electronic discussion groups on the Internet that are dedicated to moving the vision of the learning organization forward (Clausson, 1996). Senge's public presentations to large-scale audiences are handled by WYNCOM Inc., a firm based in Lexington, Kentucky, that specializes in organizing management guru or "thought leader" seminars and also handles Stephen Covey, Tom Peters and Michael Hammer (http://www.wyncom.com).

Where East meets West

While the new breed of management gurus tends to stretch well beyond the conventional boundaries of management thought for inspiration and illustration, Senge distinguishes himself by his liberal and rhetorically powerful use of philosophies and metaphors from both Eastern and Western, modern and premodern cultures. For example, the *Fieldbook* opens with an account of the common greeting of the tribes of northern Natal in South Africa, in which the greeter says the Zulu equivalent to "I see you" and the person being greeted says "I am here". This apparently reflects the spirit of *ubuntu*, which acknowledges that you are a person only because other people around you respect and acknowledge you as a person. This leads Senge and his colleagues into offering a formal acknowledgment and welcome to their readers that sets a distinctively "New Age" tone for the remainder of the book.

In trying to explain what takes place within a learning organization, Senge has resurrected the Greek term *"metanoia"* to describe a shift in mind. Senge points out that in the early (Gnostic) Christian tradition, this term took on a special meaning of awakening as a direct knowing of the highest, God (1990b: 61). *Metanoia*, to him, captures a "deeper meaning of learning" which must be grasped if we are to understand the learning organization. However, Senge is vague about the sense in which he wants to use this term. In his discussion of the discipline of "Personal Mastery", Senge makes the case that the

Power of truth, seeing reality more and more as it is, cleansing the lens of perception, awakening from self-imposed distortions of reality are different expressions of a common principle that is found in almost all of the world's great philosophic and religious systems.

(Senge, 1990b: 161)

He illustrates this claim with a litany of examples drawn from the Buddhist, Hindu, Islamic and Christian faiths. This polyglot approach mirrors Covey's universality argument discussed in Chapter 6. In Senge's hands, however, it appears to be somewhat more convincing. Perhaps Senge's Buddhist faith helps to give him a more authentic air when he is discussing multiple faiths. Certainly, of all of the management gurus, Senge is the most sympathetic to Eastern philosophies, believing that the West has much to learn from them. For example, he has observed,

In general, Westerners are deeply influenced by the philosophy of reductionism – of reducing things to a finite answer. Underlying Eastern philosophies state that one never truly understands anything, that life is a continual process of learning. You cannot say the word "learning" in Chinese without saying both "study" and "practice" constantly. You could not say, "I learned something" in Chinese. It is literally, because all you can do is practice constantly. Now that is a learning orientation!

(*Journal of European Industrial Training*, 1995: 26)

Similarly, Senge recounts his reaction to reading an extract from Hermann Hesse's book *A Journey to the East* (Hesse, 1972) included in Robert Greenleaf's book, *Servant Leadership* (1977):

As I read that passage on the airplane that evening, I cried. I knew that this man understood something that we have lost in our "transactional society", where "what's in it for me?" is the assumed bedrock of all actions. We have lost the joy of "creating", of working for something just because it needs to be done. In our frenzy to get something for ourselves, we have lost ourselves.

(Senge, 1995b: 220)

Hesse's book is the story of a party of "seekers" searching for enlightenment in the form of a particular secret spiritual order. Despite references to Eastern religions, Senge, unlike Covey, is not necessarily claiming to be advancing an essentially spiritual cause. When pressed, however, about his movement's New Age status, Senge replies:

The term carries a lot of baggage, but yes, Deming always talked about a new economic age. That was his term, and he said that the principles by which success is going to be determined in this new economy would be different. So it's New Age.

(Dumaine, 1994a: 154)

Allying himself in this way to a decidedly un-New Age figure like Deming puts Senge back into the mainstream of corporate discourse.

Not all commentators appear to be convinced, however. For example, in discussing the new breed of spiritually oriented management thinkers, *The Economist* has asserted in typically acerbic terms:

> Not only is their case not novel; some of the current knowledge theorists fail to argue convincingly. The best-known is Peter Senge who is a dedicated follower of new-age fashion. To help managers make the leap to the knowledge era, Mr. Senge encourages them to meditate (particularly during meetings), and to go on retreats where they test their physical skills, before relaxing to the bongo drums.
>
> (*Economist*, 1995b: 63)

Similarly, in a scathing review of the *Fieldbook*, Jack Gordon warns of the "awful collision" that will result in trying to wed spirituality and commerce, observing, "the dream is nothing less than to stage a post-modern wedding of God and mammon – to reconcile the poetic and spiritual aspirations of the human-potential movement with the stubbornly prosaic realities of the corporate world" (Gordon, 1995: 119).

Connecting the private and public sectors

Another distinguishing feature of Senge's message is the attention he pays to the public sector. Most management gurus focus their efforts and draw their examples from large corporations within the private sector. This strategy makes sense given that this is by far the most lucrative sector and it is the one sector to which government and not-for-profit organizations increasingly look for organizational cures and management solutions. Senge, however, has taken a wider view of the marketplace. While there is no doubt in the reader's mind that he is concerned and comfortable with the challenges facing managers within the corporate milieu, he makes frequent reference to individuals and organizations from other sectors, most particularly from the realm of public education – a particularly important area of concern for him. Indeed, he argues that the problems afflicting the latter sector may have more than a little to do with the problems afflicting the former:

> I am becoming more and more convinced that we cannot implement systems thinking by looking at business alone – we have to start earlier

in people's lives. . . . What we really need is a partnership between business and education to build learning organizations.

(Journal of European Industrial Training, 1995: 28)

Senge cites Thomas Jefferson's statement that "a democracy is only as strong as its public education" in his frequent attacks on the current state of the American public education system which Senge says is producing people who do not have the capacity to understand issues such as the causes of the budget and trade deficits and are, therefore, ripe for easy manipulation by politicians and mass media. Senge's stance and sentiments on the public sector have been recognized by Al Gore, who invited him to participate in the vice-president's "Reinventing Government" summit in the summer of 1993 (Abramson, 1994). Senge's broader appeal was reflected by the fact that at the March 1994 videoconference at which he was featured, a considerably higher proportion of public sector managers and educational administrators attended compared to the proportion who attended videoconferences featuring other management gurus.

The link with the quality movement

In common with Hammer and Covey and other management gurus, Senge goes to great lengths to point out that his concept, the learning organization, is different from and superior to the management fashions that have preceded it. Taking the moral high ground, he argues that the learning organization is too important to be characterized as just another management fashion that will inevitably be forsaken for the next great management idea. Regardless of the foibles of fashion, the learning organization, in some form or other, will endure. One means by which he sets out to insure this is to attempt strategically to align the learning organization concept with the quality movement.

Senge has made the case that the learning organization is the logical successor to the Total Quality Management (TQM) movement spawned by one of his key mentors, W. Edwards Deming. Senge states prophetically that "we're where the quality movement was in the 1940s" (Dumaine, 1994a: 148). Elsewhere, Senge has proposed that the quality movement, with its preoccupation with learning, was the "first wave" in building learning organizations. In the first wave, the primary focus of change was on frontline workers. Management's job was to champion continual improvement, remove impediments that disempowered employees, and support initiatives such as benchmarking and quality training. In the second wave, the organization shifts its attention away from employees and improving work processes to management and fostering ways of thinking and interacting that are conducive to continual learning. According to Senge, these two waves will gradually merge into a third wave in which "learning becomes institutionalized as an inescapable way of life for managers and workers (even if we bother maintaining that distinction)" (1992: 32). Senge argues that, with a few exceptions, American industry primarily operates within the first wave, adding that most American managers still lack the understanding of what is required for even the first wave of quality management practices to take root. By contrast, the second wave is well under way in Japan, driven by the introduction of the "seven new tools of management" introduced in 1979 by the Society for QC Technique Development and symbolized by the creation of Mazda's Miata sports car which took the American car market by storm (Schlossberg, 1991).

Senge positions the five disciplines of the learning organization as the means by which American managers can move into the second wave and, ultimately, surpass Japanese management. The concept can act as a unifying framework for galvanizing the quality movement which, in Senge's mind, risks being fragmented into isolated initiatives and slogans and is hamstrung by the authoritarian, command-and-control hierarchy that still predominates in the United States. Senge makes the observation that Deming's management philosophy was essentially about creating learning organizations, even though he may not have used this term. He substantiates this claim by pointing to Deming's preoccupation with intrinsic versus extrinsic rewards and by tracing Deming's "Plan, Do, Check, Act" cycle back to John Dewey, the American philosopher and educator. In making this claim, Senge attempts to build an illustrious hereditary line that stretches back to Dewey through Deming to himself as the "heir apparent" to the quality movement. To add further rhetorical weight to this claim, Senge makes frequent asides to the numerous conversations he has had with Deming.

The rhetorical community of the learning organization

An examination of evidence in the mass media that a rhetorical community has developed around Senge's rhetorical vision of the learning organization reveals that two distinctive sub-communities have been particularly vocal in their support and articulation of the vision: senior executives, and corporate trainers and human resource developers.

Senior executives

Senge is clearly aware of the rhetorical weight that a senior executive can bring to legitimating the rhetorical vision of the learning organization. Recognizing that his lack of direct industry experience could undermine the credibility of this argument, Senge makes ample and effective use of senior executives and their experiences creating and working with learning organizations. Most notably, Senge makes frequent references in his books and interviews to Bill O'Brien, the former CEO of Hanover Insurance, using him almost as a mouthpiece for the voice of direct experience and as a counterweight to Senge's academic orientation. Facing near-bankruptcy in 1969, O'Brien set out to "find out what would give the necessary organization and discipline to have work be more congruent with human nature. We gradually identified a set of core values that are actually principles that overcome the basic disease of the hierarchy" (quoted in Senge, 1990b: 181). During the 1980s, Senge joined a cadre of academically based consultants such as Chris Argyris and Lee Bolman from the Harvard Business School, who were brought into Hanover Insurance by O'Brien to help turn it into one the top financially performing companies in the insurance industry, with core values including "merit", "openness", "localness" and "leanness" (Welter, 1991: 20). Many of the real-world examples used in *The Fifth Discipline* emanate from Senge's experience as a consultant with Hanover Insurance during the 1980s and O'Brien is quoted liberally throughout the book.

In the numerous articles that have appeared about Senge and the learning organization, stirring testimonials about the potency of the learning organization concept provide additional rhetorical weight to the vision. *The Fifth Discipline* has, and continues to be, frequently cited by senior executives in magazine articles as a book that has made a big impression on them. For example, the president of Web Industries Inc., a $20-million contract manufacturer with 210 employees, has used a number of popular management books to play a major role in the company's "change-of-thinking" process. His rationale is that

> Books can help encourage change because books can be non-threatening. It's not like a new program that we want everybody to buy into; if you just start spreading books around so people have something to talk bout, those books can change how we perceive things and how we do things.
> (Brokaw, 1991: 33)

The company devoted a three-day meeting to a discussion of Senge's book. During the first day, the principles of leverage, shared vision and teamwork were discussed. The second day was used to address how people learn, and how leaders ought to lead. Only on the third day did the meeting move into the "typical discussions" about increasing sales and improving conditions. Reflecting on the meeting, the vice-president of sales observed, "that book in particular has created a vocabulary around here" (Brokaw, 1991: 31). However, the president noted that Senge's esoteric language tends to limit the appeal of the book to the senior executive group. Similarly, a CEO of a Denver-based construction company has been inspired by *The Fifth Discipline* to become a "teacher" for his organization because it articulated his objective of "keeping our souls and making money with dignity" (Filipczak, 1996: 60). Every Monday morning, he meets with about 60 of his employees in a session that usually evolves into a "learning event".

A particularly valuable source of these testimonials has been the CEOs of companies who are corporate members of MIT's Center for Organizational Learning. The Center ran a CEO leadership project, which provided a forum for inquiry into the evolving nature of leadership required to build and sustain learning organizations and to address the particular issues faced by top management, such as the evolution of corporate governance and the moral foundation of senior managers. Among the participants in this project have been CEOs or president-level executives from Harley Davidson, Philips Display Components, Shell Oil, Analog Devices and Hermann Miller (Fulmer, 1995). The president and chief executive of the latter company, which manufactures conservative office furniture, has publicly stated:

> Our profits have improved rather markedly but is there a cause-and-effect relationship? The attitudes and behaviors of our people have changed, and that leads not only to improved profits but improved performance in the long run. There's a more mature, accepting relationship among our people. You can't measure that in the short term, but it's terribly powerful in the long run.
>
> (Driben, 1995: 62)

While most of the media testimonials for Senge's work focus on what went right in organizations when the concept is implemented, I detected a few instances in which the risks of following this path were also discussed. One case, which was also featured in a short video used by Senge in a videoconference presentation, told of a steel company (GS Technologies) which, desperate for ideas as to how to turn the company around from imminent collapse, joined MIT's Center for Organizational Learning. As the company's CEO explained: "We had run out of ideas. It don't get no worse" (Dumaine, 1994a: 154). The article goes on to describe in dramatic fashion how William Isaacs, a senior researcher associated with the Center, introduced the "container", a tool developed by the Center for surfacing and processing conflict, at a meeting between the senior management and union leaders of the company. After a particularly hostile encounter, Isaacs recounts how he was able to get the two sides working together to solve some important productivity problems. As a result of this work, the company has been able to turn things around, staving off bankruptcy and rapidly increasing sales. Subsequently, however, the labor leader who had been spearheading learning organization ideas at GST has been voted out by "workers left out of the dialogue" and replaced by another labor leader who promptly passed a motion banning Senge's dialogue from the shopfloor on the grounds that it enabled the company to take advantage of workers no longer speaking with one unified voice. The moral of this fable was that "management says it made the mistake of not spreading the program fast and deep enough" (Dumaine, 1994a: 154).

Trainers and human resource professionals

With its novel emphasis on learning and development, it is perhaps not surprising that the learning organization concept has been greeted with great enthusiasm by members of the training and development community. In addition to helping to make the word "learning" not only acceptable but also fashionable within the business lexicon, Senge is alone among management gurus in at least acknowledging the role of the training and development specialist in organizational transformation efforts. Other gurus have generally been quite disparaging about this role. We should, therefore, not be surprised that the learning organization has received considerable attention from human resource and organization development professionals. For example, the 1995 National HRD Executive Survey, conducted by the American Society for Training and Development, found that 94 percent of the respondents said that it was important to build a learning organization (Gephart et al., 1996: 34). Similarly, a 1996 survey of almost 200 German companies, conducted by DEJRA Akademie with the Maisberger & Partner consulting firm, found that 90 percent consider themselves to be a learning organization, or in the process of becoming one (Gephart et al., 1996: 34).

At the same time, many are beginning to recognize that the learning organization concept can act as a double-edged sword. The increased scrutiny of the human resource development function which the learning organization promotes may result in more rewards and recognition but with these would come high performance expectations and radical changes in the way that function is carried out. For example, at the 1996 conference of the American Society of Training and Development, a participant observed that he

> Listened to numerous speakers warning trainers and developers that they had no option but to reinvent themselves. High-performance work systems, underpinned by a learning organization, may hold the key to future competitive success. But these measures will, we were told, come to nothing if the training function itself does not undergo a radical shift toward performance improvement consultancy.
>
> (Harrison, 1996: 47)

Senge argues that training and development specialists have two important roles to play in building learning organizations. First, they can help managers to design and facilitate learning processes. Second, they can guide the "diffusion of new learnings" throughout the organization. To fulfill both of these roles, Senge suggests that they will have to strike partnerships with line managers and senior managers because they lack the credibility and accountability to make learning happen themselves (Galaghan, 1991). Trainers and developers continue to grapple with what they should be doing about implementing the powerful yet elusive rhetorical vision of the learning organization. An article in *Training and Development* summarizes the discussions that took place within a focus group made up of just under 50 human resource development professionals and line managers from across the United States. The objective of the focus group was to try collectively to address the following questions: Which definitions of learning organizations made sense? What distinguishes organizational learning from individual learning? What does a learning organization look like and how can it be measured? Would training and development specialists play different roles inside a learning organization? Of the 20 definitions of the learning organization presented to the group, Senge's definition was the one that most consistently captured the hearts and minds of the participants. It is evident from the article that Senge's influence is never far away from the discussion. The authors note that when the facilitators posed the question, "If you take away from us our security-blanket copies of *The Fifth Discipline* or any book by Chris Argyris, what do we actually know about learning organizations or organizational learning?", participants responded with silence, a blank flipchart, and several top-of-the-the-head responses which "showed they know a lot about learning organization theory, but far less about how to apply it – which they readily admitted" (Calvert et al., 1994: 40).

The rhetorical vision of the learning organization

In analyzing Senge's rhetorical vision of the learning organization, I identified four major fantasy themes; these are summarized in Table 6.3. Two of the themes identified are setting themes while the others are action and character themes. Each of these will be discussed in turn.

Table 6.3 Key fantasy themes within the rhetorical vision of the learning organization

Fantasy theme	Type	Metaphors	Motive
Living in an Unsustainable World	Setting theme	Tragedy of the Commons, *Dances with Wolves*	Identification
Getting Control but not Controlling	Action theme	Dr. Karl-Henrik Robert	Transcendence
The Manager's New Work	Character theme	The Designer of the Ship	Hierarchy
Working it out within the Microworld	Setting theme	The Beer Game	Transcendence

Setting theme 1: "Living in an Unsustainable World"

In a vein similar to Covey, Senge situates organizational woes in a broader societal context. He suggests that "organizations are microcosms of the larger society. Thus, at the heart of any serious effort to alter how organizations operate lies a concern with addressing the basic dysfunctions of our larger culture" (Kofman and Senge, 1993: 7). Three fundamental dysfunctions within the culture's dominant paradigm are identified: *"fragmentation"*, which has resulted in a society that has become increasingly ungovernable and at the mercy of special interest groups and political lobbies; *"competition"*, which they argue has become the only model for change and learning, and *"reactiveness"*, whereby the evolutionarily ingrained penchant for dealing with dramatic problems rather than slow, gradual processes has made humans poorly prepared to face a "new class of systemic threats" (Kofman and Senge, 1993: 10). According to Kofman and Senge, these problems are rooted in a reductionist philosophy and mechanical thinking that has provided the basis for many of America's successes in the past. Paradoxically, they observe:

> The very same skills of separation, analysis, and control that gave us the power to shape our environment are producing ecological and social crises in our outer worlds, and psychological and spiritual crises in our inner world. When we begin to understand the origins of our problems, we begin to see that the "existential crisis" of early 20th century philosophy and the "environmental crisis" of late 20th century ecology are inseparable – caused by the co-evolution of fragmentary world views, social structures, lifestyles, and technology.
>
> (Kofman and Senge, 1993: 10–11)

Senge illustrates this paradox by pointing to the popularity of the movie *Dances with Wolves* (dir. Costner, 1990), which, with its depiction of the destruction of an indigenous culture, has resonated with Americans' sense that "they have lost a particular sensibility of what it means to live together as part of a larger natural order" (Senge, 1995b: 227). Pulled between the new and old world orders, Senge suggests that Kevin Costner's heroic lonely outsider is a character to whom an audience similarly riddled with existential and environmental doubts can well relate.

In discussing the systemic problems being faced by American organizations, Senge makes frequent reference to a system archetype called "The Tragedy of the Commons" which was first identified by ecologist Garrett Hardin (1968). This archetype is seen by Senge as especially useful for dealing directly with problems where apparently logical local decision-making can become completely illogical for the larger system. By illustration, he describes the desertification of the Sahel region in sub-Saharan Africa engendered by rampant overgrazing encouraged by unusually high rainfalls and international aid assistance. In a neat rhetorical move, Senge makes the claim that the "Tragedy of the Commons" is confined not only to ecological disasters but also to organizations. Corporations, he suggests, have many depletable "commons" to share, including financial capital, productive capital, technology, community reputation, customer good-will and the morale and competence of employees. When a company decentralizes, local divisions compete with one another for these limited resources.

In referring to the broader environmental concerns, Senge not only succeeds in grabbing the attention of readers already preoccupied with impending global ecological doom and disaster, but he also succeeds in distinguishing his message from those of other management gurus who, by and large, studiously ignore this milieu. Generally, the broader setting utilized by management gurus encompasses the competitive pressures of globalization and international trade but not environmental system dynamics. By making this connection, Senge develops a setting theme with its own built-in, mass media-fueled sense of significance and urgency. It provides an impressive and readily identifiable backdrop against which his special organizational drama can unfold. No one, therefore, can argue that the stakes are not high when creating a learning organization. This work might ultimately lead to saving the earth, let alone the organization. In his mind, there is no doubt regarding the sector from which the men with the white hats will come riding in to deal with global environmental problems. As he states,

> My deepest belief is that the way we operate the world, as a whole, is not sustainable. We're basically living off our capital and compromising the future well-being of generations to come. It's ironic that business is the most likely institution [to master change], but it has the greatest capacity to reinvent itself.
>
> (Driben, 1995: 62)

Action theme: "Getting Control, but not Controlling"

While Senge believes that it will ultimately be the private sector, and large-scale corporations in particular, that will have to develop the ability to deal with and address many of the societal woes that we are currently facing, he is quite clear that they will have to take on quite different organizational forms and be led in quite different ways in order to meet these challenges. For example, in an interview, Senge makes the following claim:

> The leadership challenges in building learning organizations represent a microcosm of the leadership challenges of our times: how do communities, be they multinational corporations or societies, productively

confront complex systemic issues where hierarchical authority is inadequate for change? None of today's most pressing issues will be resolved through hierarchical authority. In all these issues, there are no simple causes, no simple "fixes". There is no one villain to blame. There will be no magic pill. Significant change will require imagination, perseverance, dialogue, deep caring, and a willingness to change on the part of millions of people. The challenges of systemic change where hierarchy is inadequate will, I believe, push us to new views of leadership based on new principles. These challenges cannot be met by isolated heroic leaders. They will require a unique mix of different people, in different positions, who lead in different ways. Changes will be required in our traditional models.

(Senge, 1996b: 11)

In Senge's vision, organizations will increasingly have to become "localized" in that they will have to seek to extend the maximum degree of authority and power as far away from the "top" or center as possible. "Localness", a cornerstone of the learning organization, gives individuals the freedom to act, to try out their own ideas and be responsible for producing their own results. It also enables organizations to respond appropriately and in a timely fashion to rapid changes within the marketplace. Despite its obvious advantages, Senge warns that unenlightened senior managers may be unwilling to give up control of the decision-making process for fear of losing the thing they most cherish (i.e. "power") and making themselves obsolete. Moreover, they are concerned that, by pursuing localness, the organization may lose its capacity for control.

To these concerns, Senge responds, "just because no one is 'in control' does not mean that there is 'no control'" (1990b: 292). By investing in the five disciplines of the learning organization, Senge suggests that organizations can maintain control at the local level through a process of "control by learning". The improved quality of thinking and the new capacity for reflection and team learning combined with an ability to develop shared visions and understandings of complex business issues will allow learning organizations to be controlled and coordinated more effectively than their hierarchical predecessors. He adds rhetorical weight to his argument for local control by suggesting that the traditional perception that someone "up there" is in control is based on an illusion that it would be possible for anyone to master the dynamic and detailed complexity of an organization from the top. Taking on two icons of American business, Senge stridently observes:

The days when a Watson or Henry Ford or Alfred B. Sloan "fought for the organization" have long passed. The world is simply too complex to figure out from the top, and too rapidly changing to abide with the slow bureaucratic decision-making processes that come with the top-down decision-making in complex organizations. The breakdown of the authoritarian structures is universal, not only in business but in the world of public affairs as well, as can be seen only too well from the demise of the Eastern bloc governments.

(Senge, cited in Meen and Keough, 1992: 78)

While Senge's argument for local control is by no means unique among management gurus, the non-threatening and generally inoffensive way in which it is presented makes it a reasonably palatable action theme which promises some form of transcendence for both sides of the labor–management divide. Workers are presented with an essentially emancipatory vision within which they can take independent action and realize their full potential through learning, unencumbered by formal management controls imposed from above. Managers, on the other hand, can take comfort from the fact that the world is so complicated now that they cannot be expected to be held accountable. They can also rest assured that within a learning organization, control will be maintained in a constructive and tolerably orderly manner. Besides, as we shall see in the next section, Senge has some very important new work for these managers to be doing within the learning organization which is considerably more meaningful than the work that they have traditionally done within hierarchically based organizations.

While Senge is comparably sparing in his use of heroic role models, he has pointed on a number of occasions to the example set by Dr. Karl-Henrik Robert, a cancer researcher from Sweden, to indicate what can be achieved when one individual acts within the local frame of reference. Dr. Robert found himself increasingly frustrated by public debates that seemed to immobilize people from acting on environmental issues. Senge describes how, in desperation, the doctor wrote a letter stating his understanding of how natural systems worked and sent it to 20 scientists, asking for their advice and contributions. One year and 21 iterations later, he produced a pamphlet called *The Natural Step*, which outlined the basic precepts for sustainability upon which all of the scientists agreed. The scientists then sent his letter to the 10 largest companies in Sweden as well as the King of Sweden. With their support, four million copies of the pamphlet were sent to Swedish households from which over 10,000 people are now organized into networks of professionals who are actively supporting this cause. Senge concludes:

This may be how infrastructures for learning and communities of commitment will come together – a whole country or company catalyzed by a simple picture of the system to which they are a part. Perhaps this is the answer to the core leadership dilemma of our times: how can we create coordinated efforts around those systematic issues where mandated solutions from the top can never be implemented?

(Senge, 1995c: 8)

It is significant that the hero in Senge's parable should hail from a nation-state that is widely recognized for its collectivist culture. Moreover, the real hero of this heuristic drama is not Dr. Robert but the "system" that has developed as a result of his initiative.

Character theme: "The Manager's New Work"

A year prior to the publication of *The Fifth Discipline*, Senge published a paper in MIT's in-house publication, the *Sloan Management Review*, titled "The Leader's New Work" (Senge, 1990a). In the paper, Senge laid out many of the key ideas contained within the book as well as a discussion of three new "roles" that leaders would have to play in order to build a learning organization, namely, those of "designer", "teacher" and "steward". While these roles have antecedents with the ways leaders have contributed to building organizations in the past, Senge notes that they take on new meaning within the learning organization and demand new skills and tools.

Likening the organization to an "ocean liner", Senge observes that most senior executives readily relate their role to the "captain", "navigator", "helmsman", "engineer" or "social director". However, they rarely identify their role as "designer" of the ship. In this role, Senge charges senior executives with three main tasks. First, the leader must build a foundation of purpose and core values for the organization. Second, he or she must develop the policies, strategies and structures that translate these guiding ideas into business directions. Third, executives must create effective learning processes through which the policies, strategies and structures can be continually improved. To illustrate the importance of this last task, Senge makes frequent reference in his writing to the use of scenario analysis by Shell's Group Planning during the 1970s led by Arie de Geus, another influential figure in Senge's writing (De Geus, 1988). The process of "planning as learning" is dramatically portrayed as having enabled that company to anticipate and respond successfully to the emergence of the OPEC cartel while the remainder of the "seven sisters" were left scrambling.

In their role as "teachers", Senge urges executives to stop trying to be the authoritarian experts whose job is to teach the "correct" view of reality and begin to "help people restructure their views of reality to see beyond the superficial conditions and events into the underlying causes of problems – and therefore to see the new possibilities for shaping the future" (1990a: 12). Max de Pree, the retired CEO of Hermann Miller and author of the popular business book *Leadership is an Art* (1989), is frequently held up by Senge as an exemplar of an executive who was particularly effective in this role.

The third and final new role of the leader, "leader as steward", is, according to Senge, the subtlest role and is almost solely a matter of attitude. The leader's sense of stewardship operates on two levels: stewardship for the people they lead and stewardship for the larger purpose or mission that underlies the enterprise. Quoting Greenleaf, Senge argues that

The servant leader *is* servant first. . . . It begins with the natural feeling that one wants to serve, to serve *first*. This conscious choice brings one to aspire to lead. That person is sharply different from one who is leader first, perhaps because of the need to assuage an unusual power drive or to acquire material possessions.

(Senge, 1990a: 12)

More recently, Senge has begun to lay out roles that should be played by individuals at other levels within the learning organization. Specifically, he identifies two other leadership roles – the "local line leaders" and the "internal networkers". The former are heads of organizational units that are microcosms of the larger organization who have enough autonomy to be able to undertake meaningful change independent of the larger organization. The key role played by the local line leaders is to "sanction significant practical experiments and to lead through active participation in those experiments" (1996a: 3). In addition to playing a key role in the design and implementation of learning processes, local line leaders often become teachers once these learning processes become established. While Senge argues that there is much to be gained by taking on this role, he also warns potential local line leaders of the risks they run: "Improved results are often threatening to others, and the more dramatic the improvement, the greater the threat. Large organizations have complex forces that maintain the status quo and inhibit the spread of new ideas" (1996a: 4). Senge offers the cautionary tale of Fred Simon, a project manager on the new Lincoln Continental at Ford Motor Company and a champion of the learning organization. Through the use of such tools as Chris Argyris's "ladder of inference", Senge describes how Simon's team of engineers was able to break every internal product development record at Ford. Despite this impressive achievement, Simon was passed over for promotion and was asked to retire early. He believes that his enthusiasm for the learning organization was a factor in his early retirement. The moral that Senge draws from this story was that Simon "should have taken the time to explain the benefits of the learning organization to key people in the top ranks" (Dumaine, 1994a: 155).

The other key leadership role identified by Senge is that of the "internal networker", otherwise referred to as "internal community builder" or "seed carrier". Typically, this role is played by internal consultants, trainers, human resources staff or front-line workers like engineers, sales representatives, or shop stewards. Of critical importance is their ability to move freely around the organization and their high accessibility to many parts of the organization. According to Senge, their primary asset is their lack of power. Because they do not have any positional authority, they do not pose an obvious threat to management, but they are able to exploit the informal networks "through which information and stories flow and innovative practices naturally diffuse within organizations" (Senge, 1996a: 6). The first function of the internal networkers is to identify local line managers who have the power to take action and are predisposed to developing new learning capabilities. They then connect people of "like minds" to each other's learning efforts. Senge illustrates how this is done with the example of an informal "leaders of learning" group that was formed at Ford Motor Co. by local line leaders and internal networkers who wanted to share learnings and serve as a strategic leadership body. The individuals participating in this group saw their work as supporting continuing experiments, connecting these experiments with the interests of top management, and wrestling with organization-wide capacity building and learning.

In addition to providing a powerful action theme of "Getting Control, but not Controlling", Senge also develops a complete and well-integrated character theme that will enable individuals at various levels and within varying functions within the organization to transcend their current roles. Within this character theme, clear and inviting roles are deftly scripted and described. Each is accompanied by a few successful role models who repeatedly appear in his accounts and provide added confidence that this role is not only practicable but also well worth aspiring to.

Setting theme 2: "Working it out within the Micro World"

Early on in *The Fifth Discipline*, Senge devotes an entire chapter to an exposition of the "beer game", which was first developed in the 1960s at MIT and has been played "on five continents, among people of all ages, nationalities, cultural origins and vastly varied business backgrounds" (1990b: 41). Senge notes that, irrespective of the players' backgrounds or origins, the same crises ensue in the game with respect to the production, distribution and consumption of beer. These graphically illustrate the underlying barriers to implementing a learning organization which are the fragmentation of problem-solving, an overemphasis on competition to the exclusion of collaboration, and a tendency of organizations to experiment or innovate only when compelled to change by outside forces (Kofman and Senge, 1993). Senge argues that, in addition to making these barriers visible, "micro worlds" like the beer game can be a critical technology for implementing the disciplines of the learning organization.

"Micro world" is a term coined by Seymour Papert, a media technology professor at MIT, to describe an interactive computerized environment that simulates a real-world situation. According to Senge, micro worlds can help managers and their management teams begin to learn about their most important systemic issues by "compressing time and space" so that it becomes possible to experiment and "learn by doing" what the consequences of their decisions will be in the future and in distant parts of the organization. Increasingly sophisticated computer technology is helping to create what Senge describes as a new type of "managerial practice field" for management teams. These are places where teams will learn how to learn together while engaging their most important business issues. Drawing parallels with sports teams and the performing arts, Senge questions why it is that, unlike athletes and musicians, in most organizations "people only perform. They rarely get to practice, especially together" (Kofman and Senge, 1993: 19). Building micro worlds will help managers practice by "helping us to rediscover the power of learning through play" or, more correctly, "relevant play" (Senge, 1990b: 315).

To give substance to his argument for micro worlds and simulation games in general, Senge has provided a number of case studies of organizations that have been able to make important breakthroughs with them. Perhaps the most celebrated case is the "claims learning laboratory" built by a systems group from MIT for Hanover Insurance. Managers at Hanover felt that internal practices were contributing to claims settlements that seemed to be significantly higher than was fair (Hampden-Turner, 1992). By playing the "claims game" within this micro world, Senge shows how managers were able to pinpoint the source of the problem of escalating costs in the quality of the claims settlements that were being made. Senge recounts the all-important a-ha moment with obvious relish: "suddenly there is a wave of realization through the room: *If it weren't for all of those overpriced claims settlements, we'd all have more money to build our departments to what they really need to be!*" (1990b: 329). Later he shows with a quote by one of the participants how dependent the managers had become on their micro world: "so what if we went back to the micro world . . . and tried out some other possible strategies?" (1990b: 331). In a later account of this case, Senge informs us somewhat tersely that the takeover of Hanover Insurance by State Mutual Insurance uprooted the management support for the lab so that it never had the opportunity to demonstrate its full value in terms of the anticipatory learning it had generated (Senge and Fulmer, 1993).

In advocating micro worlds as a critical component of the learning organization vision, Senge provided managers with a powerful setting theme within which they could find a safe haven for dealing with, and regaining control of, a world that has seemingly gone out of control. In this respect, he has literally presented managers with an opportunity to transport themselves out of their immediate time and space situations to the relative comfort of a world in which problems can be properly managed and even played with alongside one's colleagues in a safe and sealed-off environment. The micro world theme acts as a powerful transcendental antidote to the "living in an unsustainable world" setting theme that emerges from Senge's writing, which stresses that collectively we have lost control of the modernist project and need to act immediately. As Senge and Fulmer somewhat invitingly promise, "by utilizing micro worlds to participate in the anticipation of these consequences, created with system dynamics, managers and their organizations can discover a new capacity for gaining control of their destinies" (1993: 33). Giving the micro world fantasy theme even more rhetorical weight is the allure of technology which, of course, will only continue to get better. Despite the factors that have prevented micro worlds from reaching their full potential (most of these being managerial rather than technological), Senge suggests that, with even more sophisticated technology, "future micro worlds for teams will allow managers to play out their real-world roles and understand more deeply how those roles interact" (1990b: 337). Ultimately, I am reminded of the 1970s science fiction movies *Westworld* and *Futureworld*, in which the virtual and real worlds become confused. My unease is not assuaged by the cheery pronouncement that, "when practice fields are cultivated in an organization for a sustained period of time, learning in simuworlds and micro worlds becomes seamlessly integrated with the real organizations they shadow" (Keys et al., 1996: 48).

Sustaining the vision of the learning organization

The critique

The learning organization continues to inspire a large and growing body of literature in both academic and practitioner journals. While much of this work seeks to build and refine the rhetorical vision of the Learning Organization, a sizable portion of it is devoted to critiquing the vision on several fronts. The first front homes in on the ambiguous, amorphous and ill-defined nature of the vision. As one commentator has observed, the learning organization has become a "very big conceptual catchall to help us make sense of a set of values and ideas we've been wrestling with, everything from customer service to corporate responsiveness and speed" (Kiechel, 1990: 133). In a review of the rapidly expanding body of literature that addresses the learning organization and organizational learning in general, Tsang (1997) has expressed concern at the growing dichotomy between what he identifies as two isolated streams of research – the prescriptive stream, which focuses upon the question "how should an organization learn?" (i.e. the learning organization) and the descriptive stream, which deals with the question of "how does an organization learn?" (i.e. organizational learning). He laments that books on the learning organization like Senge's tend to be based on the author's consulting experience rather than systematic or rigorous research. They tend to present only one model of the learning organization, which is supposed to be universally applicable, and ignores the cultural specificity and contextual constraints of their theories. Kilmann (1996) acknowledges that the learning organization literature is brimful of illustrations and vignettes from actual companies that are practicing what authors like Senge are advocating. However, he argues that "it is not enough to show executives what it's like being a learning organization, we must also provide them with the declarative and procedural knowledge for getting there" (1996: 230).

DiBella (1995) has helpfully identified three different orientations within the learning organization literature – normative, developmental and capability. The normative perspective of the learning organization exemplified best by Senge presumes that learning is a collective activity that takes place only under certain conditions or circumstances. Within the "developmental perspective", the learning organization is realized not in an absolute state but through staged evolution and occasional revolution (Dechant and Marsick, 1991; Torbert, 1994). In this respect, the learning organization is always in a state of becoming, with learning styles and processes adapting at each stage in the organization's development. According to DiBella, both of these perspectives view the learning organization as a "matter of becoming", presupposing that learning is not indigenous to organizational life. By contrast, the "capability perspective" sees all organizations as having learning capabilities that embody distinctive styles or patterns of learning (Brown and Duguid, 1991; Nevis et al., 1993). DiBella (1995) points out that, while each of these three perspectives has a different set of implications which can be in direct conflict, they contribute in a unique way to our understanding of the learning organization and organizational learning. He therefore advocates a "contingency approach" to selecting a particular perspective on the learning organization which recognizes our underlying theoretical assumptions about what organizations are and are for, and which takes account of the needs and constraints of the particular organizational context.

This contingent and multi-perspective approach to reconciling the emerging gap between the learning organization and the organizational learning literature appears to be gathering favor among many writers working within the field. Jones and Hendry, for example, suggest that "we need to hold onto the idea of 'learning organization' as a 'direction' whilst 'organizational learning', which is an aspect of the 'learning organization', is seen as a descriptive or heuristic device to explain and quantify learning activities and events" (1994: 157). Similarly, Burgoyne states that

> The learning company is an invention, not a discovery, a proposal, not an observation. Having said that, it is clearly one that manages its own learning processes to its advantage. The organizational learning process can, and indeed arguably must, exist whether it is known and managed, and to good effect or not – just as everyone has a state of health, what varies is whether it is good or bad, known or unknown.
>
> (Burgoyne, 1995b: 22)

Enthusiasm for this contingent view is, however, by no means universal. Within the field of adult and continuing education, for example, the learning organization has generated mixed reactions. While there is a general sense of encouragement that the term "learning" has finally found its place in the business lexicon, many have expressed concern that the vision ignores or does not properly apply adult learning theory and principles. For example, Fenwick objects to the conflation of individual and organizational learning within the learning organization in which "the workplace appoints itself as the individual's educator, personal development counsellor and even spiritual mentor" (1998:141). The learning organization meets the worker's needs only if these are not in conflict with the organization's needs. This results in a bias toward instrumental versus other forms of learning that may be equally valid and important to the worker.

A number of writers have questioned the ethical and moral basis of the rhetorical vision of the learning organization. In an editorial essay, Victor and Stephens point to the moral questions raised by what they observe to be the "dark side" of such new organizational forms as the learning organization (1994: 481). Specifically, they question the morality of the incessant demand that is placed on workers continually to adapt and innovate, which puts undue pressures on the many individuals who derive a great deal of comfort from the predictability and routine offered by more traditional organizational forms. They also suggest that learning organizations have a negative impact upon interpersonal relations, observing that "these high-velocity, high-commitment workplaces – flash in the pan collectives – offer no ongoing relationships, no safe haven, no personal space" (1994: 481). Burgoyne has acknowledged that "some of the ideas associated with the aspirations for new forms of learning company are being used to sugar the pill of the delayering, downsizing organization" (1995b: 22). He also fears that the abuse of such ideas poses the greatest threat to the emergence of a genuinely more progressive form of organization. Similarly, Watkins and Marsick (1994) have identified a number of barriers that have prevented organizations from realizing the vision of the learning organization. They point to the culture of disrespect and fear that has taken hold of a part-time, temporary and overtaxed workforce which is suffering from a combination of learned helplessness and "truncated learning" engendered by the "ghosts of learning efforts that never took root because they were interrupted or only partially implemented" (Watkins and Marsick, 1994: 240).

Other commentators have been critical of the lack of attention paid by the proponents of the learning organization to questions of power, politics and ideology within organizations. For example, Foley (1994) claims that pursuit of such ideals as the "learning organization" is a myth that disguises a process whereby global capitalism is reorganizing itself. Along similar lines, Coopey has suggested that,

> Despite the rhetoric, the Learning Organization seems to be placed within a unitarist framework of relationships, a utopia to be ushered in through the pursuit of shared goals in a climate of collaborative high trust and a rational approach to the resolution of differences.
>
> (Coopey, 1995: 196)

He predicts that, because proponents of the learning organization have stressed the control and plurality of the learning process rather than the question of who should and should not exercise that control, the learning organization might be destined to become yet another mechanism through which managerial control is improved under dramatically changed external circumstances.

This tendency for organizations to take a new perspective like the learning organization, which challenges old patterns of thinking and behavior and incorporates it in a way that turns it into another tool of control, is also noted by Hawkins. He observes that

> [Senge] provides us with exciting ways of perceiving organizations and their problems systematically from new paradigm and post-Cartesian epistemologies, and yet consistently writes with a mechanical perspective about gaining leverage to the organizational learning in a way that dualistically separates us from that which we are trying to control.
>
> (Hawkins, 1994: 72)

Dovey (1997) acknowledges that the profound changes that are offered by the learning organization are seldom achieved in practice, primarily because of the reluctance or inability of corporate leaders to confront the central issue of the transformation of power relations within their organization. However, he is optimistic that the promise of the learning organization as a potentially powerful and radical strategic option can still be realized if leaders are willing to be guided by a theory of radical humanism that embraces notions of resistance and struggle in the processes of organizational transformation.

Perhaps the most articulate response to these criticisms has come not from Peter Senge, who has not taken these directly on in the literature, but from John Burgoyne, one of the co-creators of the "Learning Company" concept. Burgoyne (1995a) speculates that the popularity of such movements as Excellence, Quality and Collective Learning is directly linked to the underlying shift in the predominant forms of work, at least at the "frontiers of practice" within advanced capitalist societies. Specifically, he is concerned with the shift from "mentofacture" (i.e. knowledge work and post-industrialization) to "spiroculture" (i.e. the creation of meaning and identity). Management fashions function as "transitional myths" which, because they make sense in both worlds, help to make the transition possible. Burgoyne's primary concern is how this transition has been manifested in how we conceptualize Learning-From-Experience (LFE) within the workplace. He suggests that LFE is undergoing a necessary change in conceptualization from one of the individual learning alone by discovering the dynamics of a concrete environment as presented in Kolb's "learning cycle" (Kolb, 1984) to one of people co-creating the meaning of their shared experience of the world as presented in the collectivist rhetorical vision of the learning organization and its variants. Burgoyne identifies "meta-dialogue", that is dialogue about the basis for believing that things might be credible, true or useful, as being a crucial process and tool in facilitating learning within the learning organization. In this regard, he directly addresses the concerns regarding the conflation and subjugation of individual learning by organizational learning within the learning organization. He is also mindful of the political dimension when he acknowledges that "the prospect of dialogue as a generator of useful LFE does presuppose the willingness for, or inevitability of, a degree of power sharing both in dialogue and its consequences (action or joint meanings)" (1995a: 70). On balance, he appears to be mildly optimistic about the possibility of this coming to pass with his comment that "the post-modern pluralization of desire and motivation does level the playing field and itself represents a break-out from modernist control" (1995a: 71).

Senge's response

Senge's presence in the academic literature's critical debate about the learning organization which, to a certain extent, he has inspired could at best be described as muted and at worst negligent. His activities indicate that he has been more concerned with sustaining the rhetorical vision among his consultant and practitioner followers. Clark and Greatbatch (1999) suggest that a key activity of management gurus is to convince their followers that it is their particular ideas that offer the most relevant solution to the immediate problems which the followers are experiencing and trying to resolve. This activity is important not only during the consciousness-creating phase of a rhetorical vision but also during the subsequent consciousness-raising and consciousness-sustaining phases (Bormann et al., 1996). The preceding FTA has revealed the dramatic foundation that serves to make Senge's rhetorical vision of the learning organization such a compelling one for potential followers. But what has Senge done to insure that his rhetorical vision will continue to sustain interest and stave off the inevitable rejection of another management fashion? I think there are two features of the way in which Peter Senge has gone about organizing his rhetorical vision that are particularly salient when considering this question.

First, as was observed earlier, Senge appears to prefer to be loosely linked with numerous organizations in which he assumes a comparatively lower profile role and works in a collaborative mode. He is committed to creating new organizational forms through which he has woven an intricate web of academics, executives, consultants and practitioners who are committed to preserving and extending the vision of the learning organization. Innovation Associates and the MIT Organizational Learning Center (OLC) were the prototypes for the new organizational form that he and his colleagues are interested in creating. In 1996 Senge along with co-founder, Charlie Kiefer, sold Innovation Associates to the Arthur D. Little consulting firm, who were anxious to align their business with the rapidly ascendant learning organization concept. In an effort to extend the work of the OLC beyond its Anglo-American origins, the OLC was "re-created" in 1998 as the Society for Organizational learning (SoL). SoL is a non-profit, member-governed organization with global ambitions inspired by the peculiar brand of "chaordic thinking" of Dee Ward Hock, the creator of the organizational infrastructure that supports the Visa card organization (Waldrop, 1996).

In reading the letter inviting potential individuals and groups to join SoL, Senge and the other two chairpersons – Arie de Geus and Goran Carstedt – show that they are keen to model the disciplines of the learning organization when they state: "as with all living systems, a global network cannot be controlled or pre-determined. . . . Different chapters (fractals) will pursue their own aspirations and issues and will adapt SoL's basic design to the requirements of their social cultural environment" (http://learning.mit.edu). Despite these good intentions, Senge is cautious about SoL's ability to disseminate the learning organization vision across the globe, observing that "the challenge for all of us at SoL is to manage growth, commitment, community, and scope without watering down the principles that make organizational learning a valuable objective for organizations of all types" (Fulmer and Keys, 1998: 41).

This change of direction was further reflected in the themes of the 1997 and 1998 "Systems Thinking in Action" conferences that were respectively billed as "From Learning Organizations to Learning Communities" and "Learning Communities: Building Enduring Capability". According to the 1997 conference brochure, this theme was selected to emphasize the growing importance of the communal nature of learning because "organizations don't learn: people do". A "learning community" is defined in the brochure as "a diverse group of people working together to nurture and sustain a knowledge-creating system through improving theory and method, enhancing people's capabilities, and producing practical results". Peter Senge's keynote speech at this conference promised to help participants discover what it was like to be part of an integrated learning community. Learning communities are viewed as being a, if not *the*, "natural pattern of organizing" and, as such, they represent a whole new territory with which to continue to develop the work of the five disciplines. The 1998 conference brochure solemnly predicted that "the corporations and organizations of tomorrow are those that can grasp the importance of learning communities and begin building the foundational capabilities for continued success."

In addition to his organization building activities, Senge continues to display a remarkable affinity for publicly reflecting on how and why the learning organization was socially constructed as the next management fashion. In recounting what motivated him to write *The Fifth Discipline*, he recalls:

It sort of hit me one morning about three years ago while I was meditating that the learning organization was going to be a hot area in business. I had already watched a fad cycle come and go related to work I had been doing for years with Innovation Associates. We had been teaching courses in personal mastery and leadership since 1979, and we all sat on the sidelines and watched as other people wrote about vision, empowerment and alignment – ideas that we had been teaching for years. That morning as I meditated it dawned on me that it was not O.K. to sit on the sidelines this time. It was time for a book on the subject of learning organizations, and I wanted to get it out before the whole world was talking about them. I didn't want to define the territory; it is really too broad for one book. My hope was to establish a point of view of learning organizations that might serve as a reference point.

(Senge, cited in Galaghan, 1991: 38)

As it turned out, the book has become *the* rather than merely *a* reference point for work on the learning organization, selling over 650,000 copies worldwide (Webber, 1999). Senge is, however, typically ambivalent about the success of the book, commenting "I am not even sure that it's such a good idea for the field that this book has been as popular as it has" (cited in Fulmer and Keys, 1998: 34).

Senge also appears to be quite philosophical about the prospect of the learning organization falling out of favor, accepting it as part of the natural cycle in management thinking in which managers embrace new ideas, explore them and move on to the next one (Griffith, 1995). While he is not the first management guru to express concern about his or her concept being consigned to the pile of "last year's models", his public statements suggest that he wants his audience to be fully aware of what they are getting into when they decide to embrace the learning organization concept. Perhaps by being explicitly reflexive about the management fashion enterprise and his role within it, Senge hopes that his followers may be more likely to resist the inevitable rejection phase of the cycle and persist with his concepts long after they cease to remain fashionable. The idea being that the learning organization is too important to be treated as another passing fad.

In a rhetorical turn reminiscent of Tom Peters' opening comments in his book, *Thriving on Chaos*, about there not being any "excellent companies" (Peters, 1987), Senge has stated a number of times that there is, in fact, no such thing as a "learning organization". Instead, he states that:

The learning organization is a thing we create in language. Like every linguistic creation, this category is a double-edged sword that can be empowering or tranquilizing. The difference lies in whether we see language as a set of labels that describe a pre-existing reality, or as a medium in which we can articulate new models for living together.

(Kofman and Senge, 1993: 16)

His unapologetically normative perspective suggests that Senge is more than aware that he is trying to create and sustain a rhetorical vision. When pressed to define the learning organization, he has responded by saying that the learning organization is essentially a vision adding: "This isn't pie-in-the-sky stuff. I believe nothing motivates change more than a clear vision" (cited in Meen and Keough, 1992: 58). There is no apparent attempt on his part to use a rhetorical sleight-of-hand by having his audience confuse his essentially normative vision with a descriptive vision. However, in the media accounts of the learning organization these two visions frequently become blurred and confused.

This confusion is further exacerbated by his attempts to respond to demands by practitioners to make the learning organization more concrete and to lay out the steps that are required to create one. His first attempt to address this challenge, *The Fifth Discipline Fieldbook* (Senge et al., 1994) received a mixed reception from the practitioner community with the general consensus being that, while it contained some interesting and provocative ideas, it was still not sufficiently practical. Five years later, Senge and his colleagues produced the book *The Dance of Change* which was tellingly subtitled "The Challenges of Sustaining Momentum in Learning Organizations" (Senge et al., 1999). The term "dance of change" refers to what the authors suggest is the inevitable interplay between "growth processes" (i.e. the five disciplines) and "limiting processes" (i.e. the ten challenges that tend to accompany any change process). These challenges are grouped into three categories: (a) challenges of initiating change ("We don't have time for this stuff!"; "We have no help!"; "This stuff isn't relevant"; "They're not walking the talk!"), (b) challenges of sustaining momentum ("This stuff is ——!"; "This stuff isn't working!"; "They're acting like a cult!"); and (c) challenges of systemwide redesign and rethinking ("They never let us do this stuff!"; "We keep reinventing the wheel!"; "Where are we going?"). To overcome these challenges, Senge urges managers to replace the predominant "company-as-machine" model with a "company-as-living-organism" model, concluding somewhat blandly, "we need to think less like managers and more like biologists" (Webber, 1999: 180). While Senge is by no means a "has-been" in the management guru arena, his publisher must be relieved that this long-promised sequel has finally materialized. It will be interesting to see whether this latest book, given the media attention it receives, will have the dramatic qualities required to reignite and sustain interest in the learning organization vision over the longer haul.

Summary

In this chapter we have observed that, although by no means unique or original, Peter Senge's vision of the learning organization has proven to be remarkably popular and persuasive. While he shares some of the common characteristics of management gurus (i.e. a solid academic pedigree combined with a gift and predilection for self-promotion), there are also a number of features that distinguish him. These include a distinctive anti-guru persona and a determinedly decentralized and collaborative approach to organizing his activities. He has disseminated a New Age message that attempts to integrate Eastern and Western philosophies that can appeal to both managers and employees in the private, public and not-for-profit sectors. Most notably, senior executives and those working in the field of human resource development appear to have been most vocal in their support for Senge's vision of the learning organization.

In examining this rhetorical vision, four key fantasy themes were described and identified. These included "Living in an Unsustainable World" (setting theme), "Getting Control but not Controlling" (action theme), "the Manager's New Work" (character theme) and "Working it out in the Micro World" (setting theme). This chapter has suggested that it is the dramatic qualities of his socially rooted vision – that is, its ability to inspire followers to see themselves actively engaged in building a learning organization – that have helped Senge's vision stand out from other competing conceptions. Senge's collectivist vision of the learning organization continues to hold lingering generative power for researchers and practitioners alike because of its underlying social master analogue. The vision resonates with a substantial constituency of individuals who are seeking a higher level of meaning and purpose in the work that they do and with the people they work with. Only by working together in a common cause can an individual truly realize his or her full self.

The learning organization concept has come under considerable critical scrutiny. The idea has been attacked on instrumental, theoretical, moral and political grounds. While Senge and his colleagues have not responded directly to this critique, they have sought to clarify and reaffirm that the learning organization is an aspiration and, as such, it should defy precise definition and implementation directives. They have also endeavored to expand the vision to encompass learning communities that supersede and transcend the barriers and resistance that have been encountered in many organizations. This has required innovative changes to the organizational forms that support the rhetorical vision to insure that it extends well beyond its traditional North American base. In the process, Peter Senge has shown himself to be an adept and agile sanctioning agent who, by putting into practice much of what he preaches, has been able to sustain widespread interest in his rhetorical vision.

7   Discussion

Putting on a tie makes me puke. Putting on a black suit makes me want to puke even more. And hanging out with a bunch of pompous old white male bastards who run large corporations doesn't do a lot for me.

(Tom Peters quoted in *Report on Business Magazine*, 1993: 13)

On a brightly lit stage is a tall figure dressed in black. His head is shaved. Bangles jangle around his wrist. He is talking about Lenin, the Pope making a CD and the niche marketing of a magazine called Legshow. His subject is management but not management, as we know it. Welcome to the funky world of Kjell Nordström and Jonas Ridderstråle.

(Stuart Crainer, *Business Life*, 2000: 20)

Introduction

In the introductory chapter I suggested that I had three main purposes for writing this book. First, I wanted the study to build on and add to the emergent theoretical debate about guru theory. It was an area that traditionally had been neglected yet it appeared to be teeming with intellectual promise. Second, I wanted to expand the available empirical material that could inform this emergent theoretical debate. I observed in the literature a general paucity of good, systematic and detailed empirical case studies of individual management fashions. Third, I wanted to develop a rhetorical critique that might engage both practitioners and academics in a critical dialogue about the sources of the underlying appeal of these and other management guru-inspired management fashions and to reflect on the quality of managerial and organizational learning which they have been responsible, either directly or indirectly, for generating.

In this chapter I want to take the first two of these three purposes and assess how, in particular, this study may have contributed to fulfilling them. I shall also discuss some of the limitations of the study that may have restricted its ability to make a fuller contribution. In light of these limitations, I shall identify some potentially fruitful directions and areas for future research. The chapter begins by looking at the empirical contributions of the study. It then reviews its theoretical contributions, assessing what the study may have added to the emerging theoretical debate and what still needs to be done.

The three rhetorical visions compared

The three previous chapters provided detailed rhetorical critiques of organizational improvement programs that attracted some of the largest followings during the 1990s in North America. While a number of critiques have already been conducted of the reengineering movement (e.g. Grey and Mitev, 1995; Grint, 1994; Wilmott, 1994), the effectiveness and the learning organization movements have not previously been analyzed in any systematic fashion. With the exception of Wolfe (1998) and Argyris (2000), Stephen Covey has eluded academic scrutiny. Likewise, although the concept of the learning organization has attracted a great deal of attention, I am not aware of a study that has looked at either Peter Senge or the movement that has developed around him.

The cases allowed for comparisons to be made of the shape and form of the three managerial movements that arose during approximately the same time period. Historically, researchers have tended to treat management fashions indiscriminately. One fad is very much like another. These three case studies have, however, revealed some important differences as well as some important similarities between them and it is these that will be described in this section. The key rhetorical elements of each of these management fashions are summarized in Table 7.1.

Beginning with the sanctioning agents of each management fashion, it is clear from the reading of the public discourse that the credibility and charismatic qualities of the management guru's persona can serve as a very powerful legitimizing agent for a management fashion. Most of the journalistic accounts of these management fashions pay particular attention to the background and personal presence of the guru, to the point that the fashion and the guru appear to be inseparable in the reader's mind. This is evidenced by the remarkable symmetry one finds between the articles one identifies in business media databases when one uses either the management fashion or the management guru as the key search term. It appears that we can use them almost interchangeably. Finding an article about the learning organization that does not mention Peter Senge or reengineering without referring to either Michael Hammer or James Champy proves challenging.

Given the central role of the management guru in legitimizing or guaranteeing the management fashion, it is intriguing to observe the diverse personae that have been constructed around each management guru. In one corner stands Michael Hammer, a truculent and outspoken provocateur who appears to take great delight in shocking and terrorizing his audience. In the opposite corner stands Stephen Covey, a considerably more solemn

Table 7.1 The key rhetorical elements of three major management fashions of the 1990s

Technical term	Case 1	Case 2	Case 3
Rhetorical vision	Reengineering	Effectiveness	The Learning Organization
Symbolic cues	*The Reengineering Revolution* *Reengineering Management*	*The Seven Habits* *First Things First* *Principle-Centered Leadership*	*The Fifth Discipline*
Sanctioning agent(s)	Michael Hammer James Champy	Stephen Covey	Peter Senge
Master analogue	Pragmatic	Righteous	Social
Setting themes		"Back to the Farm"	"Living in an Unsustainable World" "Working within the Microworld"
Character themes		"Finding True North"	"The Manager's New Work"
Action themes	"Preservation of Self" "Redemption of Self" "Representation of Self"	"Working from the Inside Out"	"Getting Control But Not Controlling"
Fantasy type	"Restoration"	"Restoration" "Fetching Good"	"Fetching Good Out of Evil"

and deliberate presence who measures every word as though worth its weight in gold, gliding determinedly through his sermon. In an entirely different ring stands Peter Senge, the unassuming Ivy Leaguer, who projects a studiously anti-guru persona through his soft-spoken, high-pitched voice and donnish attire.

It appears, therefore, that there is no one ideal persona on which aspirant gurus should model themselves. Academics have tended to cast all management gurus in the image of Tom Peters. They are caricatured as loud, passionate zealots who sweat a lot and are constantly foaming at the mouth as they preach their own particular brand of fire and brimstone. While it appears that one's prospects of achieving full-blown guru status are overwhelmingly advantageous if one happens to be a white, middle-aged American male with an academic pedigree, the study has revealed a wide range of oratorical and writing styles among the four management gurus described in the case studies. It has shown that we need to conduct more finely tuned analyses of speech in order to ascertain what it is about their writing and presentation styles that makes them so persuasive.

One thing that is clear from the analysis, however, is that if one does have guru aspirations, it is important to develop a persona that is distinctive, quickly recognizable and easily related to. The public personae of gurus are by no means complex and intricate. In fact, gurus appear to devote considerable attention toward showing their potential and existing followers how similar they are to them in terms of their background, daily experiences and dreams. Moreover, it is important for the gurus to stick with and continually to reinforce their persona. Guru followers, like pop star fans, are generally intolerant of image overhauls and identity makeovers. In an age of fear and uncertainty about the future, one has to be able to rely on one's guru for some sense of continuity. As we shall see in the next chapter, this need for consistency, predictability and reliability places significant constraints upon the guru which are neither frequently appreciated nor grounds for envy.

In addition to divergent personae, each management guru has gone about the task of organizing his rhetorical vision in entirely different ways. Stephen Covey has maintained close control of his vision by internalizing all of the associated consulting activities. He has exerted further control by supplying a dazzling array of products which all serve to reinforce the Covey brand. The original organizational platform for his rhetorical vision, the privately held Covey Leadership Center, proved to be remarkably effective even in the face of explosive sales growth. His more recent platform, the publicly held Franklin Covey Company, was created in order to move the venture to a whole new level of endeavor. However, to date the merger has not gone well. In order to make it work, Covey has had to forfeit considerable control over the enterprise. It will be interesting to see what impact this restructuring has on the power and reach of the effectiveness vision.

By contrast, Peter Senge has professed and evinced a far more collaborative and fluid approach to organizing. He has developed loose and tight associations with numerous organizations while maintaining his links with the Massachusetts Institute of Technology. Unlike Covey, he has not tried to commodify the learning organization vision in any systematic way. This has been left to a few fringe organizations with which Senge has only a limited and tangential connection. Nor has he attempted to brand the learning organization as his original vision. Far from it, he has stressed his debt to other thinkers and the importance of fostering collective ownership of the vision in order to guarantee the vision's long-term viability. Commentators are keener to place Senge in the leadership role than Senge appears willing to assume.

Michael Hammer has severed his link with the Harvard Business School and has set up his own corporation, which continues to present public and private seminars in an increasingly global operation. James Champy has moved from being the head of his own consulting firm to holding a senior position in a much larger transnational service corporation. He continues to write as an independent contributor to a number of management and IT trade journals. Both Hammer and Champy have made no apparent effort to create and impose a monopoly on the lucrative consulting business that emanated from the reengineering movement. Although Hammer trademarked the name, reengineering became fair game for consultants belonging to either the large transnational consultancies or to sole operators. In a recent television documentary, however, Hammer acknowledges that he would have become a considerably richer man had he attempted to control the reengineering brand (Snoddy, 1999).

Identifying and analyzing the rhetorical communities that have formed and coalesced around each of these visions is a process fraught with methodological difficulties. In this study we have used as a surrogate the individuals who have been singled out by the gurus and the media as being typical followers. Bearing in mind this important limitation, we can make the following broad observations. Covey's rhetorical vision has had perhaps the broadest audience base upon which to draw. With its focus on individual responsibility and accountability, and its emphasis upon the integration of work and home lives, Covey's effectiveness movement includes executives, middle managers and employees at all levels within both private and public sector organizations. The reengineering vision, on the other hand, found particular favor among senior executives and consultants from the private sector (most notably those in information technology and finance functions), who were lured by the promise of dramatic performance improvements and cost savings. The learning organization has attracted most interest from senior executives from all three sectors who are driven by more ostensibly altruistic concerns. It also particularly appealed to human resource developers and training managers who were keen to move learning processes higher up the crowded corporate agenda.

While there is undoubtedly considerable overlap between the rhetorical communities that have coalesced around these visions, it is apparent that the content of the vision and the marketing and communication strategies employed by the gurus and their supporting organizations have created quite different communities in terms of membership and the degree and levels of commitment they evince. We need to pay considerably more attention to the people who follow these fashions, what attracts them initially, what motivates them to persist with a vision, and how the vision influences their values and practices in the workplace and elsewhere. We also need to be aware of and conceptualize a whole range of levels of commitment to gurus from a state of total dedication through to one of open hostility. The study shows that managers do not blindly follow one management fashion and then another as they are frequently characterized as doing in media and academic accounts. In many cases they are not given an option to do this, as the fashion is mandated from the top. Theirs is not to reason why but to find a way to translate the fashion into some kind of operational reality.

However, this perception too can also be overplayed. I have come across a number of managers who are advocates of a particular guru or fashion even though their organization demonstrates no interest in it and, indeed, is unlikely ever to show an interest in it. These individuals follow a particular guru or management fashion not because the organization has mandated that they should, but because they have found that the vision speaks compellingly to their individual personality and situation, and resonates with their individual values. This possibility was graphically demonstrated to me when a small group of managers came up to me after I had given a seminar in which I was highly critical of the reengineering movement. They warmly thanked me for reasserting the values of the quality movement, even though I had in fact not mentioned it explicitly in the presentation. It reminded me of something that I have should have already known. Even within seemingly homogeneous groups, individuals are attracted to and animated by different ideas. Why should management fashions be different?

Turning to the content of these three management fashions, each could be placed at different points along a continuum that measures the relative weight placed by the vision upon organizational versus individualistic change. At one end of the continuum, the reengineering vision is almost entirely preoccupied with organizational design and process issues. Individuals are there primarily to fill roles that are created by revamped business processes. At the other end of the continuum, Covey's effectiveness vision focuses entirely on individual transformation, suggesting, but not articulating in any substantial way, that organizational change will necessarily follow if individuals take responsibility for themselves and cease to worry about wider organizational issues. With the emphasis placed on creating learning organizations, it would be natural to assume that Peter Senge's vision lies at the organizational end of the spectrum. However, closer inspection reveals that, with his five disciplines which include both "Systems Thinking" and "Personal Mastery", Senge has attempted to create a vision that integrates both individual and organizational transformation; it is therefore best conceptualized as spreading either way along the continuum.

One reason that these three case studies were selected was that they were viewed as being good exemplars of the three master analogues which Bormann and his colleagues have found to run through all of the rhetorical visions in America that they have analyzed. In this study I have suggested that the reengineering vision is rooted in a pragmatic master analogue because the primary reason for pursuing that vision is that the potential follower has no choice other than to pursue it. To ignore reengineering would mean certain extinction. Covey's vision of effectiveness, by contrast, is rooted in a righteous master analogue, which stresses that followers should pursue the vision because it is the right thing to do. The vision is, after all, founded on principles that are universal and indisputable. Peter

Senge's vision of the learning organization is rooted in a social master analogue which urges followers collectively to pursue the vision because it is a good thing to do. In working together to create the common goal of a learning organization, individuals can transcend their differences and find inner peace.

In focusing on the illustrative power of each of the three case studies, it is likely that the exclusivity of each master analogue has been overstressed. In actual fact, one can observe elements of the other two master analogues in each of this study's three visions. In stressing the relative superiority of each of their visions, Covey and Senge are, to a certain extent, basing their appeal on pragmatic grounds. That is, they urge you to consider their vision because you really have no choice but to follow it. In a complex and troubled world, you must take action in order to survive. Here is one way out. Similarly, by placing some emphasis on the validity of their respective visions, Hammer, Champy and Senge partially base their appeals on righteous grounds. The vision has proven to be successful, so why not pursue it? Finally, I have observed Hammer, Champy and Covey stressing the social benefits, particularly in terms of teamwork and community building, that can be reaped as a result of pursuing their respective visions. In sum, elements of the three master analogues can be traced in each of the rhetorical visions that have been analyzed in this study. However, I would argue that one master analogue quite clearly predominates within each vision.

In light of the fact that each rhetorical vision is undergirded by a different primary master analogue, we should not be surprised to learn that the building-blocks or fantasy themes of each vision vary in number, mix and type. While strong setting and action themes were identified in both the effectiveness and learning organization visions, no singularly powerful setting or action theme was identified within reengineering. The effectiveness movement derived considerable rhetorical energy from the frontier mythology of America's agrarian past. The learning organization, on the other hand, drew on two settings at quite different scales – the global system under environmental threat and the considerably more intimate sanctuary of the computer-simulated micro world. Covey appealed to his audience's desire to return to the past when things were better, when there was some level of certainty and trust between people. Senge, on the other hand, appeals to his audience's desire to move ahead into the future, to turn their backs on the mistakes of the past and to embrace liberating technology.

With respect to character themes, both the reengineering and the learning organization visions focus heavily on the changing roles of the manager. The learning organization vision stresses the positive aspects associated with the new manager's roles within this new vision. Taking the "carrot option", the vision portrays managerial roles in which managers garner respect not through fear and manipulation but because of their personal integrity and intellect. The reengineering vision, by contrast, emphasizes the negative characteristics of the conventional recalcitrant middle manager and then offers a path of salvation for those bold enough to take it. This "stick option" stresses the Darwinian consequences of staying with their current roles within their organizations. What is intriguing is that, while Senge and Hammer and Champy use radically different means to motivate managers to reinvent their roles and take two quite disparate tacks, the end results are strikingly similar. The "model managers" who embrace the respective reengineering and the learning organization visions are not all that dissimilar, even though their titles and labels might be different. For Hammer and Champy they are "process owners", "coaches" and "leaders". For Senge they are "local line leaders", "internal networkers" and "leaders". They have rid themselves of the shackles of bureaucratic control and are leading their newly empowered workgroups with a potent mixture of vision, integrity and passion.

The effectiveness vision draws largely on characters outside of the corporate world for its inspiration. These include well-known historical figures from around the world as well as high-profile contemporary Americans who are widely recognized as being successful. Using these types of individuals as exemplars is a conventional tactic that is practiced widely in popular books about leadership. What Covey does to particularly good effect, however, is to supplement these stock figures with moving accounts of the experiences of "regular folk" who have become effective by following the "Seven Habits". Using famous successful people attracts the potential follower's attention, but intersplicing these with tales of ordinary people who are much like the potential followers adds considerable credibility to the effectiveness vision and provides added confidence that they will succeed should they decide to embrace the vision. So successful has this gambit been, that the individual testimonial has become a central feature of Covey's proselytizing strategy to the point that his most recent book was composed entirely of stories of "Seven Habits" followers.

Considerable commonality was found between the action themes identified in the effectiveness and the learning organization visions. Both Covey and Senge adopt a variant of a stage model to show how individuals can progress by following some clearly articulated scripts in order to transform their current situations. Covey's pilgrimage is considerably more spiritual and individually driven than the one laid out for followers of the learning organization vision. Senge's vision tends to take into active account the individual's changing organizational context and constraints. His action theme is considerably less formulaic and more contingent than Covey's. Followers of Covey's vision can be considerably more assured about the journey that they will embark upon. The steps are laid out in a logical succession. All the individual has to do is to adhere to and persist with them and the vision of effectiveness will be realized. By contrast, a much greater leap of faith is required for the follower of the learning organization. Even if the individual practices the five disciplines, there are no guarantees that the nirvana of the learning organization will be reached. While this might seem a more realistic promise, the relative vagueness of Senge's action theme is something that he and his colleagues have consistently been criticized for by practitioner audiences who are anxious to get a handle on the "how-to" of the learning organization. The ambiguity can, however, work in the guru's favor. Providing that interest in pursuing the rhetorical vision can be maintained, the followers will continue to seek out help in finding their way. With each book comes the possibility of finally comprehending what needs to be done.

The study also showed that the Burkean motives of identification, transcendence and hierarchy were significant components of all three rhetorical visions, though they were associated with different types of fantasy theme. Based on the rhetorical analysis conducted on the three management fashions, it was apparent that the critical first step for the guru is to make sure that managers can quickly find themselves within the vision. Getting managers to *identify* either with a strong setting theme (i.e. a dysfunctional organization or a mythical past) or a character theme (i.e. a regular overworked, underresourced manager) within a vision appears to be an effective means for establishing a rhetorical link with the guru's audience.

Having created some measure of identification on the part of the follower, the guru has then to insure that their followers can be clear about how they can *transcend* their current situations or the roles that they play. This can be achieved through a powerful action theme that might take the form of a step-by-step model or a series of phases of activity that leads to some kind of logical conclusion. Alternatively, a strong character theme can help to provide a powerful means of showing potential and committed followers the way ahead. The key to animating the transcendental motive in the followers is to show them that you know where they are now and where they need to be. You can do this by providing instructions or by pointing to the experiences of role models to which they can relate.

At the same time, the manager needs to be clear that, through transcendence, he or she can continue to progress and move forward through some kind of *hierarchical* system within the new organizational form. The rhetorical vision must not force them to lose ground within the organization. Strong character themes are particularly effective in giving the manager confidence and reassurance that things will turn out well if they decide to participate fully in the rhetorical vision. There are plenty of people like themselves who have embraced the rhetorical vision and have prospered as a result. Perhaps they have had to move to another organization to move up the hierarchy and perhaps the hierarchy does not look as clear-cut as it might have been for their forebears, but it is there nonetheless. Similarly, it may not be immediately apparent to them how they will, in fact, be better off at the end of the day, but the role models give them hope and strength. It is a fight worth fighting for.

Bormann (1982a) has identified two major fantasy types originating in the Puritan settlements of the New World that have proven to be a remarkably resilient feature of American public discourse in the last 300 years. The "restoration" fantasy type urges Americans to harken back to the perfect society originally envisaged by the founding fathers. It has been traced by researchers in numerous religious, political and social movements and can be clearly seen in Michael Hammer and James Champy's call to make America great again. It is also readily apparent in Stephen Covey's plea for Americans to turn away from the predominant "personality ethic" and to embrace the "character ethic" which was a hallmark of the American nation in its formative years. Interestingly, Senge makes only limited reference to America's past, preferring instead to look ahead at creating new models of community and society.

The "fetching good out of evil" fantasy type that Bormann has also identified dwells on the positive community building forces that can be harnessed when Americans are under threat. This motif can be clearly detected in Covey's vision of effectiveness. The personal testimonials of individuals who have embraced the Seven Habits follow a familiar cycle of a fall from grace, hitting rock bottom, finding their way out with the aid of the Seven Habits, and redeeming themselves in the eyes of their family, friends and community. This fantasy type is also very pronounced within Senge's learning organization, albeit on a much larger scale. The vision places heavy emphasis upon the need for collective action in the face of an overwhelming global environmental threat. The demons that Senge deals with are not individually created but are generated by the complex systems of production and consumption that have given a few a great deal and a great many much less. Questions of inequality aside, these systems are not environmentally sustainable in the long term. While the outlook may be bleak, Senge ultimately presents an optimistic vision in which communities will pull together to rise to this seemingly overwhelming task and transcend their current plight. In this way society will redeem itself.

All three visions clearly resonate with the deep cultural proclivities of the American psyche. In this study I have begun to trace some of these points of resonance but I sense that there is a much greater opportunity for a deeper and more extensive investigation, particularly from scholars who are more heavily immersed in American history and cultural studies. This work would also seek to delineate the cultural specificity of these visions, helping non-American scholars assess to what extent the rhetorical visions are truly universal. Appreciating that looking to the past and to the broader national culture is crucial for furthering our understanding of contemporary, supposedly future-oriented, managerialist rhetorical visions. It is a critical first step in a research program that holds considerable promise.

Assessing Fantasy Theme Analysis

What FTA adds

The review of the of the management guru and management fashion literature revealed a body of research that, though still relatively limited, was rapidly gathering momentum. Not surprisingly, given its infancy, it remains relatively undertheorized and empirically underexplored. This study has attempted to contribute to active theory development by introducing a method of rhetorical criticism that has previously not been used to analyze the management guru and management fashion phenomenon. Clark (1995) demonstrated the explanatory power of the theatrical metaphor in his dramaturgical analysis of the consultant–client relationship. This study was launched to extend this method beyond face-to-face interaction and to encompass the mass-mediated realm of the guru–follower relationship. With its traditional preoccupation and proven track-record in investigating large and small group communication processes, many of which were analogous to the management fashion-setting process, SCT and FTA appeared to hold considerable promise.

SCT has provided a theoretical framework that was helpful in describing and understanding each of the three management fashions examined in this study. It proved to be sufficiently general to accommodate the distinctive qualities of each fashion and was flexible enough to capture the dynamic qualities of each fashion. It has provided us with a much-needed theoretical framework through which we can conduct comparisons between management fashions. With this framework in place, we can begin systematically to examine management fashions from the recent and more distant past. It may also provide us with a means to assess the likelihood of a new management fashion taking off in a significant way. FTA could, if you like, provide an "early warning system" for emergent management fashions. Before we become too enthused about this prospect, however, we should recognize that rhetorical criticism is almost always more successful in analyzing the potency of rhetorical visions after rather than before the fact.

In conducting FTA, I found the translation between theory and the data to be a relatively natural and a genuinely iterative process. I also felt that my interpretations were neither forced, nor constrained, nor overly prescribed. The FTA method enabled me to draw upon my experience and insights to build a distinctively individual yet rigorous and methodical critique. It is a technique that strikes a welcome balance between the thoroughness and rigor demanded of the social sciences and the artistry and ingenuity expected in the humanities. By the same token I recognize that methods which strive to straddle this intellectual divide can be readily disowned by both traditions and, therefore, anyone who uses these methods can place themselves in a precarious position.

The emphasis that FTA places upon analyzing the content of the "message" of the rhetorical vision enables one to assess the contributions that all of the agents of the management fashion industry make to its construction. While this study has singled out the influential role of the management guru in constructing the rhetorical vision of the management fashion, it has also incorporated the perspectives of other agents within the industry including academics, agents, consultants and journalists who also make important contributions. FTA's concern with delineating the rhetorical community that supports and follows the rhetorical vision also insures that the consumer or follower's contribution to the construction of the rhetorical vision is not ignored either. FTA also produces critiques to which both academics and practitioners can readily relate. Because the technique is not overly challenging or philosophically complex to grasp, the reader can quickly understand the major points that are being made in the critique. It tends to be an inclusive rather than an exclusive method of rhetorical criticism.

What FTA misses

In Chapter 3 I reviewed five indictments that had been leveled by critics of SCT and the FTA method. I concluded that Bormann and his colleagues have done a reasonably thorough job in addressing three of these indictments. They have labored to clarify the basic presuppositions upon which the theory is based; they have clearly demonstrated that the theory can extend well beyond small group to mass communications; and they have bent over backwards to show that SCT is not merely a relabeling of old concepts with trivial jargon that lacks precision and clarity. There are, however, two indictments that I feel I have not been able to resolve entirely satisfactorily even after using the theory and method to analyze four case studies including a pilot study. The first of these is that SCT's insights are researcher-dependent and not theory-dependent. The second is that, while SCT presents a developed epistemology, it is ontologically underdeveloped.

In a critique of an earlier piece of my work that utilized FTA, a reviewer expressed the concern that, although he found the paper interesting and insightful, he was not entirely convinced that the analysis of the basic themes of the guru's work was a result of the application of the methodology presented. He suggested that I could have arrived at the same findings using a more commonplace or conventional analysis. Not being entirely sure what that more commonplace analysis might be, I decided to persist with the fantasy theme methodology because I personally have been quite comfortable working with it. I have found that, while it is a technique that is no longer being employed as widely as it once was, it provides a theoretical framework and a vocabulary for capturing what I was observing from my own direct experience. More decisively, it has helped me to say what I wanted to say about management gurus and management fashions.

This is by no means the one or even the best way in which to conceptualize this phenomenon, but it was certainly the method that helped me move forward the most in my thinking in a way that I found exciting and energizing. In short, it enabled me to identify themes in the gurus' work that were not immediately apparent from my initial reading. However, I recognize that ultimately, enthusiasms notwithstanding, the method will, and should, be judged by the reader on the credibility, coherence and authenticity of the account that is rendered as a result of applying it.

Moving to the other indictment, which I believe has not been fully addressed in either this or any other study, SCT and the FTA method still lack a clearly formulated and articulated philosophical base. In common with most communication and rhetorical theorists, Bormann and his colleagues assume that rhetoric is essentially "epistemic". That is, they assume that rhetoric actively creates knowledge and that, in turn, creates reality and truth. By leaving the ontological questions unasked and unanswered, SCT and FTA are open to the charges of skepticism and relativism. This possibility has been raised by another reviewer who questioned: "Isn't the argument assuming a rather conventional (and dubious) form – that the ideas appeal because the ideas appeal?" My stock response to this question is that it is the dramatic quality of those ideas that make them so compelling to the audience. The problem with this is it does not address the issue of why the quality of drama is so important for humans. We know it to be intuitively true and we also know that we can distinguish between "good" and "bad" drama. But how do we go about articulating the underlying reasons for this? This question will be taken up later in this chapter.

In this study I have attempted to address this concern by proposing an exploratory rapprochement between the thinking of Ernest Bormann and Kenneth Burke. Both writers work within the dramatistic tradition and both bring two complementary strengths to the table. Bormann is a pragmatic theorist who has built up an impressive body of empirical research. Burke, on the other hand, is a strong philosopher who has done the most to tackle the tricky ontological questions posed by dramatism. Bormann's method is helpful in identifying the basic building-blocks of a rhetorical vision but somewhat equivocal when it comes to identifying what basic psychological need it might be serving for an individual. I recognize that there is something intrinsically persuasive about a particular theme and want to say something about the roots of its potency. Burke's motives provide a language for capturing these and ascribing a motive to a particular fantasy theme.

I have not come across any other attempts at a conceptual merger between Bormann and Burke, which is surprising given their dramatistic leanings. However, I think this is something worth pursuing. One potentially fruitful avenue to follow might be to problematize the concept of the master analogue. Bormann is frustratingly vague about what this is, what function it plays and why there are only three of them. He is even less clear about how they should be identified. Intuitively, they strike me as being potentially very powerful ways of distinguishing between different types of rhetorical vision. However, it is quite apparent that they require considerably greater elucidation. Perhaps, in light of Bormann's reluctance to develop this concept further, Burke's canon might be the place to look for this.

Another related criticism that has been leveled at my SCT/FTA-related work is that it tends to privilege the role of the guru at the expense of the other actors in the organizational drama, most especially the audience. As one reviewer remarked, "I have troubles with explanations that attribute the appeal of ideas to the cleverness of the presenter and the sleepiness of the audience. Isn't it also possible that these ideas work for the audience?" One of the appeals of FTA is its emphasis on analyzing the message rather than any particular agent. I tried to keep this in mind throughout my analysis but will admit that, almost inevitably, I found it difficult on occasion to separate out in my own mind what was in fact the "message" and what was the guru's text.

I would say, however, that the rhetorical visions described in this study derive their persuasive power precisely because they do, in fact, "work" for the audience. That is, they directly address the here-and-now needs of managers, be they material, psychological, emotional or existential. The aesthetic qualities of the ideas cannot solely account for the popularity of a particular management fashion. They have to find a significant degree of resonance with the audience. This implies some kind of active and not purely passive participation on the part of the audience. Therefore, it is important to demonstrate that a substantial rhetorical community has, in fact, organized itself around the rhetorical vision and to be clear about the motives of the individuals for doing this. This is an area that needs to be further developed on both theoretical and empirical planes.

Extending the analysis

This study was essentially an exploratory exercise that also acted as something of an experiment. It took a well-developed and widely used method of rhetorical criticism and applied it to a research phenomenon that was still relatively new terrain for management and organizational scholars. With this in mind, I would suggest that this experiment has been sufficiently encouraging to warrant further exploration both theoretically and empirically, as discussed in the preceding section.

An important theoretical line of inquiry

Perhaps the single most important line of theoretical inquiry that would be worth exploring is the project of integrating SCT/FTA within the broader dramatistic or dramaturgical tradition of social theory. In their published work, Bormann and his colleagues make little or no reference to other scholars who have been inspired by the theatrical metaphor. Most notably, the two widely acknowledged figureheads of the dramaturgical method, Burke and Goffman are, for some reason, both ignored. This apparent aberration can perhaps be better understood when one considers that, rather than being a unified body of theory, dramatism is best characterized as a "genre". As Littlejohn has observed, dramatism "still remains basically an 'interest group' or coalition of theories that share a metaphor rather than any particular set of theoretical terms or principles" (1992: 189). Bormann's dramatistic method of rhetorical criticism is one of four interest groups or "subgenres" of dramatism that have influenced organizational and management researchers. The other subgenres include Burke's dramatistic system (Burke, 1968, 1969), Goffman's dramaturgy (Goffman, 1960, 1974) and Turner's social drama analysis (Turner, 1974, 1982). Burke's work has inspired organizational studies by Mangham and Overington (1983 and 1987), Cheney (1983) and Case (1999). Goffman has influenced numerous impression management studies (e.g. Clark, 1995; Clark and Salaman, 1996; Rosenfeld et al., 1995). Turner's work has spawned studies of rituals within organizations by Rosen (1988) and Elmes and Costello (1992).

The most obvious strength of the dramatistic method is that it is rooted in a metaphor that can be readily and universally understood. It is also a metaphor that most people find intrinsically interesting – it speaks to the actor, playwright and critic in us all. Encouraging individuals to look at life as theater and vice versa is, therefore, not a task that is fraught with difficulty though it can, on occasion, create some bemusement. Dramatism's primary area of concern is also deceptively straightforward. It inquires into the processes by which social reality is put together or, as Goffman has stated in typically frank fashion: "What is it that is going on here?" (Goffman, 1974: 8). Unfortunately, the method's strengths also prove to be the sources of its greatest weakness. Ease of grasp of the method's basic precepts and questions is often confused with full proficiency. Like film noir, the dramatistic genre is widely known and appreciated, but extremely difficult to master.

The dramatistic perspective is plagued by the fundamental question about the "ontological status" of the idea of life as theater. This has not been helped by the fact that the two leading exponents take two quite different lines on this question. For Goffman, life is *like* theater: for Burke, life *is* theater (Mangham, 1990). Combs and Mansfield note that "the basic problem is whether or not the dramaturgical perspective is an organization of social conduct, and therefore *imposed* on reality or whether it is a description of actual conduct, and therefore inheres in reality" (1976: xxviii). If the former is the case, then the image may be only a convenient metaphor of considerable heuristic value. If the latter is true, then the "bisociation" of theater and social life may add a new level of insight to social inquiry.

In accounting for the continued confusion, Overington and Mangham suggest that, because the theatrical metaphor has become so inculcated in common, everyday discourse, it has assumed for many an ontological rather than an epistemological status. They note that "this collapse of *a way of knowing what the world is* into an affirmation of *what it is* presents difficulties for the use of theatre as a perspective, so great a penetration into everyday speaking has it made" (Overington and Mangham, 1982: 174). Perinbanayagam asserts that drama is not something that just occurs in theaters and which a few sociologists want to compare social life to; rather it is a description of certain ways of doing and being that can occur in both places. In fact, he observes that "there are many occasions in the theatre when people purport to put on a play which, on inspection, turns out not to have enough drama! Conversely, one can see more than enough of it in some episodes of everyday life" (Perinbanayagam, 1982: 263). While the ontological-epistemic confusion continues to permeate and, to a certain extent, hamper the dramatistic genre, I concur with Overington and Mangham's view that

> the theatrical perspective can serve as a general metaphor for human social conduct in the same way that functionalism or systems theory has been presented . . . [T]he theatrical perspective is one among many analytic frameworks that may be applied to grasping human social life.
> (Overington and Mangham, 1982: 174)

Another criticism expressed about the dramatistic perspective is the claim that it is not a general theory but is specific to the structure of modern post-industrial societies and reflects the inherent "inauthenticity" of such societies (Young, 1990). The claim that people are merely actors is not disputed, but the "theatrical condition" is seen as being peculiar to one type of social structure. In defence, Combs and Mansfield point out that the "phony" is a social type that has a long and undistinguished history in modern and premodern societies. They also question whether or not the inauthentic actor is any less an actor-in-role than the authentic one. Ultimately, however, the only way to eliminate the confusion about the specificity and generality of the theatrical metaphor will be to place the dramaturgical perspective in a larger sociological and philosophical framework.

Burke and Goffman and their followers have tended to limit their attention to the conduct of small-scale social interactions. This inattention, however, does not preclude the possibility of the method encompassing broader levels of social reality. Burke stressed that the pentad (act; agent; agency; purpose and scene) can function equally well as a tool for analyzing a specified event, work or speaker as well as for analyzing a rhetorical campaign or a social movement. Overington and Mangham make the case that the theatrical metaphor is ready-made for providing a general framework "that allows us to run up and down the social scale without changing key" (1982: 184). It is only in recent years, however, that the dramaturgical perspective has begun to be applied to some of the larger processes of social life such as the mass media and politics.

Young (1990) suggests that dramaturgy should be actively utilized to understand broader levels of social reality than mere face-to-face interactions. In particular, we should shift and broaden our attention to encompass the "dramaturgical society", which he defines as one in which "the technologies of social science, mass communication, theatre, and the arts are used to manage attitudes, behaviours, and feelings of the population in modern mass society" (1990: 71). In this "short take" society, role performances are frequent, varied, episodic and devoid of permanent inclusive relationships. Mangham (1996) has characterized Young's conception of dramaturgy not as a metaphor, but as an ideology that is "used in its repressive modes, to construct a fraudulent social world" (Young, 1990: 215).

With its focus on the "chaining" of fantasies between small groups and large groups through the technologies of mass communication, the SCT/FTA method would seem to be well placed to investigate and elucidate the dynamics of communication processes within the dramaturgical society. Bormann and his colleagues have been an important force in insuring that rhetorical criticism recognizes that "the capacities of the different media present rhetorical opportunities and choices, some unique to themselves, and some shared with public speech and other media" (Medhurst and Benson, 1984: vii). In this regard, the SCT/FTA method could provide an important bridge for dramaturgically oriented researchers to mesh and integrate their traditional preoccupation with the immediate theater of organization with the broader yet by no means less influential mass-mediated theater.

Further empirical lines of inquiry

These case studies were conducted in order to provide a deeper description of the discourse related to management fashions and to sketch out the beginnings of an exploratory framework within which to better understand the management fashion and management guru phenomenon. The obvious next step for empirical research would be to extend this dramatistic method to other management fashions, especially those that have emerged prior to the 1990s. For example, Fantasy Theme Analyses could be conducted of the Total Quality Management, Excellence, Quality Circles, Management by Objectives, Theory X and Theory Y and even the Scientific Management movements. It would be especially interesting to see what master analogues might be identified for each of these and other popular movements. Similarly, in building up a collection of Fantasy Theme Analyses of management fashions, it would be worthwhile examining patterns that might be detected in the predominance of action, setting or character themes. This might help us to determine, for example, if certain themes tend to predominate during different stages of the economic cycle. In addition, we might wish to identify what are the recurrent fantasy types of managerial discourse and whether or not any new fantasy types have emerged over time.

In this study the focus has been on trying to understand the processes by which a management fashion is articulated, disseminated and legitimated with specific reference to the role of the management guru. Given the media's pivotal role in this process, business media documents as well as the gurus' original texts have served as the primary sources of data. While this has proven to be a rich and varied source of data, it has inevitably limited the range and scope of the study.

One obvious area where we need to extend our empirical reach is to collect primary data from the consumers of management fashions. In the literature review, studies by Huczynski (1991, 1993a) and Watson (1994) were singled out as lone yet commendable attempts to ascertain through interviews how managers themselves actually made sense of management gurus and management fashions. More recent studies conducted by Knights and McCabe (1998a, 1998b) illustrate the utility of conducting ethnographic analyses of the impact of management fashions as they are adopted and implemented within organizations.

In addition to focusing on the consumer of management fashions, we also need to gain a fuller and more sophisticated understanding of the institutional linkages and arrangements that exist between the various producers of management fashions. Management consultants have become a focal point of attention for critically oriented researchers who are interested in the production, dissemination and consumption of management knowledge, especially in Europe (Alvarez, 1997). For example, Kieser (1999) has explored the strategies by which consultants create management fashions in order to increase demand for their services. Engwall and Eriksson (1999) have investigated the relationships and interaction between CEOs from the top ten corporations in Sweden and the increasingly Americanized Swedish consulting industry.

Other institutional actors within the management fashion industry are also being subjected to increased scholarly scrutiny. For example, a recent study by Clark and Greatbatch (1999) draws on interviews with five management gurus to develop an explanation of guru impact and success informed by Actor Network Theory. They identify the role of the book editor as one that is particularly significant and requires further exploration. From my own experience I would add the distinctive roles played by the speaker's bureau, the seminar production agency and the meeting manager in the management fashion industry. Detailed studies of each of these would, I am sure, yield some important new insights that would also help to fill out our understanding of this relatively under-analyzed industry.

A forthcoming collection of critical essays each focusing on different actors within the "management advice industry" promises to make an important contribution to bringing together and synthesizing the now significant body of work that has recently been done (Clark and Fincham, forthcoming).

Symbolic Convergence Theory (SCT) and Fantasy Theme Analysis (FTA) have been applied exclusively to American phenomena. This study is no exception to this tradition, although it has encompassed media accounts from other countries, most notably Canada, the United Kingdom and New Zealand. Bormann has developed SCT with the aim of making it a theory that can be generalized to all cultural contexts. It would, therefore, make sense to conduct Fantasy Theme Analyses in other national and regional contexts to see how generalizable the theory actually is. My sense would be that, with the globalization of the mass media and the widening influence of managerialism, the theory and the method may be more generalizable than it might have been previously. I am hoping to have the opportunity to address this question by conducting some case studies of management movements as they develop in national contexts other than the United States.

Finally, I think that there may be potential to conduct empirical research that is guided by SCT and FTA on other management and organizational phenomena, beyond management fashions and management gurus. SCT-informed empirical studies have been conducted by communication scholars on phenomena as diverse as political communication, social movements and interpersonal and small group communication. One area that would be particularly interesting to explore would be to examine the linkage between internal and external communication processes within an organization and even within an industry. For example, why is it that certain strategic visions gain widespread acceptance and buy-in within an organization or industry while many others are ignored or, at best, given grudging lip-service? How do strategic visions spread between organizations? Can we discern distinctive stages of consciousness-raising, sustaining and maintaining followed by decline and decay? What are the processes by which new managerial or technological ideas are brought into the organization? Which individuals prove to be the most influential and what rhetorical strategies and tactics do they adopt to influence others? These and other related organizational communication questions would be worth pursuing using an FTA that is informed by Symbolic Convergence Theory.

Summary

In this chapter we reviewed what this study might have contributed toward the emergent research field that is examining the management fashion and management guru phenomenon. On the empirical front, it was noted that the study had provided three detailed case studies of management fashions which, upon closer scrutiny, had revealed some important similarities and differences in terms of their shape and form. Management gurus were central figures in all three. They played critical roles in creating, disseminating and legitimating the rhetorical vision of the fashion. The means by which the management guru did this, however, varied considerably, as did the constituency of the followers of the vision. This initial exploration has been sufficiently encouraging to suggest that the method may be further extended to comparative analyses of management fashions in broader historical and geographical frames.

On the theoretical front, it was concluded that, notwithstanding the impressive track-record of the SCT/FTA method, considerable work needs to be done in order to clarify and refine its philosophical base. To this end, it was felt that a conscious effort should be made to situate and integrate the method within the dramatistic tradition. The method is subject to many of the same longstanding ontological and epistemological problems that are shared by the various subgenres within this minor, loosely aligned yet promising avenue of research.

8   Conclusion

With its focus on gossip, new-age therapies and tawdry scandals, the daytime television circuit seems an unlikely source of management expertise. Nevertheless, demand for a new course led by talk-show host Oprah Winfrey at Northwestern University's respected Kellogg Graduate School of Management, near Chicago, has proved overwhelming.

(Watts, 1999: 45)

What's wrong with a phenomenon that brings comfort to so many people? That's a bit like asking what's wrong with a lobotomy, a steady diet of happy pills. The rise of charismatic authority figures is always disconcerting, especially when they malign rationalism and exhort us to abandon critical thinking in order to realize spiritual growth. Pop gurus prey on existential anxieties and thrive when our fear of being alone and mortal in an indifferent universe is stronger than our judgement. No one who seeks worship, however covertly, deserves respect. Argue with them, please.

(Kaminer, 1997: 60)

Introduction

At the outset, I mentioned that one of the primary motives for writing this book was to attempt to facilitate what I felt was a much needed yet all too rare dialogue between academics and practitioners about management gurus and management fashions. I hoped that the rhetorical critiques that are presented in this book might serve to stimulate discussion about the sources of the underlying appeal of these and other management guru-inspired management fashions. I also hoped to encourage some critical reflection on the quality of managerial and organizational learning that management fashions have been responsible for generating, either directly or indirectly. I have come across numerous practitioners who share the same kinds of concerns and are asking the same kinds of questions about the management guru and management fashion phenomenon as many of my academic colleagues. In light of these common interests, it is somewhat unfortunate that there has been little evidence of these two communities talking across their respective boundaries. I hoped that this study might provide some stimulus, or at least raw material, to enable such a dialogue to take place.

This chapter will begin with a consideration of the challenges and pitfalls of trying to engage practitioners and academics in such a debate. We are only beginning to scratch the surface of such an endeavor and have considerable work to do; however, some valuable lessons have already been learned. I shall also look ahead and make some observations about how the management guru and management fashion phenomenon might evolve during the first decade of the new millennium based on the recent emergence of a few significant trends. The chapter and the book will close by considering the most appropriate role for the academic in the management fashion industry and how that role might best be played.

Fostering a dialogue between academics and practitioners

Of the three main purposes that were set out for this book, this is the one that I have perhaps made least progress with. Partly this is a reflection of the fact that it is an unrealistic and, frankly, arrogant ambition for one individual to pursue in isolation. Despite its lack of practicality, however, it did prove to be a remarkably motivating and enduring ambition, even though it remains essentially unfulfilled.

Despite the obvious lack of direct success in this realm, I can claim a small measure of indirect success. As I was conducting this study I was invited to speak about my research on the management guru and management fashion phenomenon at numerous practitioner-oriented events. The first thing that struck me when I participated in these events was how well attended they tended to be. The topic obviously held considerable appeal, even though it did not fit that well into any traditional management category and it did not promise any immediate skills transfer. It had general but not specific significance. The second thing that struck me was how genuinely interested the participants seemed to be in the topic. It invariably generated considerable and animated discussion, some of it hostile, most of it constructive. Invariably, the participants appeared to be deeply concerned and disenchanted by their organization's management fashion habit and the negative impact it had had upon morale and productivity. They were less concerned with the influence of the management guru, whom they largely saw as a constructive rather than a sinister force in promoting different organizational possibilities.

As I began to formulate the dramatistic critique of management gurus and management fashions, I began to introduce various components of it into each session. With equal parts of surprise and delight I found that the practitioners were not only receptive but also quite enthusiastic about Fantasy Theme Analysis. They appeared to grasp quickly the key concepts and the central idea of the method. Most significantly, however, were the few participants who would invariably come up to me after the session and say something along the lines of "And I thought I was the only one who thought this way."

My first instinct upon hearing this was one of pleasure and instant gratification. Perhaps this was something akin, albeit on a comparatively miniature scale, to the adulation that the management gurus command when they speak to the mass audience. Further reflection, however, made me start to appreciate the dilemma that gurus inevitably face. By telling people what they already instinctively know, you can indeed connect with many people – in their case, a staggering number of people. However, in the process, are you forced to give up the critical distance so prized by the academic? In other words, if the only way to connect with practitioners is to "tell them what they already know", are you any closer to fostering a genuine dialogue? Perhaps the answer lies in trying to commence the dialogue by locating this point of contact and, having gained some measure of trust and respect, consciously challenging it in the hope of finding new points of contact. Keeping out of the guru's trap is something that is, no doubt, easier to talk about than to pull off in practice (Jackson, 1996a; Lee, 1991; Reed, 1990).

The road ahead

I am frequently and quite reasonably asked "what's next?" by individuals who know about my scholarly enthusiasms. Indeed, one would have thought that, having studied management fashions and management gurus for the past six years, I would have learned enough to be quietly confident about predicting what new management fashions will be grabbing the corporate imagination in a substantial way over the next five to ten years. Unfortunately, when questioned this way, I find myself compelled to disappoint those wanting to have a flutter on the "next big thing" in management. I can, however, make a few observations about some recent trends within the management advice industry that are likely to become more significant in the next few years.

In the last two to three years it has become apparent that no single management guru has monopolized the attention of the business media in the same way that Michael Hammer, James Champy, Stephen Covey or Pete Senge did at their peaks during the 1990s. The business bookshelves in the high street and airport bookstores are as well stocked as they have ever been, but no one or two authors currently dominate either business book sales or media attention. There have been isolated surges of interest in concepts like 'Emotional Intelligence', that have brought its creator, Daniel Goleman, widespread recognition in the international arena. However, as yet he has received nothing like the attention that was garnered by the gurus who were discussed in this study (Goleman, 1995, 1998).

Similarly, minor management fashions such the Balanced Scorecard (Kaplan and Norton, 1996), Core Competencies (Hamel and Prahalad, 1994), Shareholder Value Analysis (Rappaport, 1997) and Economic Value Added (Ehrbar, 1998) have given their creators, Robert Kaplan, David Norton, Alfred Rappaport and Joel Stern influential but by no means massive followings. These are essentially economic, bottom-line focused concepts that have been primarily targeted at senior executives, company directors and financial analysts and have held only limited appeal for more operationally minded middle managers and front-line employees. Moreover, the proponents of these concepts are by no means charismatic figures who crave the limelight of the mass media. They are primarily interested in connecting with the highest level executives from Fortune 500 companies. Consequently, none of these management fashions has forged a managerial movement on the scale of the Excellence, TQM, reengineering and the learning organization movements.

Looking at the two most recent management fashions that have generated substantial followings in the past two years, it is interesting to note that neither of them has been led by a single all-powerful management guru figure. Knowledge Management certainly had a number of key expert figures such as Ikujiro Nonaka and James Quinn, who wrote influential books (Nonaka and Tekeuchi, 1995; Quinn, 1992), but neither of these assumed a leadership role in the way that James Champy and Michael Hammer did for the reengineering movement, for example. Similarly, e-Business or e-Commerce as it is alternatively referred to, is a management fashion that is currently dominating if not monopolizing the attention span of business journalists and corporate leaders throughout the world without the benefit of an obvious management guru sitting at the helm (*Fortune*, 2000).

The major influence that we saw being exerted by transnational consulting firms in promoting Knowledge Management has become even more apparent with the e-Business management fashion. In particular, the 'big five' management consulting firms – Andersen Consulting, Cap Gemini Ernst & Young, Deloitte Consulting, KPMG and PriceWaterhouseCoopers – as well as the major IT consulting firms like EDS, IBM and UNISYS, have been instrumental in leading the e-business charge throughout the developed world and beyond. Traditionally, these consulting firms were to some extent dependent upon management gurus for creating and promoting new management fashions. Now it seems quite possible that these global consulting firms have eclipsed the management guru and have gained ascendancy in the management fashion industry. They are also engaged in a worldwide dogfight to determine which of them will lead the way in the future. At present it is difficult to pick up a magazine or walk through an airport anywhere in the world without seeing an advertisement for one of these firms' brands of e-commerce. We may well look back at the 1980s and the 1990s as the decades of the management guru. It seems likely that these may be superseded by a decade in which the worldwide consulting firm assumes the guru mantle and rules the management waves, leaving the independent management gurus and the business schools bobbing in their wake.

Another related development that I think will have an important if currently largely unknown impact upon the management fashion phenomenon is the Internet. The Internet has the potential to disseminate new management fashions at an increasingly rapid rate. Already we have seen how the increasingly globalized business media, supported in large part by the Internet, have had a significant impact in reducing both the production and the consumption cycles for management fashions. The gurus themselves have used the Internet to good effect in promoting their wares. Most notably, the Franklin Covey Company is a model business-to-consumer e-business operation. Taken to its logical conclusion, management fashions could become almost instantaneous, fleetingly "famous", only to be quickly relegated to a disposable and peculiarly managerial form of popular art. The primary problem then, as now, will not lie with the media that support the management fashion but in getting the attention of an overly stimulated and an increasingly sophisticated and distracted audience. This will tax even the most rhetorically skilled management consultant and will place a heavy premium on getting the dramatic qualities of the management fashion exactly right.

We have noted the importance that many management followers place on having face-to-face, physical proximity to the management guru. This is graphically reflected in the exhorbitant registration fees that are charged and collected to attend management guru seminars. To what extent the Internet will address and be able to capitalize on this perhaps archaic yet fundamentally human need remains to be seen. Similarly, how significant the guru–follower relationship will be to a younger generation of managers raised on a steady diet of electronic interaction and digital exchange will also be a point of interest.

The more idealistically inclined proponents of the Internet point to its liberating potential and democratizing effects. Universal access to information undermines the informational power exerted by those in authority, including management gurus. The same could also be said, of course, for consultants and business school professors. With the Internet everyone has the potential to become their own guru, consultant or professor. The less idealistic proponents of the Internet point, however, to the increased dependency of followers upon a few experts and gurus to make sense of the information explosion that is unleashed by the Internet. Perhaps the Internet's much-vaunted capacity to remove the barriers of physical distance will serve merely to reduce the potential number of relevant sources of management thinking and to create an even stronger dependence upon a few dominant voices. As a former colleague of mine once said in order to dramatize the threat that the Internet posed to our cosy existence,

"Why would anyone want to get a degree from our place when they can get one from Harvard?"

Curtain call

In this study numerous roles have been identified and cast in the production of the three biggest corporate "blockbusters" of the 1990s: reengineering, effectiveness and the learning organization. Because of his central role in creating each of these organizational dramas, the management guru's role as playwright has attracted the bulk of the attention. During the course of the study, we have also looked at the roles played by the protagonists and antagonists, the producers, the auxiliaries, the chorus, extras and behind-the-scenes people. But what of the role of the academic in this organizational drama? For many, the appropriate role might be to stay at home and miss the show. However, I believe that academics should ideally be playing the role of "critic" to the guru's playwright. As Bormann has argued,

> If the critic can illuminate how people arrange themselves into social hierarchies, how they acted to achieve the goals embedded in their dreams, and how they were aroused by the dramatic action and the dramatis personae within the manifest content of their rhetoric, his or her insights will make a useful contribution to understanding the movement and its adherents.
>
> (Bormann, 1972: 400)

In our quest to become effective critics, I believe we can learn some valuable lessons from the leading practitioners from the world of the arts.

First, effective critics ignore popular culture at their peril. The dynamic and complex link between "high" and "low" culture is not only recognized but also actively celebrated in the arts. We have to recognize that popular movements in management like reengineering, TQM and Excellence, while essentially transitory and superficial in nature, are nevertheless important areas to research. This is because they tell us a lot about managers and management and they have a real and frequently deleterious impact on the lives of those who work in the organizations that embrace them.

Second, effective critics try to know as much about the audiences they are communicating to as they do about the artists they are criticizing. This book is one of a number of studies that have set about providing a rhetorical critique of what the "artists" are trying to say to their audience. However, in order to complete this critique, we must begin to explore more fully how the audience actually interprets the artist and his or her work. We have lamentably few good analyses of what roles management gurus actually play for practicing managers, let alone how they affect them. These studies together with anecdotal evidence suggest that, on an individual level at least, managers tend to be quite ambivalent in their attitudes toward management gurus, yet substantial book sales and widespread and far-reaching organizational change efforts suggest otherwise.

Third, effective critics find the media and make the points that will enable them to connect their critiques to the needs and preoccupations of their readers. As academic researchers, we have to make a concerted effort to reach practitioners and compellingly engage them with rhetorical critiques that are informed by all that is good about the academic tradition. Namely, the desire to look beyond the obvious and taken-for-granted, the determination to see the task through to its full extent, the importance given to considered self-reflection and a genuine concern with improving the human condition. Perhaps, in future, we should endeavor to connect with other groups, with particular attention to the senior executives who are the primary sponsors of the gurus and their prescriptions.

Dramatism is one methodological framework that is particularly suitable for management researchers who are interested in fulfilling the role of critic because it is both a technique of analysis of human interaction and a method for assessing social theories of human conduct (i.e. a meta-method) (Overington, 1977). It allows "its practitioners to tell stories about organizational mystifications, and in the process, teach their audiences both how to locate mystifications and to relate persuasive accounts of them" (Mangham and Overington, 1983: 232). The crux of any work that we do in this area as critics will ultimately rest on the plausibility of our accounts. Plausibility is, of course, ultimately in the eyes of the audience for those accounts.

As social scientists we have learned to hone the rhetoric of our accounts to other social scientists. As we demystify the rhetoric of the management gurus, we can selectively learn from that rhetoric how to make our accounts more plausible to the audience of practicing managers who need to hear what we have to say. In this way we can take our place with the others at curtain call.

References

Abrahamson, E. (1991) "Managerial Fads and Fashions: The Diffusion and Rejection of Innovations", *Academy of Management Review* 16, 3: 586–612.

Abrahamson, E. (1996a) "Management Fashion", *Academy of Management Review* 21, 1: 254–285.

Abrahamson, E. (1996b) "Technical and Aesthetic Fashion", in B. Czarniawski and G. Sevon (eds.) *Translating Organizational Change*, Berlin: de Greuter, 117–137.

Abrahamson, E. (1997) "The Emergence and Prevalence of Employee Management Rhetorics: The Effects of Long Waves, Labor Unions, and Turnover, 1875 to 1992", *Academy of Management Journal* 40: 491–533.

Abrahamson, E. and Fairchild, G. (1999) "Management Fashion: Lifecycles, Triggers, and Collective Learning Processes", *Administrative Science Quarterly* 44: 708–740.

Abrahamson, E. and Rosenkopf, L. (1993) "Institutional and Competitive Bandwagons: Using Mathematical Modeling as a Tool to Explore Innovation Diffusion", *Academy of Management Review* 18, 3: 487–517.

Abramson, M. (1994) "Return of the Management Gurus", *Government Executive* 26, 11: 72–73.

Accountancy (1999) "The Top 10 Technologies: The Applications", March, 187, 3: 12–13.

Across the Board (1995) "Reengineering: A Light That Failed?", March: 27–31.

Across the Board (1999) "The Major Leaguers", 36, 9: 21–22.

Aldag, R.J. (1997) "Moving Sofas and Exhuming Woodchucks: On Relevance, Impact, and the Following of Fads", *Journal of Management Inquiry* 6, 1: 8–16.

Alvarez, J.L. (1991) "The International Diffusion and Institutionalization of the New Entrepreneurship Movement: A Study in the Sociology of Organizational Knowledge". Unpublished doctoral dissertation, Harvard University.

Alvarez, J.L. (ed.) (1997) *The Diffusion and Consumption of Business Knowledge*, New York: St. Martin's Press.

Alvarez, J.L. and Mazza, C. (2000) "Haute Couture and Prêt-à-Porter: The Popular Press and the Diffusion of Management Practices", *Organization Studies* 21, 3: 567–588.

Alvesson, M. (1990) "On the Popularity of Organizational Culture", *Acta Sociologica* 33, 1: 31–49.

Argyris, C. (1998) "Empowerment: The Emperor's New Clothes", *Harvard Business Review*, May/June: 98–105.

Argyris, C. (2000) *Flawed Advice: How Managers Can Know They're Getting Good Advice and When They're Not*, New York: Oxford University Press.

Argyris, C. and Schon, D.A. (1977) *Theory in Practice*, San Francisco: Jossey-Bass.

Argyris, C. and Schon, D.A. (1978) *Organizational Learning: A Theory in Action*, Reading, MA: Addison-Wesley.

Bales, R.F. (1970) *Personality and Interpersonal Behavior*, New York: Holt, Rinehart & Winston.

Bank Marketing (1988) "Relationship Selling Must Focus on 'Emotional Bank Accounts'", April: 10.

Barley, S.R. and Kunda, G. (1992) "Design and Devotion: Surges of Rational and Normative Ideologies of Control in Managerial Discourse", *Administrative Science Quarterly* 37: 363–399.

Barley, S.R., Meyer, G.W. and Gash, D.C. (1988) "Cultures of Culture: Academics, Practitioners and the Pragmatics of Normative Control", *Administrative Science Quarterly* 33: 24–60.

Barrier, M. (1990) "Back in the Shark Tank", *Nation's Business* 78, 3: 50–51.

Barry, D. and Elmes, M. (1997) "Strategy Retold: Toward a Narrative View of Strategic Discourse", *Academy of Management Review* 22, 2: 429–452.

Bart, V. and Stephens, C. (1994) "The Dark Side of the New Organizational Forms: An Editorial Essay", *Organization Science* 5, 4: 479–482.

Bass, B.M. (1986) "Evolving Perspectives on Charismatic Leadership", in J.A. Conger and R.N. Kanungo (eds.) *Charismatic Leadership: The Elusive Factor in Organizational Effectiveness*, San Francisco: Jossey-Bass, 40–77.

Bateson, G. (1973) *Steps to an Ecology of Mind*, New York: Ballantine Books.

Batra, R. (1988) *Surviving the Great Depression of the 1990's*, New York: Dell.

Bauman, Z. (1987) *On Modernity, Post-Modernity and Intellectuals*, Cambridge, U.K.: Polity Press.

Beaumont, P.B. (1985) "The Diffusion of Human Resource Management Innovations", *Relations Industrielles* 40, 2: 243–256.

Bell, D. (1995) "Paradigms Lost, Paradigms Found", *Report on Business Magazine*, July: 23–29.

Bendix, R. (1956) *Work and Authority in Industry: Ideologies of Management in the Course of Industrialization*, New York: Harper & Row.

Berger, P.L. (1967) *The Social Reality of Religion*, Harmondsworth, U.K.: Penguin.

Berger, P.L. and Luckmann, T. (1966) *The Social Construction of Reality*, New York: Doubleday.

Berger, P.L., Berger, B. and Kellner, H. (1973) *The Homeless Mind: Modernization and Consciousness*, New York: Random House.

Beugré, C.D. (1998) "Implementing Business Process Reengineering: The Role of Organizational Justice", *Journal of Applied Behavioral Science* 34, 3: 347–361.

Bion, W.R. (1961) *Experiences in Groups*, London: Tavistock.

Black, E. (1965) *Rhetorical Criticism: A Study in Method*, Madison, WI: Wisconsin Press.

Black, E. (1980) "A Note on the Theory and Practice of Rhetorical Criticism", *Western Journal of Speech Communication* 44: 331–336.

Blackburn, A. (1996) "BPR: New Wine Which Missed the Bottle?", *Management Services*, May: 18–21.

Blair, H., Taylor, S.G. and Randle, K. (1998) "A Pernicious Panacea: A Critical Evaluation of Business Re-engineering", *New Technology, Work and Employment* 13, 2: 116–128.

Blanchard, K. and Johnson, S. (1983) *The One Minute Manager*, New York: Morrow.

Bloom, H. (1992) *The American Religion: The Emergence of the Post-Christian Nation*, New York: Simon & Schuster.

Boje, D.M., Rosile, G.A. and Dennehy, R. (1997) "Re-storying Reengineering: Some Deconstructions and Postmodern Alternatives", *Communication Research* 24, 6: 631–668.

Bongiorno, L. (1993) "Corporate America, Dr. Feelgood Will See You Now", *Business Week*, December 6: 52.

Bormann, E.G. (1972) "Fantasy and Rhetorical Vision: The Rhetorical Criticism of Social Reality", *Quarterly Journal of Speech* 58: 396–407.

Bormann, E.G. (1973) "The Eagleton Affair: A Fantasy Theme Analysis", *Quarterly Journal of Speech* 59: 143–159.

Bormann, E.G. (1976) "General and Specific Theories of Communication", in J.L. Golden, G.W. Berquist and W.E. Coleman (eds.) *The Rhetoric of Western Thought*, Dubuque, IA: Kendall, 431–449.

Bormann, E.G. (1977) "Fetching Good out of Evil: A Rhetorical Use of Calamity", *Quarterly Journal of Speech* 63: 130–139.

Bormann, E.G. (1980) *Communication Theory*, New York: Holt.

Bormann, E.G. (1982a) "Fantasy and Rhetorical Vision: The Rhetorical Criticism of Social Reality", *Quarterly Journal of Speech* 58: 396–407.

Bormann, E.G. (1982b) "A Fantasy Theme Analysis of the Television Coverage of the Hostage Release and the Reagan Inaugural", *Quarterly Journal of Speech* 68: 133–145.

Bormann, E.G. (1982c) "Fantasy and Rhetorical Vision: Ten Years Later", *Quarterly Journal of Speech* 68: 288–305.

Bormann, E.G. (1983) "Symbolic Convergence: Organizational Communication and Culture", in L. Putnam and M.E. Paconowsky (eds.) *Communication and Organizations: An Interpretative Approach*, Beverly Hills, CA: Sage, 99–122.

Bormann, E.G. (1985) *The Force of Fantasy*, Carbondale, IL: Southern Illinois University.

Bormann, E.G. (1996) Unpublished Bibliography of Fantasy Theme Analysis and Symbolic Convergence Theory.

Bormann, E.G., Cragan, J.F. and Shields, D.C. (1994) "In Defense of Symbolic Convergence Theory: A Look at the Theory and its Criticisms after Two Decades", *Communication Theory* 4, 4: 259–294.

Bormann, E.G., Cragan, J.F. and Shields, D.C. (1996) "An Expansion of the Rhetorical Vision Component of the Symbolic Convergence Theory: The Cold War Paradigm Case", *Communication Monographs* 63, March: 1–28.

Bormann, E.G., Kroll, B.S., Watters, K. and McFarland, D. (1984) "Rhetorical Visions of Committed Voters in the 1980 Presidential Campaign: Fantasy Theme Analysis of a Large Sample Survey", *Critical Studies in Mass Communication* 1: 287–310.

Bouw, B. (1998) "A Highly Effective Person Brings His Seven Habits on the Road", *Financial Post*, November 11: C4.

Boyett, J.H. and Boyett, J.T. (1998) *The Guru Guide: The Best Ideas of the Top Management Thinkers*, New York: John Wiley.

Brewis, J. (1996) "The 'Making' of the 'Competent' Manager: Competency Development, Personal Effectiveness and Foucault", *Management Learning* 27, 1: 65–86.

Brickley, J.A., Smith, C.W. and Zimmerman, J.L. (1997) "Management Fads and Organizational Architecture", *Journal of Applied Corporate Finance* 10, 2: 24–39.

Brimelow, P. (1989) "How Do You Cure Injetilance?", *Forbes*, August 7: 42–44.

Brokaw, L. (1991) "Books that Transform Companies", *Inc.* 13, 7: 30–36.

Brooke, J.L. (1996) *The Refiner's Fire: The Making of Mormon Cosmology, 1644–1844*, Cambridge U.K.: Cambridge University Press.

Brown, J.S. and Duguid, P. (1991) "Organizational Learning and Communities of Practice", *Organization Science* 2: 40–57.

Brownlie, D. and Saren, M. (1995) "On the Commodification of Marketing Knowledge: Opening Themes", *Journal of Marketing Management* 11: 619–627.

Bryman, A. (1992) *Charisma and Leadership in Organizations*, London: Sage.

Burdett, J.O. (1994) "TQM and Re-engineering", *TQM Magazine* 6, 2: 7–13.

Burgoyne, J.G. (1995a) "Learning from Experience: From Individual Discovery to Meta-Dialogue via the Evolution of Transitional Myths", *Personnel Review* 24, 6: 61–72.

Burgoyne, J.G. (1995b) "Feeding Minds to Grow the Business", *People Management* 1, 19: 22–25.

Burgoyne, J.G. and Jackson, B.G. (1997) "The Arena Thesis: Management Development as a Pluralistic Meeting Point", in J.G. Burgoyne and M. Reynolds (eds.) *Management Learning*, London: Sage, 55–70.

Burgoyne, J.G. and Reynolds, M. (1997) "Introduction", in J.G. Burgoyne and M. Reynolds (eds.) *Management Learning*, London: Sage, 1–16.

Burke, K. (1931) *Counter-Statement*, New York: Harcourt, Brace.

Burke, K. (1962) *A Rhetoric of Motives*, Cleveland, OH: World Publishing Company.

Burke, K. (1968) "Dramatism", in *The International Encyclopedia of the Social Sciences,VII*, New York: Macmillan, 445–452.

Burke, K. (1969) *A Grammar of Motives*, Berkeley: University of California Press.

Burrell, G. (1989) "The Absent Centre: The Neglect of Philosophy in Anglo-American Management Theory", *Human Systems Management* 8: 307–312.

Burrell, G. (1997) *Pandemonium: Towards a Retro-Organization Theory*, London: Sage.

Butler, C. (1997) "What's the Big Deal About Stephen Covey?", *Sales and Marketing Management* 149, 4: 20–23.

Butman, J. (1997) *The Book that's Sweeping America or Why I Love Business!*, New York: John Wiley.

Byrne, J.A. (1986) "Business Fads: What's In and What's Out?", *Business Week*, January 20: 52–61.

Byrne, J.A. (1992) "Management's New Gurus", *Business Week*, August 31: 44–52.

Byrne, J.A. (1993) "Bidding Farewell to a Guru – at $395 a Pop", *Business Week*, August 30: 43.

Byrne, J.A. (1994) "The Craze for Consultants", *Business Week*, July 25: 61–66.

Byrne, J.A. (1996) "Has Outsourcing Gone Too Far?, *Business Week*, April 1: 26–28.

Calgary Herald (1998) "Motivational Guru Gets His Message Across", February 2: C1.

Calvert, G., Mobley, S. and Marshall, L. (1994) "Grasping the Learning Organization", *Training and Development* 48, 6: 39–43.

Camerer, C. and Knez, M. (1996) "Coordination, Organizational Boundaries and Fads in Business Practices", *Industrial and Corporate Change* 5, 1: 89–113.

Campbell, J. (1979) "Jimmy Carter and the Rhetoric of Charisma", *Central States Speech Journal* 30: 174–186.

Campbell, R.H. and Skinner, A.S. (eds.) (1976) *An Inquiry into the Nature and Causes of the Wealth of Nations*, Oxford: Clarendon Press.

Carroll, D.T. (1983) "A Disappointing Search for Excellence", *Harvard Business Review* 61, 6, November/December: 78–88.

Case, P. (1995) "Reengineering the End of History: A Critique of Business Process Reengineering", CRICT Discussion Paper No. 52, Brunel University, U.K.

Case, P. (1999) "Remember Re-Engineering?: The Rhetorical Appeal of a Management Salvation Device", *Journal of Management Studies* 36, 4: 419–442.

Casey, D.R. (1983) *Crisis in Investing: Opportunities and Profits in the Coming Great Crash*, New York: Simon & Schuster.

Cassell, C. and Symon, G. (eds.) (1995) *Qualitative Methods in Organizational Research: A Practical Guide*, London: Sage.

Caulkin, S. (1997) "The Great Consultancy Cop-Out", *Management Today* March: 32–37.

Chambers, V. (1997) "Bonding Business", *Newsweek*, October 6: 58.

Champy, J. (1995) *Reengineering Management*, New York: HarperBusiness.

Champy, J. (1998a) "Get Ready for More Reengineering", *Sales and Marketing Management* 150, 3: 26–27.

Champy, J. (1998b) "Japan's 'Burning Platform'", *Forbes*, June 15: 67–68.

Champy, J. (1999) "E-commerce Winners and Losers", *Sales and Marketing Management* 151, 7: 32–41.

Champy, J. and Nohria, N. (2000) *The Arc of Ambition*, New York: Perseus.

Chapman, C. (1998) "Just Do It", *The Internal Auditor* 55, 3: 38–41.

Chen, C.C. and Meindl, J.R. (1991) "The Construction of Leadership Images in the Popular Press: The Case of Donald Burr and People Express", *Administrative Science Quarterly* 36: 521–551.

Cheney, G. (1983) "The Rhetoric of Identification and the Study of Organizational Communication", *Quarterly Journal of Speech* 69: 143–158.

Chesebro, J.W. (1988) "Epistemology and Ontology as Dialectical Modes in the Writings of Kenneth Burke", *Communications Quarterly* 36: 175–191.

Chipman, D. (1993) "A Glossary of Managerese", *Across the Board* 30: 39–47.

Church, E. (1999) "Hammer's Theory Hits on the Internet", *Globe and Mail*, April 16: B23.

Clark, T. (1995) *Managing Consultants: Consultancy as the Management of Impressions*, Buckingham: Open University Press.

Clark, T. and Fincham, R. (eds.) (forthcoming) *Critical Consulting*, Oxford: Blackwell.

Clark, T. and Greatbatch, D. (1999) "Translating Actors' Interests: How Management Gurus Understand Their Impact and Success". Paper presented at the 15th EGOS Annual Colloquium, Warwick, U.K.

Clark, T. and Greatbatch, D. (2000) "Mantaining Audience Affiliation through Storytelling: The Case of Management Gurus". Paper presented at the 16th EGOS Annual Colloquium, Helsinki, Finland.

Clark, T. and Salaman, G. (1996) "The Management Guru as Organizational Witchdoctor", *Organization* 3, 1: 85–107.

Clark, T. and Salaman, G. (1998a) "Telling Tales: Management Gurus' Narratives and the Construction of Managerial Identity", *Journal of Management Studies* 35, 2: 137–161.

Clark, T. and Salaman, G. (1998b) "Re-imagining the Corporation: Guru Theory

Narratives, the 'New Organization' and the Heroic Leader", unpublished paper.

Clausson, J. (1996) "Peter Senge's Ideas Live on via Learning-Org", *Quality Progress* 29, 9: 153–162.

Clemons, E.K. (1995) "Using Scenario Analysis to Manage the Strategic Risks of Reengineering", *Sloan Management Review*, 36, 4: 61–71.

Cleverly, G. (1971) *Managers and Magic*, London: Longman.

Clutterbuck, D. and Crainer, S. (1990) *Makers of Management*, London: Macmillan.

Combs, J.E. and Mansfield, M.W. (1976) *Drama in Life*, New York: Hastings House.

Conger, J.A. and Kanungo, R.N. (1987) "Toward a Behavioural Theory of Charismatic Leadership in Organizational Settings", *Academy of Management Review* 12, 4: 637–647.

Conlin, M. (1999) "Religion in the Workplace", *Business Week*, November 8: 81–86.

Conlon, G. (1996) "The 25 Power Brokers", *Sales and Marketing Management*, July: 49–62.

Connors, R., Smith, T. and Hickman, C. (1994) *The Oz Principle: Getting Results through Individual and Organizational Accountability*, New York: Prentice-Hall.

Coopey, J. (1995) "The Learning Organization: Power, Politics, and Ideology", *Management Learning* 26, 2: 193–213.

Corbett, E.P.J. (1990) *Classical Rhetoric for the Modern Student*, New York: Oxford University Press.

Coser, L.A., Kadushin, C. and Powell, W.W. (1982*)* *The Culture and Commerce of Publishing*, Chicago: The University of Chicago Press.

Covey, S.R. (1982) *The Divine Center*, Salt Lake City, UT: Deseret.

Covey, S.R. (1988) "The Centered Life", *Executive Excellence*, May: 3–6.

Covey, S.R. (1989) *The Seven Habits of Highly Effective People: Powerful Lessons in Personal Change*, New York: Simon & Schuster.

Covey, S.R. (1990a) "An Inside-Out Approach", *Executive Excellence*,October: 3–4.

Covey, S.R. (1990b) *Principle-Centered Leadership*, NewYork: Simon & Schuster.

Covey, S.R. (1993) *Spiritual Roots of Human Relations*, Salt Lake City, UT: Deseret.

Covey, S.R. (1996) "Goodbye Ego", *Incentive*, January: 17.

Covey, S.R. (1997) *The Seven Habits of Highly Effective Families*, New York: Golden Books.

Covey, S.R. (1999) *Living the Seven Habits*, New York: Simon & Schuster.

Covey, S.R., Merrill, A.R. and Merrill, R.R. (1994*)* *First Things First: To Live, to Love, to Learn, to Leave a Legacy*, New York: Simon & Schuster.

Cragan, J.F. (1981) "The Origins and Nature of the Cold War Rhetorical Vision, 1946–1972: A Partial History", in J.F. Cragan and D.C. Shields (eds.) *Applied Communication Research: A Dramatistic Approach*, Prospect Heights, IL: Waveland Press, 47–66.

Cragan, J.F. and Shields, D.C. (eds.) (1981) *Applied Communication Research: A Dramatistic Approach*, Prospect Heights, IL: Waveland Press.

Cragan, J.F. and Shields, D.C. (1992) "The Use of Symbolic Theory in Corporate Strategic Planning", *Journal of Applied Communication Research* 20: 199–218.

Cragan, J.F. and Shields, D.C. (1995) *Symbolic Theories in Applied Communication: Bormann, Burke and Fisher*, Cresskill, NJ: Hampton Press.

Crainer, S. (1996a) *Key Management Ideas: Thinkers That Changed the Management World*, London: Pitman.

Crainer, S. (1996b) "The Rise of Guru Scepticism", *Management Today*, March: 48–51.

Crainer, S. (1997) "The Gurus: Tom Peters", *Management Today*, May: 74–77.

Crainer, S. (1998a) "Brain Gain", *Management Today*, April: 68–70.

Crainer, S. (1998b) "The Gurus and Their Ghosts", *Globe and Mail*, November 15: B15.

Crainer, S. (2000) "Vikings Inc.", *Business Life*, April: 20–24.

Creedon, J. (1998) "God with a Million Faces", *Utne Reader*, August: 42–48.

Cresswell, J.W. (1998) *Qualitative Inquiry and Research Design: Choosing Among Five Traditions*, Thousand Oaks, CA: Sage.

Cummings, S. (1999) "A Counter-History of Management". Unpublished doctoral dissertation, Warwick University Business School, U.K.

Cunningham, I. (1989) "The 59 Second Academic: A Time of the Signs?", *Management Education and Development* 20, 1: 39–44.

Czarniawska-Joerges, B. (1995) "Rhetoric and Modern Organizations", *Studies in Cultures, Organizations and Societies* 1: 147–152.

Czarniawska, B. (1997) *Narrating the Organization: Dramas of Institutional Identity*, Chicago: The University of Chicago Press.

Dances with Wolves [Film] (1990) Director Kevin Costner. Majestic Film and Tig Productions.

Davenport, T. (1993) *Process Innovation*, Boston, MA: Harvard Business School Press.

Davies, H. (1997) "Without Humility", *New Statesman* 10, 436: 45–46.

De Geus, A. (1988) "Planning as Learning", *Harvard Business Review*, March/April: 70–74.

De Geus, A. (1997) "The Living Company", *Harvard Business Review*, March/April: 51–59.

De Mause, A. (1977) "Jimmy Carter and the American Group Fantasy", *Journal of Psychohistory* 7: 151–173.

De Pillis, M.S. (1991) "Mormonism Becomes a Mainline Religion", *Dialogue*, Winter: 59–68.

De Pree, M. (1989) *Leadership Is an Art*, New York: Doubleday.

Dechant, K.K. and Marsick, V.J. (1991) "In Search of the Learning Organization: Toward a Conceptual Model of Collective Learning". Proceedings of the Eastern Academy of Management, Hartford, CT.

Deming, W.E. (1986) *Out of the Crisis*, Cambridge, U.K.: Cambridge University Press.

DiBella, A.J. (1995) "Developing Learning Organizations: A Matter of Perspective", *Academy of Management Journal*, Best Papers Proceedings: 287–290.

Director (1997) "The Good Book Triumphs", 50, 12: 62.

Dixon, M. (1986) "The Guru Factor: Ancient Wisdom with a Novel Twist", *Financial Times*, July 17: 14.

Dixon, N.M. (1994) *The Organizational Learning Cycle: How We Can Learn Collectively*, London: McGraw-Hill.

Dodsworth, T. (1986) "Why America is Just Wild about Wisdom", *Financial Times*, July 14: 14.

Dovey, K. (1997) "The Learning Organization and the Organization of Learning", *Management Learning* 28, 3: 331–349.

Driben, L.I. (1995) "The Pied Piper of Learning", *Chief Executive* 101: 62–63.

Du Gay, P. and Salaman, G. (1992) "The Cult(ure) of the Customer", *Journal of Management Studies* 29: 615–633.

Du Gay, P., Salaman, G. and Rees, B. (1996) "The Conduct of Management and the Management of Conduct: Contemporary Managerial Discourse and the Constitution of the 'Competent Manager'", *Journal of Management Studies* 33, 3: 263–282.

Dumaine, B. (1989) "What the Leaders of Tomorrow See", *Fortune*, July 3: 48–62.

Dumaine, B. (1994a) "Mr. Learning Organization", *Fortune*, October 17: 147–157.

Dumaine, B. (1994b) "Why Do We Work?", *Fortune* 130, 13: 196–201.

Durkheim, E. (1938) *The Rules of Sociological Method*, trans. by S.A. Solovay and J.H. Mueller and edited by G.E. Catlin, Chicago, IL: The University of Chicago Press.

Eadie, W.F. (1982) [Review of Cragan and Shield (eds.) (1981) *Applied Communication Research: A Dramatistic Approach*], *Journal of Applied Communications Research* 10: 75–78.

Economist (1994a) "Good Guru Guide: Take Me to Your Leader", January 7: 21–26.

Economist (1994b) "In Defence of the Guru", February 26: 18.

Economist (1994c) "Re-engineering Europe", February 26: 63.

Economist (1995a) "Management Theory: The Advent of the Euroguru", March 11: 66–67.

Economist (1995b) "The Knowledge", November 11: 63.

Economist (1996a) "Confessor to the Boardroom", February 24: 74.

Economist (1996b) "Andersen's Androids", May 4: 72.

Economist (1997) "The Anti-Management Guru", April 5: 64–65.

Economist (2000) "Fading Fads", April 22: 62–63.

Edwards, C. and Peppard, J.W. (1994) "Business Process Redesign: Hype, Hope and Hypocrisy?", *Journal of Information Technology* 9: 251–266.

Ehrbar, A. (1998) *EVA, Economic Value Added: The Real Key to Building Wealth*, New York: John Wiley.

Elmes, M. and Costello, M. (1992) "Mystification and Social Drama: The Hidden Side of Communication Skills Training", *Human Relations* 45, 5: 427–445.

Encyclopedia of Religion (1987) New York: Macmillan.

Engwall, L. and Eriksson, C.B. (1999) "Advising Corporate Superstars: CEOs and Consultancies in Top Swedish Corporations". Paper presented at the 15th Annual EGOS Colloquium, Warwick, U.K.

Ezzamel, M., Lilley, S. and Wilmott, H. (1994) "A Survey of Management Practices", *Management Accounting*, July/August: 10–12.

Farnham, A. and Kover, A. (1996) "In Search of Suckers", *Fortune*, October 14; 30–47.

Farrell, T.B. (1980) "Critical Modes in the Analysis of Discourse", *Western Journal of Speech* 44: 300–314.

Farrell, T.B. (1982) [Review of Cragan and Shield (eds.) ((1981) *Applied Communication Research: A Dramatistic Approach*], *Quarterly Journal of Speech* 68: 96–97.

Fast Company (1997) "Loose Lips Burn Ships", 9: 50–51.

Fenwick, T. (1998) "Questioning the Learning Organization", in S. Scott, B. Spencer and A. Thomas (eds.) *Learning for Life*, Toronto, ON: Thompson, 140–152.

Ferguson, A. (1997) "Now They Want Your Kids", *Time* 150, 13: 64–65.

Filipczak, B. (1996) "The CEO and the 'Learning Organization'", *Training* 33, 6: 60.

Fincham, R. (1995) "Business Process Reengineering and the Commodification of Managerial Knowledge", *Journal of Marketing Management* 11: 707–719.

Fincham, R. (1996) "Management as Magic: Reengineering and the Search for Business Salvation". Paper presented at the 14th Annual International Labour Process Conference, Lancashire Business School.

Fincham, R. (1999) "The Consultants' Offensive: Reengineering – from Fad to Technique", *New Technology, Work and Employment* 14, 1: 32–44.

Fisher, A. (1997) "Tom Peters, Professional Loudmouth", *Fortune* 136, 12: 273–276.

Flesch, R. (1974) *The Art of Readable Writing*, New York: Harper & Row.

Foley, G. (1994) "Adult Education and Capitalist Reorganization", *Studies in the Education of Adults* 26, 2: 121–143.

Fort, T.L. (1997) "Religion and Business Ethics: The Lessons from Political Morality", *Journal of Business Ethics* 16, 3; 263–270.

Fortune (2000) "Doing Business the e-Commerce Way", 141: 6.

Foss, S.K. (1989) *Rhetorical Criticism: Exploration and Practice*, Prospect Heights, IL: Waveland.

Foss, S.K., Foss, K.A. and Trapp, R. (1985) *Contemporary Perspectives on Rhetoric*, Prospect Heights, IL: Waveland.

Foucault, M. (1977) *Discipline and Punish*, Harmondsworth, U.K.: Penguin.

Fowler, R. (ed.) (1987) *A Dictionary of Modern Terms*, London: Routledge & Kegan Paul.

Freeman, F.H. (1985) "Books that Mean Business: The Management Best Seller", *Academy of Management Review*, 10, 2: 345–50.

Fulmer, R.M. (1995) "Building Organizations that Learn: The MIT Center for Organizational Learning", *Journal of Management Development* 14, 5: 9–14.

Fulmer, R.M. and Keys, J.B. (1998) "A Conversation with Peter Senge: New Developments in Organizational Learning", *Organizational Dynamics*, Autumn, 27, 2: 33–41.

Furlong, C. (1994) "Buzzword Management", *B.C. Business*, November: 27–35.

Furusten, S. (1999) *Popular Management Books*, London: Routledge.

Galaghan, P.A. (1991) "The Learning Organization Made Plain", *Training and Development* 45: 37–44.

Garratt, B. (1990) *Creating a Learning Organization: A Guide to Leadership, Learning and Development*, New York: Simon & Schuster.

Garratt, B. (1995) "An Old Idea that Has Come of Age", *People Management* 19: 25.

Garvin, D.A. (1993) "Building a Learning Organization", *Harvard Business Review*, July/August: 78–91.

Gee, J.P., Hull, G. and Lankshear, C. (1996) *The New Work Order: Behind the Language of the New Capitalism*, St. Leonards, NSW: Allen & Unwin.

Gephart, M.A., Marsick, V.J., Van Buren, M.E., Spiro, M.S. and Senge, P. (1996) "Learning Organizations Come Alive", *Training and Development* 50, 12: 34–46.

Gergen, K.J. (1971) *The Concept of Self*, New York: Holt, Rinehart & Winston.

Gergen, K.J. (1991) *The Saturated Self*, New York: Basic Books.

Gergen, K.J. (1992) "Organization Theory in the Postmodernist Era", in M. Reed and M. Hughes (eds.) *Rethinking Organization Theory*, London: Sage, 207–226.

Gibson, R. (ed.) (1997) *Rethinking the Future*, London: Nicholas Brealey.

Giddens, A. (1991) *Modernity and Self-Identity*, Cambridge, U.K.: Polity Press.

Gill, J. and Whittle, S. (1993) "Management by Panacea: Accounting for Transience", *Journal of Management Studies* 30, 2: 281–295.

Glaser, B.G. and Strauss, A.L. (1967) *The Discovery of Grounded Theory: Strategies for Qualitative Research*, Chicago: Aldine Publishing.

Goffman, E. (1960) *The Presentation of Self in Everyday Life*, New York: Doubleday Anchor.

Goffman, E. (1974) *Frame Analysis: An Essay on the Organization of Experience*, New York: Harper & Row.

Golden, J.L., Berquist, G.F. and Coleman, W.E. (eds.) (1976) *The Rhetoric of Western Thought*, Dubuque, IA: Kendall.

Goldratt, E.M. and Cox, J. (1984) *The Goal*, London: Gower.

Goldratt, E.M. and Cox, J. (1986) *The Race*, New York: North River.

Goleman, D. (1995) *Emotional Intelligence*, New York: Bantam.

Goleman, D. (1998) *Working with Emotional Intelligence*, New York: Bantam.

Goodnight, G., Thomas, E. and Pulakos, J. (1981) "Conspiracy Rhetoric: From Pragmatism to Fantasy in Public Address", *Western Journal of Speech Communication* 45, 299–316.

Gordon, J. (1995) [Review of Senge et al. (1994) *The Fifth Discipline Fieldbook*], *Training* 32, 1: 119.

Gordon, J. (1996) "A Devil's Dictionary of Business Buzzwords", *Training*, February: 33–37.

Gordon, J. (1999) "Duct Tape for the Soul", *Forbes* 163, 6: 240.

Grayson, M. (1997) "Stuck on Strategy", *Hospitals and Hospital Networks* 71, 19: 74–76.

Greenleaf, R.K. (1977) *Servant Leadership: A Journey into the Nature of Legitimate Power and Greatness*, New York: Paulist Press.

Grey, C. and Mitev, N. (1995) "Re-engineering Organizations: A Critical Appraisal", *Personnel Review* 24: 6–18.

Griffin, E.M. (1997) *A First Look at Communication Theory*, New York: McGraw-Hill.

Griffith, V. (1995) "Corporate Fashion Victim", *Financial Times*, April 12: 15.

Grint, K. (1994) "Reengineering History: Social Resonances and Business Process Reengineering", *Organization* 1, 1: 179–201.

Grint, K. (1997) *Fuzzy Management: Contemporary Ideas and Practices at Work*, London: Oxford University Press.

Grint, K. and Case, P. (1998) "The Violent Rhetoric of Reengineering: Management Consultancy on the Offensive", *Journal of Management Studies* 35, 5: 557–577.

Grint, K. and Willcocks, L. (1995) "Business Process Re-engineering in Theory and Practice: Business Paradise Regained?", *New Technology, Work and Employment* 10, 2: 89–98.

Gronbeck, B.E. (1990) "Dramaturgical Theory and Criticism: The State of the Art (or Science?)", *Western Journal of Speech Communication* 44: 315–330.

Grover, R. (1999) "Gurus Who Failed Their Own Course", *Business Week*, November 8: 121–122.

Gubernick, L. (1995) "The Happiness Hucksters", *Forbes* 156, 8: 82–88.

Guest, D.E. (1990) "Human Resource Management and the American Dream", *Journal of Management Studies* 27, 4: 377–397.

Hamel, G. and Prahalad, C.K. (1994) *Competing for the Future*, Boston, MA: Harvard Business School Press.

Hammer, M. (1990) "Reengineering Work: Don't Automate, Obliterate", *Harvard Business Review* 67, 4: 104–112.

Hammer, M. (1996) *Beyond Reengineering: How the Process-Oriented Organization Is Changing Our Work and Our Lives*, New York: HarperBusiness.

Hammer, M. (1997) "Beyond the End of Management", *Executive Excellence*, September: 5–6.

Hammer, M. (1999) "Reengineering at Net Speed", *Informationweek* 730: 176.

Hammer, M. and Champy, J. (1989) "Help Wanted: Heroes and Visionaries Preferred", *Retail Control* 57, 5: 7–17.

Hammer, M. and Champy, J. (1993) *Reengineering the Corporation: A Manifesto for Business*, New York: HarperBusiness.

Hammer, M. and Stanton, S.A. (1995) *The Reengineering Revolution: A Handbook*, New York: HarperBusiness.

Hammer, M. and Stanton, S. (1999) "How Process Enterprises *Really* Work", *Harvard Business Review*, November/December: 108–118.

Hampden-Turner, C. (1992) "Charting the Dilemmas of Hanover Insurance", *Planning Review* 20, 1: 22–26.

Hansen, K.J. (1981) *Mormonism and the American Experience*, Chicago: The University of Chicago Press.

Hardin, G. (1968) "The Tragedy of the Commons", *Science*, December 13: 1243–1248.

Hare, A.P. and Blumberg, H.H. (1988) *Dramaturgical Analysis of Social Interaction*, New York: Praeger.

Harrar, G. (1994) "The Tools of Success", *Enterprise*, October: 12–19.

Harrington, B., McLoughlin, K. and Riddell, D. (1998) "Business Process Re-engineering in the Public Sector: A Case Study of the Contributions Agency", *New Technology, Work and Employment* 13, 1: 43–50.

Harrison, R. (1995) *The Collected Papers of Roger Harrison*, London and New York: McGraw-Hill.

Harrison, R. (1996) "A Role-Over Week for Training As We Know It", *People Management* 2, 14: 47–48.

Hart, R.P. (1986) "Contemporary Scholarship in Public Address", *Western Journal of Speech Communication* 50: 283–295.

Hart, R.P. (1989) *Modern Rhetorical Criticism*, Glenview, IL: Scott, Foresman/Little, Brown.

Hartnoll, P. (1980) *A Concise History of the Theatre*, London: Thames & Hudson.

Hawkins, P. (1994) "Organizational Learning: Taking Stock and Facing the Challenge", *Management Learning* 25, 1: 71–82.

Heath, R. (1986) *Realism and Relativism: A Perspective on Kenneth Burke*, Macon, GA: Mercer University Press.

Heelas, P. (1996) *The New Age Movement*, Oxford: Blackwell.

Hensley, C.W. (1975) "Rhetorical Vision and the Persuasion of a Historical Movement: The Disciples of Christ in Twentieth Century American Culture", *Quarterly Journal of Speech* 61: 250–264.

Hesse, H. (1972) *A Journey to the East*, New York: Bantam.

Hilmer, F.G. and Donaldson, L. (1996) *Management Redeemed: Debunking the Fads that Undermine Corporate Performance*, East Roseville, NSW: Free Press Australia.

Hitt, M.A. and Ireland, R.D. (1987) "Peters and Waterman Revisited: The Unending Quest for Excellence", *Academy of Management Executive* 1, 2: 91–97.

Hodder, I. (1993) "The Interpretation of Documents and Material Culture", in

N. Denzin and Y. Lincoln (eds.) *Handbook of Qualitative Research*, Thousand Oaks, CA: Sage, 393–402.

Hogarty, D.B. (1993) "The Future of Middle Managers", *Management Review*, September: 51–53.

Holland, D. and Kumar, S. (1995) "Getting Past the Obstacles to Successful Reengineering", *Business Horizons* 38, 3, 79–86.

Horner, W.H. (ed.) (1990) *The Present State of Scholarship in Historical and Contemporary Rhetoric*, Columbia, MS: University of Missouri Press.

Huczynski, A.A. (1991) "Management Gurus". Unpublished doctoral thesis, Department of Social and Economic Research, Glasgow University.

Huczynski, A.A. (1993a) *Management Gurus*, London and New York: Routledge.

Huczynski, A.A. (1993b) "Explaining the Succession of Management Fads", *International Journal of Human Resource Management* 4, 2: 444–463.

Huczynski, A.A. (1994) "Business School Faculty as Gatekeepers of Management Ideas: An Exploratory Study". Unpublished manuscript, Glasgow Business School.

Iacocca, L. and Novak, W. (1984) *Iacocca: An Autobiography*, New York: Bantam Books.

Inc. (1994) "Inc. 500 Special Issue".

Inc. (1995) "Sales and the Seven Habits", December: 117.

Independent (1995) "Economic Prophet of the Information Age", December 11: 13.

Insights Quarterly (1994) "The Unfinished Revolution: Why Management Must Be Reengineered", 6, 2: 14–21.

Institute of Personnel Development (1994) "The Way We Were: 1969–1994", *Personnel Management*, mid-December: 23–41.

Ivie, R.L. (1987) "The Complete Criticism of Political Rhetoric", *Quarterly Journal of Speech* 73: 98–107.

Jackson, B.G. (1994a) "Management Gurus and Business Fads: Boon or Bust for University Continuing Education?". Proceedings of the Annual Conference of the Canadian Association for University Continuing Education, Vancouver, BC.

Jackson, B.G. (1994b) "The Management Guru as Guarantor: The Implications and Challenges for Management Research". Paper presented at the British Academy of Management 1994 Annual Conference, Lancaster University, U.K.

Jackson, B.G. (1996a) "Guru's Line Is It Anyway? An Exploratory Genealogy", *SCOS Notework* 14, 1: 12–16.

Jackson, B.G. (1996b) "Reengineering the Sense of Self: The Manager and the Management Guru", *Journal of Management Studies* 33, 5: 571–589.

Jackson, B.G. (1999) "The Goose That Laid the Golden Egg? A Rhetorical Critique of Stephen Covey and the Effectiveness Movement", *Journal of Management Studies* 36, 3: 353–378.

Jackson, B.G. (2000) "A Fantasy Theme Analysis of Peter Senge's Learning Organization", *Journal of Applied Behavioral Science* 36, 3: 191–207.

Jacoby, S.M. (1991) "Masters to Managers: An Introduction", in S.M. Jacoby (ed.) *Masters to Managers: Historical and Comparative Perspectives of American Employers*, New York: Columbia University Press, 1–20.

Jaffe, D.T. and Scott, C.D. (1998) "Reengineering in Practice: Where Are the People? Where Is the Learning?", *Journal of Applied Behavioral Science* 34, 3: 250–267.

Johansson, H.J., McHugh, P., Pendlebury, J.A. and Wheeler, W.A. (1993) *Business*

Process Reengineering: Break-Point Strategies for Market Dominance, Chichester: John Wiley.

Johnson, B., Natarajan, A. and Rappaport, A. (1985) "Shareholder Returns and Corporate Excellence", *Journal of Business Strategy* 6, 2: 52–62.

Jones, A.M. and Hendry, C. (1994) "The Learning Organization: Adult Learning and Organizational Transformation", *British Journal of Management* 5: 153–162.

Jones, M. (1994) "Don't Emancipate, Exaggerate: Rhetoric, Reality and Reengineering", in S. Smithson, O. Ngwenyama and I.L. Degross (eds.) *Transforming Organizations with Information Technology*, North Holland: Elsevier Science B.V.

Jones, T.C. (1997) "Social Organization of Management Knowledge: A Philosophy, a Guru, and an Institute". Unpublished paper, University of the West of England at Bristol, Faculty of Economics and Social Science.

Journal of European Industrial Training (1995) "Interview with Peter Senge", 19, 6: 26–29.

Kaminer, W. (1997) "Why We Love Gurus", *Newsweek*, October 20: 60.

Kaplan, R.S. and Norton, D.P. (1996) *The Balanced Scorecard: Translating Strategy into Action*, Harvard: Harvard Business School Press.

Kendall, J.E. (1993) "Good and Evil in the Chairman's 'Boiler Plate': An Analysis of Corporate Visions of the 1970s", *Organization Studies* 14, 4: 571–592.

Kennedy, C. (1991) *A Guide to the Management Gurus*, London: Business Books Limited.

Kennedy, C. (1994a) *Managing with the Gurus*, London: Century Business Books.

Kennedy, C. (1994b) "A Day with Michael Hammer", *Director*, April: 13–14.

Kennedy, C. (1996) "Carry on Consultants", *Director*, June: 11–13.

Kennedy, C. (1997) "When Life's a Beach, Who Needs Business?", *Director*, July: 60–62.

Kets de Vries, M.F.R. and Miller, D. (1984) "Group Fantasies and Organizational Functioning", *Human Relations* 37, 2: 111–134.

Keys, J., Fulmer, R.M. and Stumpf, S.A. (1996) "Micro Worlds and Simuworlds: Practice Fields for the Learning Organization", *Organizational Dynamics*, Spring, 24, 4: 36–50.

Kiechel, W. (1990) "The Organization That Learns", *Fortune*, March 12: 133–136.

Kieser, A. (1997) "Rhetoric and Myth in Management Fashion", *Organization* 4, 1: 49–74.

Kieser, A. (1999) "Consultants and Management Fashions". Paper presented at the Conference on Management Consultants and Management Knowledge, Reading, U.K.

Kilmann, R.H. (1984) "Beyond the Quick Fix: Why Managers Must Disregard the Myth of Simplicity as a Direct Route to Organizational Success", *Management Review* 73, 11: 24–37.

Kilmann, R.H. (1996) "Management Learning Organizations: Enhancing Business Education for the 21st Century", *Management Learning* 27, 2: 203–237.

Kinni, T.B. (1994) "The Reengineering Rage: Powerful New Improvement Process or Pet Rock?", *Industry Week*, February 7: 11–14.

Kleiner, A. (1992) "The Gurus of Corporate Change", *Business and Society Review*, Spring: 39–42.

Knights, D. and McCabe, D. (1998a) "When 'Life is But a Dream': Obliterating Politics Through Business Process Reengineering", *Human Relations* 51, 6: 761–798.

Knights, D. and McCabe, D. (1998b) "What Happens When the Phone Goes Wild? Staff, Stress and Spaces for Escape in a BPR Telephone Banking Work Regime", *Journal of Management Studies* 35, 2: 163–194.

Knowlton, C. (1989) "The Buying Binge in Business Books", *Fortune* 119, 4: 101–103.

Koester, J. (1982) "The Machiavellian Princess: Rhetorical Dramas for Women Managers", *Communication Quarterly* 30: 165–172.

Kofman, F. and Senge, P.M. (1993) "Communities of Commitment: The Heart of Learning Organizations", *Organizational Dynamics* 32, 5: 5–23.

Kofman, F., Repenning, N. and Sterman, J. (1994) "Unanticipated Side Effects of Successful Quality Programs: Exploring a Paradox of Organizational Improvement", MIT Sloan School of Management Working Paper.

Kolb, D.A. (1984) *Experiential Learning*, Englewood Cliffs, NJ: Prentice-Hall.

Kondratieff, N.D. (1935) "The Long Waves in Economic Life", *Review of Economic Statistics* 17: 105–115.

Kotcheff, T. (1974) *The Apprenticeship of Duddy Kravitz* [Film], Malofilm Group.

Krell, T.C. (1981) "The Marketing of Organizational Development: Past, Present and Future", *Journal of Applied Behavioral Science* 17, 3: 309–323.

Lawlor, J. (1996) "Getting into the Habit: Stephen Covey is Bringing his Message of Integrity and Empathy to Sales Training", *Sales and Marketing Management* 148, 5: 68–71.

Lee, M. (1991) "Playing the Guru: Inequality of Personal Power", *Management Education and Development* 22, 4: 302–309.

Legge, K. (1995) *Human Resource Management: Rhetorics and Realities*, Basingstoke, Hants: Macmillan Business.

Lessem, R. (1991) *Top Quality Learning: Building a Learning Organization*, Oxford: Basil Blackwell.

Leverment, Y., Ackers, P. and Preston, D. (1998) "Professionals in the NHS: A Case Study of Business Process Re-engineering", *New Technology, Work and Employment* 13, 2: 129–139.

Lilley, S. (1997) "Stuck in the Middle with You?", *British Journal of Management* 8: 51–59.

Lindholm, C. (1990) *Charisma*, Oxford: Basil Blackwell.

Littlejohn, S.W. (1992) *Theories of Human Communication*, Belmont, CA: Wadsworth.

Lorenz, C. (1986) "The Guru Factor: Europe Warms to Business Punditry", *Financial Times*, July 2: 18.

Lowrekovich, S.N. (1996) "Reengineering: Is it Safe and Is It Really New?", *Industrial Management*, May/June: 1–2.

Luckmann, T. (1967) *The Invisible Religion: The Problem of Religion in Modern Society*, New York: Macmillan.

Lyman, S.M. and Scott, M.B. (1975) *The Drama of Social Reality*, New York: Oxford University Press.

McConville, D.J. (1994) "Money Talks", *Industry Week*, November 7: 44–48.

McGill, M.E. (1988) *American Business and the Quick Fix*, New York: Henry Holt.

MacKay, H. (1988) *Swim with the Sharks without Being Eaten Alive*, New York: Morrow.

McKinley, W., Sanchez, C.M. and Schick, A.G. (1995) "Organizational Downsizing: Constraining, Cloning, Learning", *Academy of Management Executive* 9, 3: 32–44.

Maglitta, J. (1994) "In Depth: Michael Hammer", *Computerworld*, January 24: 84–86.

Mahoney, A.I. (1997) "Senge, Covey, and Peters on Leadership Lessons", *Association Management* 49, 1: 62–66.

Maidique, M.A. (1983) "The New Management Thinkers", *California Management Review* 26, 1: 151–161.

Mangham, I.L. (1978) *Interactions and Interventions in Organizations*, Chichester: John Wiley.

Mangham, I.L. (1986) *Power and Performance in Organizations*, Oxford: Basil Blackwell.

Mangham, I.L. (1990) "Managing as Performing Art", *British Journal of Management* 1: 105–115.

Mangham, I.L. (1996) "All the World's a ...", *Studies in Cultures, Organizations and Societies* 12, 2: 9–13.

Mangham, I.L. and Overington, M.A. (1983) "Dramatism and the Theatrical Metaphor", in G. Morgan (ed.) *Beyond Method*, Beverly Hills, CA: Sage, 219–233.

Mangham, I.L. and Overington, M.A. (1987) *Organizations as Theatre: A Social Psychology of Dramatic Appearances*, Chichester: John Wiley.

Marchetti, M. (1999) "Stephen Covey's Win–Lose Merger", *Sales and Marketing Management* 151, 3: 20.

Mariotti, J. (1998) "The Challenge of Change", *Industry Week* 247, 7: 140.

Marsick, V.J. and Watkins, K.E. (1990) *Informal and Incidental Learning in the Workplace*, London: Routledge.

Mauss, A.L. (1994) "Refuge and Retrenchment: The Mormon Quest for Identity", in M. Cornwall, T.B. Heaton and L.A. Young (eds.) *Contemporary Mormonism: Social Science Perspectives*, Urbana: University of Illinois Press, 24–42.

Medhurst, M.J. and Benson, T.W. (eds.) (1984) *Rhetorical Dimensions in Media: A Critical Casebook*, Dubuque, IA: Kendall/Hunt.

Meen, D.E. and Keough, M. (1992) "Creating the Learning Organization", *McKinsey Quarterly*, Winter, 1: 58–79.

Merriam, S.B. (1995) *A Guide to Research for Educators and Trainers of Adults*, Malabar, FL: Krieger.

Meyer, J.W. and Rowan, B. (1977) "Institutional Organizations: Formal Structure as Myth and Ceremony", *American Journal of Sociology* 83: 340–363.

Meyer, J.W. and Scott, W.R. (1983) *Organizational Environments: Ritual and Rationality*, Beverly Hills, CA: Sage.

Micklethwait, J. and Wooldridge, A. (1996) *The Witch Doctors*, London: Heinemann.

Miles, M.B. and Huberman, A.M. (1994) *Qualitative Data Analysis: An Expanded Sourcebook*, Thousand Oaks, CA: Sage.

Mitroff, I.I. and Bennis, W. (1989) *The Unreality Industry*, New York: Oxford University Press.

Mohrmann, G.P. (1982a) "An Essay on Fantasy Theme Criticism", *Quarterly Journal of Speech* 68: 109–132.

Mohrmann, G.P. (1982b) " Fantasy Theme Criticism: A Peroration", *Quarterly Journal of Speech* 68: 306–313.

Monin, N. and Monin, J. (1998) "Rhetoric and Managerial Discourse: A Rhetorical Analysis of a Text by Henry Mintzberg". Paper presented at the Third International Conference on Organizational Discourse, Kings College, London, U.K.

Morgan, J. (1997) "Rethinking and Radical Change Don't Come Easy", *Purchasing* 122, 10: 31–32.

Naisbitt, J. (1984) *Megatrends: Ten New Directions Transforming Our Lives*, New York: Warner Books.

National Underwriter (1995) "Habits of Effective Risk Managers", December 25: 9.

Neal, A.G. and Groat, H.T. (1984) [Review of Naisbitt (1984) *Megatrends*], *Contemporary Sociology* 13, 1: 120–122.

Nevis, E.C., DiBella, A.J. and Gould, J.M. (1993) "Organizations as Learning Systems", MIT Sloan School of Management Working Paper.

New Encyclopaedia Britannica (15th edn) (1993) Chicago.

New Scientist (1967) "Ariadne", 35, 562: 559.

New Statesman (1996) "Managing to Look Attractive: Tony Blair and Bill Clinton are in Love with Management Theory", 125, 4309: 24.

Newstrom, J.W. and Pierce, J.L. (1989) "The Potential Role of Popular Business Books in Management Development Programmes", *Journal of Management Development* 8, 2: 13–24.

Nichols, M.H. (1952) "Kenneth Burke and the New Rhetoric", *Quarterly Journal of Speech* 38: 133–144.

Nirenberg, J. (1997) *Power Tools: A Leader's Guide to the Latest Management Thinking*, New York: Prentice-Hall.

Nohria, N. and Berkley, J.D. (1994) "Whatever Happened to the Take-Charge Manager?", *Harvard Business Review*, January/February: 128–137.

Nonaka, I. (1991) "The Knowledge-Creating Company", *Harvard Business Review*, November/December: 96–104.

Nonaka, I. and Tekeuchi, H. (1995) *The Knowledge Creating Company*, Oxford: Oxford University Press.

Norton, B. and Smith, C. (1998) *Understanding Management Gurus in a Week*, London: Hodder & Stoughton.

Oberle, J. (1990) "Quality Gurus: The Men and their Message", *Training* 27, 1: 47–52.

O'Connor, E.S. (1995) "Paradoxes of Participation: Textual Analysis and Organizational Change", *Organization Studies* 16, 5: 769–803.

Oliver, N. (1990) "Just-in-time: The New Religion of Western Manufacturing". Proceedings of the British Academy of Management Conference, Glasgow, U.K.

Osborn, M. (1986) [Review of Bormann (1985) *The Force of Fantasy*], *Communication Education* 35: 204–205.

O'Shea, J. and Madigan, C. (1997) *Dangerous Company*, New York: Random House.

Ouchi, W.G. (1981) *Theory Z: How American Business Can Meet the Japanese Challenge*, Reading, MA: Addison-Wesley.

Overington, M.A. (1977) "Kenneth Burke and the Method of Dramatism", *Theory and Society* 4: 131–156.

Overington, M.A. and Mangham, I.L. (1982) "The Theatrical Perspective in Organizational Analysis", *Symbolic Interaction* 5, 2: 173–186.

Oxford English Dictionary (1989) Prepared by J.A. Simpson and E.S.C. Weiner, Oxford: Clarendon Press.

Parkinson, N. (1957) *Parkinson's Law*, Harmondsworth: Penguin.

Pascale, R.T. (1990) *Managing on the Edge*, New York: Touchstone.

Pascale, R.T. and Athos, A.G. (1981) *The Art of Japanese Management*, New York: Warner Books.

Pauchant, T.C. (1991) "Transferential Leadership: Towards a More Complex Understanding of Charisma in Organizations", *Organization Studies* 12, 4: 507–527.

Pedler, M., Burgoyne, J. and Boydell, T. (1991) *The Learning Company*, London: McGraw-Hill.

Pedler, M., Burgoyne, J. and Boydell, T. (1997) *The Learning Company* (2nd edn), London: McGraw-Hill.

Performance (1995) "Q and A with Michael Hammer", March: 25–28.

Perinbanayagam, R.S. (1982) "Dramas, Metaphors, and Structures", *Symbolic Interaction* 5, 2: 259–276.

Peter, L.J. and Hull, R. (1969) *The Peter Principle*, New York: Morrow.

Peters, T.J. (1987) *Thriving on Chaos*, New York: Alfred A. Knopf.

Peters, T.J. (1993) "Tom Peter's New Rules of Disorder Supplant the Quest for Excellence", *Report on Business Magazine*, January 29: 13.

Peters, T.J. and Waterman, R.H. (1982) *In Search of Excellence: Lessons from America's Best Run Companies*, New York: Harper & Row.

Pierce, J.L. and Newstrom, J.W. (eds.) (1990) *The Manager's Bookshelf*, New York: HarperCollins.

Pinault, L. (2000) *Consulting Demons: Inside the Unscrupulous World of Global Corporate*, New York: HarperCollins.

Poole, M.S. (1990) "Do We Have Any Theories of Group Communication?", *Communication Studies* 41, 3: 237–247.

Porter, L.W. (1976) "The White House Transcripts: Group Fantasy Events Concerning the Mass Media", *Central States Speech Journal* 27: 272–279.

Postman, N. (1985) *Amusing Ourselves to Death*, New York: Viking Penguin.

Powell, W.W. and DiMaggio, P.J. (eds.) (1991) *The New Institutionalism in Organizational Analysis*, Chicago: The University of Chicago Press.

Prince, C.J. (1998) "Fast, Right, Cheap and Easy", *Chief Executive* 131: 40–43.

Quinn, J.B. (1992) *The Intelligent Enterprise: Knowledge and Service-Based Paradigm for Industry*, New York: The Free Press.

Quinn, J. (1995) "Mr. Covey Goes to Washington", *Incentive*, April: 9.

Ramsay, H. (1996) "Managing Sceptically: A Critique of Organizational Fashion", in S.R. Clegg and G. Palmer (eds.) *The Politics of Management Knowledge*, London: Sage, 154–171.

Rappaport, A. (1997) *Creating Shareholder Value: A Guide for Managers and Investors*, New York: The Free Press.

Ray, C.A. (1986) "Corporate Culture: The Last Frontier of Control?", *Journal of Management Studies* 23, 3: 286–297.

Reed, M. (1990) "From Paradigms to Images: The Paradigm Warrior Turns Post-Modernist Guru", *Personnel Review* 19, 3: 35–40.

Rein, I.J., Kotler, P. and Stoller, M.R. (1987) *High Visibility*, New York: Dodd, Mead & Co.

Repenning, N.P. (1996) "Modelling the Failure of Productivity Improvement Programs", MIT Sloan School of Management Working Paper.

Revans, R.W. (1980) *Action Learning: New Techniques for Management*, London: Blond & Briggs.

Reynolds, M. (1998) "Bright Lights and the Pastoral Idyll: Social Theories Underlying Management Education Methodologies". Paper presented at the Leeds–Lancaster Conference on Emergent Fields in Management, Leeds, U.K.

Rigby, D.K. (1993) "How to Manage the Management Tools", *Planning Review*, November/December: 8–15.

Rigby, D.K. (1998) "What's Today's Special at the Consultant's Cafe?", *Fortune* 138, 5: 162–163.

Rippin, A. (1994) "Total Quality Management and Organizational Nostalgia". Paper presented at the 12th Standing Conference on Organizational Symbolism, Calgary, Canada.

Rose, N. (1991) *Governing the Soul*, London: Routledge.

Rosen, M. (1988) "'You Asked For It': Christmas at the Bosses' Expense", *Journal of Management Studies* 25, 5: 463–480.

Rosenfeld, P., Giacalone, R.A. and Riordan, C.A. (1995) *Impression Management in Organizations*, London: Routledge.

Rostow, W.W. (1978) *The World Economy: History and Prospect*, New York: Macmillan.

Roszak, T. (1969) *The Making of a Counter Culture*, Garden City, New York: Anchor Books.

Rubin, R.B., Rubin, A.M. and Peiele, L.J. (1993) *Communication Research: Strategies and Sources*, Belmont, CA: Wadsworth.

Ruff, H.J. (1979) *How to Prosper During the Coming Bad Years*, New York: Times Books.

Schaaf, D. and Kaeter, M. (1994) *Business Speak*, New York: Warner Books.

Schickel, R. (1985) *Intimate Strangers*, Garden City, NY: Doubleday.

Schlossberg, H. (1991) "Author: Consumers Just Can't Wait to be Satisfied", *Marketing News* 25, 3: 13–14.

Scott, R.L. (1967) "On Viewing Rhetoric as Epistemic", *Central States Speech Journal* 27: 258–266.

Scott, W.R. (1995) *Institutions and Organizations,* Thousand Oaks, CA: Sage.

Security Management (1992) "Thrill Seekers Find Their Quarry", September: 62–64.

Seglin, J.L. (1999) "The Sequel Syndrome", *Inc.* 21, 10: 97.

Senge, P.M. (1990a) "The Leader's New Work: Building Learning Organizations", *Sloan Management Review* 32, 1: 7–23.

Senge, P.M. (1990b) *The Fifth Discipline: The Art and Practice of the Learning Organization*, New York: Doubleday Currency.

Senge, P.M. (1992) "Building Learning Organizations", *Journal for Quality and Participation* 15, 2: 30–38.

Senge, P.M. (1995a) "Making a Better World", *Executive Excellence* 12, 8: 18–19.

Senge, P.M. (1995b) "Robert Greenleaf's Legacy: A New Foundation for Twenty-First Century Institutions", in L.C. Spears (ed.) *Reflections on Leadership*, New York: John Wiley, 217–240.

Senge, P.M. (1995c) "Learning Infrastructures", *Executive Excellence* 12, 2: 7–8.

Senge, P.M. (1996a) "Rethinking Leadership in the Learning Organization", *The Systems Thinker* 7, 1: 1–8.

Senge, P.M. (1996b) "Leading Learning Organizations", *Executive Excellence* 13, 4: 10–12.

Senge, P.M. (1997) "The Tragedy of Our Times", *The Systems Thinker*, August: 9–10.

Senge, P.M. and Fulmer, R.M. (1993) "Simulations, Systems Thinking and Anticipatory Learning", *Journal of Management Development* 12, 6: 21–33.

Senge, P.M., Roberts, C.B., Ross, R.B., Smith, B.J. and Kleiner, A. (1994) *The Fifth Discipline Fieldbook*, New York: Doubleday Currency.

Senge, P. M., Kleiner, A., Roberts, C.B., Roth, G. and Ross, R.B. (1999) *The Dance of Change*, New York: Doubleday Currency.

Sennett, R. (1998) *The Corrosion of Character: The Personal Consequences of Work in New Capitalism*, New York: W.W. Norton.

Shapiro, E.C. (1995) *Fad Surfing in the Boardroom*, Reading, MA: Addison-Wesley.

Shapiro, E.C. (2000) "Managing in the Cappucino Economy", *Harvard Business Review*, March/April: 177–183.

Sharpe, T. (1984) "The Day I Saw John Fenton or 'By the Inch It's a Cinch'", *Management Education and Development* 15, 1: 14–16.

Shellenbarger, S. (1995) "Work and Family: Books That Give You Some Perspective on Life's Demands", *Wall Street Journal*, December 27: 13.

Shepherd, G. and Shepherd, G. (1984) "Mormonism in Secular Society: Changing Patterns in Official Ecclesiastical Rhetoric", *Review of Religious Research* 26, 1: 28–42.

Shields, D.C. (1981) "The St. Paul Fire Fighters' Dramatis Personae: Concurrent and Construct Validation for the Theory in Use Rhetorical Vision", in J.F. Cragan and D.C. Shields (eds.) *Applied Communication Research: A Dramatistic Approach*, Prospect Heights, IL: Waveland Press, 235–270.

Simons, H.W. and Melia, T. (eds.) (1989) *The Legacy of Kenneth Burke*, Madison, WI: The University of Wisconsin Press.

Smith, A. (1976) *An Inquiry into the Nature and Causes of the Wealth of Nations*, eds. R.H. Campbell and A.S. Skinner, Oxford: Clarendon Press.

Smith, H.R. (1994) *The 10 Successful Laws of Time and Life Management*, New York: Warner Books.

Smith, T.K. (1995a) "Call Them Microsofties", *Fortune*, May 15: 22.

Smith, T.K. (1995b) "What's So Effective about Stephen Covey?", *Fortune*, December 12: 116–126.

Snoddy, R. (1999) *Masters of the Universe, Part 1* [Film], Channel 4 documentary.

Soeters, J.L. (1986) "Excellent Companies as Social Movements", *Journal of Management Studies* 23, 3: 299–312.

Spell, C.S. (2000) "Where Do Management Fashions Come From, and How Long Do They Stay?" *Journal of Management History* 5, 6: 334–348.

Stake, R.E. (1993) "Case Studies", in N. Denzin and Y. Lincoln (eds.) *Handbook of Qualitative Research*, Thousand Oaks, CA: Sage, 236–247.

Stark, R. (1994) "Modernization and Mormon Growth: The Secularization Thesis Revisited", in M. Cornwall, T.B. Heaton and L.A. Young (eds.) *Contemporary Mormonism: Social Science Perspectives*, Urbana, IL: University of Illinois Press, 13–23.

Starkey, K. (ed.) (1996) *How Organizations Learn*, London: International Thomson Business Press.

Starkey, K. (1998) "What Can We Learn From the Learning Organization?", *Human Relations* 51, 4: 531–547.

Stephenson, W. (1953) *The Study of Behaviour*, Chicago: University of Chicago Press.

Stern, W. (1995) "Did Dirty Tricks Create a Best Seller?", *Business Week*, August 7: 30–33.

Stewart, T.A. (1993) "Reengineering: the Hot New Managing Tool", *Fortune*, August 23: 1–6.

Stewart, T.A. (1996) "It's a Flat World After All", *Fortune*, August 19: 197–198.

Strang, D. and Macy, M.W. (1999) "'In Search of Excellence': Fads, Success Stories and Communication Bias". Proceedings of the Academy of Management Meeting in Chicago.

Stuller, J. (1992) "The Guru Game: Who's the Next Peter Drucker?", *Across the Board* 29, 12: 16–22.

Sturdy, A. (1995) "An Insecure Business: IT Strategy Consultancy in U.K. Financial Services". Paper presented at the British Academy of Management, Sheffield, U.K.

Successful Meetings (1993) "Listening with Empathy", March: 122–125.

Swift, G. (1983) *Waterland*, Oxford: Heinemann New Windmills.

Taylor, J.A. (1995) "Don't Obliterate, Informate! BPR for the Information Age", *New Technology and Employment* 10, 2: 99–109.

Taylor, W.H. and Jackson, B.G. (1996) "Reengineering Continuing Education: Repositioning our Workplace for the Future", Proceedings of the 43rd Annual Conference of the Canadian Association for University Continuing Education in Fredericton, New Brunswick.

Thackray, J. (1993) "Fads, Fixes and Fictions", *Management Today*, June: 40–42.

Thomas, A.B. (1989) "One Minute Management Education: A Sign of the Times?", *Management Education and Development* 20, 1: 23–38.

Thomas, K. (1973) *Religion and the Decline of Magic: Studies in Popular Beliefs in Sixteenth- and Seventeenth-Century England*, Harmondsworth, U.K.: Penguin.

Thompson, J.B. (1995) *The Media and Modernity*, Cambridge, U.K.: Polity Press.

Thrift, N. (1997) "Soft Capitalism", *Cultural Values* 1, 1: 29–58.

Time (1996) "Time's 25 Most Influential Americans", June 17: 14–39.

Tirbutt, E. (1989) "The Business Book Business", *Accountancy* 103, 1148: 90–94.

Tomasko, R.M. (1996) "The Catch 22 of Reengineering", *Across the Board*, May: 12.

Torbert, W.R. (1994) "Managerial Learning, Organizational Learning: A Potentially Powerful Redundancy", *Management Learning* 1: 57–70.

Townley, B. (1995) *Reframing Human Resource Management*, London: Sage.

Training (1992) "Q and A with Stephen Covey", December: 37–42.

Training and Development (1994) "The Future of Workplace Learning and Performance", 48, 5: S36–51.

Treacy, M. and Wiersema, F. (1995) *The Discipline of Market Leaders*, New York: Addison-Wesley.

Tsang, E. (1997) "Organizational Learning and the Learning Organization: A Dichotomy between Descriptive and Prescriptive Research", *Human Relations* 50, 1: 73–90.

Tudor, A. (1974) *Image and Influence*, London: Allen & Unwin.

Turner, V. (1974) *Dramas, Fields, and Metaphors*, Ithaca and London: Cornell University Press.

Turner, V. (1982) *From Ritual to Theatre: The Human Seriousness of Play*, New York: PAJ Publications.

Twitchell, J.B. (1992) *Carnival Culture*, New York: Columbia University Press.

Van Maanen, J. (1983) *Qualitative Methodology*, London: Sage.

Verespej, M.A. (1995) "Reengineering Isn't Going Away", *Industry Week* 244, 4: 42.

Victor, B. and Stephens, C. (1994) "The Dark Side of the New Organizational Forms: An Editorial Essay", *Organization Science* 5, 4: 479–481.

Waldrop, M.M. (1996) "The Trillion Dollar Vision of Dee Hock", *Fast Company*, October/November: 75–81.

Wall, S. and McKinley, R. (1998) "Wall-to-Wall Change", *Across the Board* 35, 5: 32–38.

Wall Street Journal (1995) "Managers Beware: You're Not Ready", January 24: B1.

Watkins, K.E. and Marsick, V.J. (1994) *Sculpting the Learning Organization*, San Francisco: Jossey-Bass.

Watson, T.J. (1986) *Management, Organization and Employment Strategy*, London: Routledge.

Watson, T.J. (1994) "Management 'Flavours of the Month': Their Role in Managers' Lives", *International Journal of Human Resource Management* 5, 4: 893–909.

Watts, T. (1999) "MBA Students Flock to Oprah the Entrepreneur", *BRW*, November 12: 45.

Webb, E.J., Campbell, D.T., Schwartz, R.D. and Sechrest, L. (1966) *Unobtrusive Measures: Nonreactive Research in the Social Sciences*, Chicago: Rand McNally & Co.

Webber, A.M. (1999) "Learning for a Change", *Fast Company*, May: 178–188.

Weber, M. (1947) *The Theory of Social and Economic Organization*, Glencoe, IL: The Free Press.

Weber, M. (1958) *The Religion of India*, Glencoe, IL: The Free Press.

Wellemeyer, M. (1987) "Books Bosses Read", *Fortune*, April 27: 145–148.

Wells, J. (1995) "Guru to the Great", *Report on Business Magazine*, July: 11–18.

Welter, T.R. (1991) "The Source of Strength: Roots and Reach", *Industry Week* 240, 20: 20–24.

Wheatley, M.J. (1992) *Leadership and the New Science*, San Francisco, CA: Berett-Koehler.

Whitford, D. (1996) "Therapist to a New Economy", *Inc.*, September: 76–84.

Whyte, W.H. (1957) *The Organization Man*, New York: Doubleday Anchor.

Wilkerson, J.L. (1997) "The Future is Virtual HR", *HR Focus* 74, 3: 15.

Wilkinson, A. and Wilmott, H. (1995) *Making Quality Control*, London: Routledge.

Wilmott, H. (1993) "Strength is Ignorance: Managing Culture in Modern Organizations", *Journal of Management Studies* 30, 4: 515–552.

Wilmott, H. (1994) "Business Process Reengineering and Human Resource Management", *Personnel Review* 23, 3: 34–46.

Wilmott, H. (1995) "Will the Turkeys Vote for Christmas? The Re-engineering of Human Resources", in G. Burke and J. Peppard (eds.) *Examining Business Process Re-engineering*, London: Cranfield University School of Management, 306–315.

Wolfe, A. (1998) "White Magic in America", *New Republic* 4, 336: 26–34.

Wood, S.J. (1989) "New Wave Management?", *Work, Employment and Society* 3, 3: 379–402.

Wooldridge, A. and Kennedy, C. (1996) "Can Covey Convert the World?", *Director*, May: 52–56.

Workforce (1997) "Covey Leadership Centre and Franklin Quest Agree to Merger", March: 12.

Wren, D.A. (1972) *The Evolution of Management Thought*, New York: Ronald Press.

Wurman, R.S. (1989) *Information Anxiety*, New York: Doubleday.

Yin, R.K. (1989) *Case Study Research: Design and Methods*, Newbury Park, CA: Sage.

Young, T.R. (1990) *The Drama of Social Life: Essays in Post-modern Social Psychology*, New Brunswick: Transaction.

Zilbergeld, B.A. (1984) "A One-Minute Essay, More or Less, on the One-Minute Books", *Psychology Today*, August: 6–7.

Index

Note: numbers in *italics* refer to tables